A Long Awakening to Grace

"*A Long Awakening to Grace* shows the transformative power of an open heart and questing spirit. Faith buoys Linda Marshall through decades of family pain and tragedy caused by a mysterious genetic condition. Over the course of this inspiring journey, love opens the way for profound healing."

–Susan J. Tweit,
author of *Walking Nature Home: A Life's Journey*

"One of my physician colleagues, when asked how he dealt with 'such depressing neuromuscular diseases,' replied, 'I have the greatest job in the world because I get to work with heroes every day.' This remarkable memoir chronicles one such hero's quest to find an answer to a genetic riddle that had severely impacted her family for decades. The story is moving, meaningful, and inspiring, and reading it has made me a better doctor. It is a tremendous resource for other families in similar situations."

–John T. Kissel, M.D.; Chair, Department of Neurology;
Director, Division of Neuromuscular Medicine;
Ohio State University Wexner Medical Center.

"Linda's memoir is more than just a retelling of her life story. This work of nonfiction functions on so many levels. In addition to being a brilliantly insightful spiritual exploration and narrative about a rare genetic disorder, it's the quintessential story of the American woman born in the 1940s, growing up in the 1950s, and dealing with stifling gender roles imposed on American women of that era."

–April Wilson, M.A. in English, M.S. in Education
author of five novels and college educator

A Long Awakening to Grace

by

Linda A. Marshall

Copyright © 2017 by Linda A. Marshall
Cover design © 2017 by Danny Manglesdorf
Formatting by April Barnswell
All rights reserved.

Emergings Press
P.O. Box 752063
Dayton, OH 45459

No part of this publication may be reproduced, stored in a retrieval system, or transmitted in any form or by any means without the prior written permission of the author. The only exception is brief quotations to be used in book reviews.

Visit www.LindaAMarshall.com to contact the author.

Author photograph by Rick Guidotti of Positive Exposure: https://positiveexposure.org/. Photographs in Chapter 31 and 32 by Rick Guidotti of Positive Exposure.

Butterfly logo By Evan MacDonald (The Noun Project) [CC BY 3.0 (http://creativecommons.org/licenses/by/3.0)], via Wikimedia Commons

ISBN-13: 978-1974442621
ISBN-10: 1974442624

Library of Congress Control Number: 2017913415
CreateSpace Independent Publishing Platform, North Charleston, SC

Published in the United States of America
First Printing August 2017

Dedication

This memoir is dedicated to my children,
Doug and Nicole,
and to our messenger,
Alexandra

Author's Note

My story is written from my perspective, the events told as I experienced and made meaning of them. My prayer journals, records, and correspondence helped to refresh my memory of many details. To respect privacy, some names have been changed. The dialogue reflects accurately what was said and is retold to the best of my memory in order to evoke feeling and meaning.

Portions of Chapter 32 of this memoir first appeared in *Sophia's Table: Women's Wisdom in Five Voices*, "Our Last Conversation," 2013, pages 43-46.

A portion of the proceeds from the sale of *A Long Awakening to Grace* will be donated to:

> The Myotonic Dystrophy Foundation
> 1004A O'Reilly Avenue
> San Francisco, CA 94129
> www.myotonic.org

Table of Contents

PART I – PREPARATION 1
   Ready or Not 3
   Self-betrayal 9
   Marriage—An Unwise Agreement 23
   The Worst Kind of Loneliness 32
   Trust 37
   Intuition 46
   Sustenance 56
   Intuition Confirmed 65
   Call 76
   Guerilla Warfare 88
   Struggle 96
   Darkness Descends 107

PART II - AWAKENING 119
   Finding a Better Way 120
   Changing 129
   Shattered 140
   Clashing 147
   Living Forward 158
   Facing Reality 168
   Daunted 175
   Survival Skills 179
   Meeting 192
   Evolving 198
   Acceptance 208
   Secrets 220

PART III – EMERGING 231
    Summoning Courage 232
    Surrender 241
    Grace Unfolding 248
    Fire Walk 253
    Mama Bear 263
    Doug's Story 269
    Nicole's Story 279
    The Mystery 289
Epilogue: Awakening to "The Better Way" 298
Acknowledgements 302
Footnotes 305
Resources 306
Author's Biography 308

PART I – PREPARATION

*If you have a deep desire to move forward,
a way is being prepared for you.*

~Bryant McGill

Ready or Not

Late July 1999

*Opportunity doesn't make appointments,
you have to be ready when it arrives.*

~Tim Fargo

Nicole, my daughter, phoned to tell me she had broken up with her baby's father. Finally I was free to offer to serve as her support person. She accepted and on my first trip with her to her monthly ultrasound appointment, the clinic nurses seemed excited to see someone accompanying her. I shrank inside, not knowing how to respond. I had been struggling with how much to be involved in my daughter's chaotic life. *How much responsibility does a mother have for an adult child making poor choices?* The nurses led Nicole to the ultrasound room and asked me to wait in the short hall off the main corridor.

The empty hallway was quiet except for the muffled voices inside the ultrasound room and the occasional squeak of rubber-soled shoes rushing along the walkway. With my head down and my arms crossed over my stomach, I leaned against the wall, agonizing about Nicole's situation. *How did we arrive here?* A flurry of memories of the day she was born passed through my mind.

That sunny June 4 morning, I arose early, took a shower, washed my hair, and rolled it in giant rollers to obtain a classic bouffant. I had experienced contractions during the night with no pain. In case I gave birth to my second child that day, I would be prepared. As I started drying my hair, the pain began. When I called the doctor, his wife answered and sounded alarmed when I told her my contractions were three minutes apart. "Get to the hospital NOW!" she ordered.

I donned a blue net cap to hold my rollers in place while Buddy called his parents. Neighbors agreed to watch Doug, almost three years old, until Buddy's parents arrived from Cincinnati. We drove the twenty minutes from our home in Germantown to Middletown Regional Hospital. While Buddy signed me in, an attendant wheeled me to the prep room, the pain with my contractions growing more intense.

The attendant parked me outside the door to await my turn. A young man sporting a mustache and curly dark hair worn Afro-style approached me. He squatted alongside the wheelchair and inquired about my contractions. Then he said, "You look familiar." He recognized me even with rollers in my hair.

"You look familiar to me, too."

As it turned out, Terry had been a student in my college-prep typing class during the time I taught business education courses at Carlisle High School. Now he was studying to be a nurse. Excited to see me, he came into the delivery room to assist.

The doctor told me the anesthesiologist was on his way. I asked, "From where?" If he was coming from home, I was sure he wasn't going to make it. I cried out with another intense contraction.

The doctor took my legs out of the stirrups and held them together. Terry took my hand and began coaching my breathing. My hands cramped into a claw-like position. Terry said, "Relax. Remember how you used to tell us to relax in typing class?"

I raised an eyebrow and gave him a skeptical look. "I think this is a little different." We both chuckled. He continued to coach my breathing, and it helped. If I had been astute enough to seek out a doctor who supported natural childbirth, I could have easily given birth without anesthetic. But natural childbirth was rare in 1971.

The anesthesiologist arrived and had no sooner administered the saddle block than my daughter slipped out into the doctor's hands. My experience with her was so different than Doug's birth. I went through hours of labor with him. I still tease Nicole about being in a hurry.

I was thrilled to have a daughter and looked forward to the opportunity to develop a loving relationship with her. I wanted to be different from the critical, disapproving mother who had raised me.

My hospital roommate and I hit it off immediately. We bragged to the nurses about how cute our babies were and asked them to take our pictures holding them. We acted as though the nurses had never seen such beautiful babies.

Nicole possessed thick black hair like her brother before his turned blond. Doug's eyes were dark brown like his dad's, but Nicole had eyes the dark blue of deep ocean waters.

Now, twenty-eight years later, on this hot July day in 1999, I stood in a hallway waiting for Nicole to emerge from her ultrasound, pondering my failure to establish that loving relationship with her ... to create the caring, harmonious family of my childhood dreams. For twenty-two years I had lived with unanswered questions despite my desperate search to identify the reasons behind my children's puzzling behavior ... to find help to stop our family's nightmare. Years ago, I had given up all hope of ever knowing, instead agonizing as their lives went from bad to worse.

Today I wondered what Nicole's experience of giving birth would be like. She seemed so lost. How would she ever be able to care for a baby? She wasn't taking care of herself.

I didn't know how to handle being a grandmother in a situation like this. What role was I to take? I felt worn out and lost, too.

I had been contemplating all this with a heavy heart ever since Nicole told me about her pregnancy. Bringing an innocent child into our mess frightened me. I had no confidence this child would turn the situation around. All I could see was more pain and sorrow.

Breaking the chain of family dysfunction and healing family scars was a yearning I had carried in the deepest part of me since I was ten years old. At that tender age, I noticed the psychological scars my mother and her siblings bore. While they were growing up, their dad, a violent drunk, battered his wife in front of them. I learned later he also ran around with other women and infected my grandmother with sexually transmitted diseases. She divorced him while my mother, their eldest, was pregnant with me. We rarely knew his whereabouts after that.

Watching my mother and her siblings bicker at family gatherings,

I developed a strong urge to help them find *a better way* of relating. Of course, at ten I had no way of knowing what that was, but I intended to find out. My search had led to my current professional calling, and I had learned a lot about healthy relationships in my training as a therapist. But everything I learned and all the skills I had accumulated had no effect on my mother, aunts, and uncle ... or the family I helped to create. We fared worse than any of them. I felt like a miserable failure.

The birthing center at the Miami Valley Hospital (MVH) Berry Women's Building was unfamiliar territory to me. Turning Point, the chemical dependency treatment center where I worked as a family therapist, was on the other side of this large urban hospital's campus in Dayton, Ohio. MVH had an excellent reputation. I was grateful my daughter and her baby would receive quality care. It was her circumstances I hated.

While I waited in the hallway outside the ultrasound room, I grumbled internally to God, who seemed to have abandoned my daughter and me. Despite my prayers, our situation had gone from bad to worse. *Wish you would come to me with skin on so I could hear you tell me loud and clear how you would like me to handle this. I'm doing the best I can ... trying to keep my cool ... trying to give Nicole responsibility for her choices ... trying to do it with love. But I'm growing weary. I need your help. Send me a sign I can't miss.*

The door to the ultrasound room opened, and the nurse approached me. "Nicole's having contractions. She can't feel them, but we need to send her to labor and delivery."

I straightened, locking my knees to steady my trembling body. I blurted out, "Oh no. This isn't good. She isn't due for another five weeks. I'm supposed to coach her. We were going to start Lamaze classes next week. We're not ready."

Self-betrayal

1964–1966

Self-betrayal, unlike acts of betrayal that are initiated by others, are often equally if not more painful, because in the end you have to confront the truth that you ignored your own warning signals ...

~Caroline Myss

After graduation from college, I came home for the summer. While Mom helped me carry my belongings from my Ford coupe into our two-story, stucco duplex, our neighbor stopped us on the sidewalk to congratulate me. Mom cut the celebratory mood short when she said, "I worry about what's wrong with Linda. Boys don't seem to be attracted to her."

Doris said, "I've wondered about that, too."

They both turned and looked at me, pity lining their faces. Also worried about what was wrong with me, I didn't know what to say. Even though I'd had boyfriends from the time I was in sixth grade, I had never had a serious relationship. If I was attracted to a boy, I was awkward, as a high school blind date proved. He was a striking, charming guy I would have loved dating. He did his best to engage me in conversation, but I was so bashful and inhibited, I could hardly speak. He must have considered me his worst date ever.

In college, I pined for a guy from afar who didn't know I existed. The only guy I dated was more like a brother to me than a boyfriend. He touched a nerve when he talked to my roommate and called me a prude. He used the same word my mother had used, and I wondered if they were right about me. My mother's off-color jokes embarrassed me, so I told her once that I didn't find them funny. I had a bit of a pious, right/wrong attitude even as a young child. She'd said, "Oh, Linda, you're such a prude."

Girls in my day faced a limited future. Few 1960s women aspired to anything beyond those most important roles of wives and mothers, presenting a dilemma for girls like me who didn't date much. My BS in business education couldn't compete with the degree I lacked—the essential one for 1950s–60s girls—my "MRS" degree.

It's a miracle I went to college. If not for Alice, the parish worker at my church, I never would have. In my senior year of high school, she asked what I planned to do after graduation.

"I don't want to be a secretary, but that's probably what I'll do. I don't know what else to do. I can't be a nurse. I feel like vomiting when somebody else does."

"Why don't you go to college?"

I hadn't considered that option because I had no aptitude for math and science and didn't see myself as smart enough. After Russia launched Sputnik, the first artificial satellite, during my sophomore year, our government charged students with saving our country from communism. "Take math and science so we can beat the Russians in the space race."

I saw typing and shorthand classes as the only options available to me in New Bremen High School's limited curriculum. No one at school or home encouraged me to consider higher education.

High school graduation

I told Alice, "My grades aren't that good. I've only taken secretarial classes. I haven't thought about going to college. What would I major in?"

"You should think about being a parish worker like me."

Alice came to our congregation right out of college and had served as our parish worker the past five years. She assisted our pastor in the office, taught the first-year confirmation class, organized the youth fellowship program, and coordinated our teacher training and education programs.

I tucked Alice's recommendation in the back of my mind and didn't tell my parents about our conversation. I didn't think I dared ask them to send me to an expensive church-sponsored college. Carolyn, my best friend and our class valedictorian, had applied to Bowling Green State University, a less-expensive state school. BGSU seemed a more viable option. I figured I would prefer teaching secretarial courses to doing secretarial work.

I told my parents, "I want to go to Bowling Green and learn how to teach girls to become a secretary."

They still carried hope I would marry, and said, "Why do you want to go to college? You'll just get married and have kids."

It took some doing, but I convinced them a wife and mother could also teach. I learned later business education didn't suit me well, but because I didn't see myself as smart enough for another course of study, it never occurred to me to explore other options. I saw my only choices as persevering through my major or returning to my hometown to work as a secretary. Something in me longed for the larger life a college education would afford, but I was largely unaware of that deeply-buried desire. It took years before I learned to discern the path best suited for me.

After my second year teaching typing, shorthand, and office practice to high school students and two years renting rooms in private homes, I decided to move into a long, brick, three-story apartment building lining Verity Parkway in Middletown, Ohio. I would be living alone for the first time. I chided myself about my queasy stomach. *You'll be fine. You can entertain friends anytime you want.*

While I struggled to lug my furniture, stereo system, boxes of books, and clothes from my car to my new studio apartment three flights up on the top floor, a young man not much older than I reclined on the stoop in a webbed lawn chair. He wore nothing but khaki shorts, his olive skin, black hair, and hairy legs, arms, and chest exposed. I noticed his good looks.

He smiled, his dark brown eyes watching me, and said "Hi" every time I passed but made no offer to help. I excused him. After all, he didn't know me.

But another tenant, a thirtyish woman he greeted by name, passed him carrying two bulging paper grocery bags. As she climbed the stairs to the second floor, one bag broke. Soup cans, apples, and oranges plummeted down the steps toward him. He laughed and offered no help.

"What a jerk," I mumbled.

A few days later, my friends Chuck and Linda came by bearing housewarming gifts. They passed the young man, whose name I later learned was Buddy, sunning himself, always seeming to relish scrutinizing the comings and goings. Linda recognized him. "Beware of that guy sitting on the stoop downstairs. I used to work with him, and he thinks he's God's gift to women." Later, she told me he was divorced.

The next week as I passed him on his front-stoop perch, Buddy asked me out to dinner and a movie. I told him I was busy. He persisted. I resisted. For three weeks he asked, and I declined. But being pursued was a rare experience, and I liked Buddy singling me out as though I was someone special. I found that his attention served as a balm for my core childhood wound, the sting of my mother's preference for my brother.

Linda and her brother, Phil

In my earliest significant memory, I was five years old and taking a long trip with my parents and brother. We drove two hours before turning down a lane, the car tires crunching gravel. Six adults I didn't know came out of a big old farmhouse to greet us. They invited us inside, and when we entered, my mouth watered at the aroma of vegetable soup and fresh-baked bread.

After we ate, my parents and my father's distant relatives retired to the living room. The women sat on the sofa and two overstuffed chairs. The men carried kitchen chairs for themselves, forming a circle with their wives. The huge front porch blocked the diffuse light from the overcast sky, throwing a gray pall over the room.

I joined the adults and played with my doll at the edge of the living room on the wood floor beyond the area rug. I enjoyed listening to their chatter. I didn't know my brother's whereabouts. My mother's voice rose above the hum, "Phil's my favorite. I don't know why. I guess it's because he's my baby."

Hot sparks shot out from my belly to my fingers and toes. Pretending I didn't hear, I wrapped a blanket around my baby doll, held her close, and rocked her.

Because of my sensitivity, when I heard, "Phil's my favorite," a dark cloud enshrouded the sunshine in my five-year-old soul. Other children might not have been affected as I was, but I wondered why my mother didn't love me and began to question my worth. For years, my internal refrain became: *What's wrong with me?*

I developed a strategy for dealing with not being favored: "Maybe if I'm a good girl, if I please Mommy, if I'm not a bother, she'll love me." However, I found my mother difficult to please and easily bothered. Even though by age ten, I had some understanding of the childhood origins of her disgruntled, critical manner, for many years I made it all about me. I searched for affection and approval in others' faces, yearning to be favored in someone's eyes. After I climbed in bed at night, I would sift through the day counting my flaws and ways I might have offended someone. I promised myself I would do better the next day.

At age thirty-five, I read a section in Trina Paulus's book, *Hope for the Flowers*, that revealed the inadequacy of my childhood strategy. "How does one become a butterfly? You must want to fly so much that you're willing to give up being a caterpillar."[1] I saw for the first time how counting my flaws only reinforced my belief that I was an ugly worm. Yet, I sensed that inside me lived a butterfly with a deep desire to fly. I needed to find a way to fly free of my childhood baggage.

However, at twenty-three I was considered an old maid. With my mother's words still ringing in my ears, "I worry about what is wrong with Linda. Boys don't seem to be attracted to her," my interest in Buddy heightened. He was good looking after all, and he did seem attracted to me. One evening I caught a glimpse of him through my living room window as he arrived home from work. I hid behind the curtain and watched him park his turquoise Thunderbird convertible. He paused by the door and surveyed the parking lot before strolling toward our building wearing dark green slacks, a matching plaid jacket, a green flecked tie, and a yellow straw fedora. No one this handsome had ever shown interest in me. With the scarcity in my dating history, I didn't think I could afford to reject him any longer. I needed to prove to my mother she was wrong about me. And I needed to prove that to myself. So I decided to give him a chance. The first week in July, I agreed to a date.

He was on vacation, so that date led to a week of constant togetherness. I enjoyed our hugging and kissing, but amorous Buddy's hands sliding next to my breasts as we came up for air made me uncomfortable. I felt rushed but didn't say so for fear of pushing him away or proving my worries about prudishness right.

One night Buddy's voice quivered when he said he had something he needed to tell me. He said, "I'm afraid you won't want to be with me when I tell you this. I've been married before."

"I already know. Linda told me. It doesn't matter."

I shudder looking back at my lack of wisdom and experience. It didn't occur to me to ask Buddy what he had learned about his contribution to his marriage not working or what he planned to do differently in our relationship.

That weekend we traveled to meet each other's families. During our visit with his family, I sized him up as a potential good father as I watched him interact with his delightful preschool-age niece and nephew who seemed to adore him. After meeting each other's families, we declared our love. The day his vacation ended and he returned to work, a dozen red roses were delivered to my door. I breathed in their sweet fragrance as I read the note: "Thank you for helping me spend one of the most enjoyable weeks of my life. Love, Buddy."

One week later, on my twenty-fourth birthday, he gave me an engagement ring. When word reached our neighbors, they grabbed my hand and admired my ring. They expounded on what a great guy Buddy was. I told Chuck and Linda, "He's God's gift to *this* woman." It had been only six weeks since I first saw him sunning himself on that stoop.

Two weeks later we abandoned our initial plan to wait a year and began planning a Thanksgiving wedding. Buddy wanted to save money on rent by marrying sooner. I acquiesced and, to save more money, began cooking and eating at his place. We were together every possible moment.

Enchanted by romance's elixir, I threw myself headlong into this relationship, believing I had arrived as a woman. A man attracted to and wanting to marry me gave me a sense of worth. I would have to make sure nothing happened to ruin this opportunity to become "right" in my mother's and our culture's eyes. It took me years to learn my worth is inherent and can only be found by journeying within—a painful, but ultimately, liberating lesson.

I wanted to hold my wedding in the progressive church that had become important to me after I moved to Middletown in 1965. Following my first visit to the local United Church of Christ, their pastor called on me. As our conversation ended, Rev. McNamara said, "We at St. Paul's would like to be your family away from home." People at church had served as a lifeline since my elementary school days, so his invitation touched me deeply. I joined the church and attended regularly.

When I contacted the church office to make wedding arrangements, I learned premarital counseling was customary. The secretary gave me questionnaires for Buddy and me to fill out and return in preparation for a first meeting with the pastor. If I hadn't been so dead set on walking down that aisle, I might have been open to taking a closer look at the challenges we would likely face, challenges Rev. McNamara noticed immediately. In our first session, he asked how we would deal with two glaring differences—religion and education.

Looking at Rev. McNamara holding his pipe and leaning back in his swivel chair on the other side of his desk, I said, "Buddy isn't comfortable in his family's church. He wants to come to church with me."

Buddy nodded. He had stopped attending his family's conservative, fundamentalist congregation before I met him. "I never liked altar calls. They try to force you to come forward and get baptized. Your church doesn't do that, so I'm okay coming here."

Rev. McNamara puffed on his pipe.

I didn't say so, but I felt lucky to have found a man willing to attend church with me. I believed Mom and Dad's marriage and our family would have been happier if they had been active in the church.

I continued, "Only two people in my family graduated college, my cousin Wanda and me. My dad quit school after eleventh grade and worked his way up into a management position."

I looked at Buddy, "And you did the same thing, didn't you? You started out in the shop?"

He nodded.

I turned back to Rev. McNamara. "And now Buddy has the same title as my dad—Production Control Manager."

Rev. McNamara leaned forward in his chair and stared at our questionnaires on his desk as though looking for another way to approach the subject. I wanted him to express happiness for us, and when he didn't, my bubble of joy burst. I couldn't see how Buddy not having a college education created a problem.

In one last attempt to explain, I said, "My dad always provided well for our family. Buddy makes a good enough living."

I didn't know how else to respond to Rev. McNamara's concerns and was unprepared to listen to the part of me who knew he was on to something significant.

I never gave thought to values and couldn't have identified mine if asked. As a young woman, I possessed little awareness of wants and needs and had never learned to verbalize mine. I didn't know and didn't know I didn't know what I wanted in a marriage beyond one *better* than my parents'. I still had not learned to listen to my inner wisdom to discern the best course for my life. Rev. McNamara couldn't find a way into a discussion about these deeper issues.

As I learned years later when I provided counseling to couples planning to marry, they rarely comprehend the significance of red flags, no matter how glaring. The feel-good chemical cocktail of adrenaline, dopamine, serotonin, and oxytocin floods couples "in love," causing their brains to go offline. In addition, I thought marriage was mandatory for me. For lots of reasons, my pastor didn't have a chance.

But one Friday afternoon while playing domestic diva in Buddy's apartment, a major difference did begin to bother me. After putting a pot roast in the oven, I began dusting and running the sweeper. I noticed for the first time Buddy's lack of bookshelves and books. Books were my friends. Biographies and historical fiction gave me a window into the wider world and showed me how people relate to each other, providing content in my search for *a better way*. I wanted to be able to discuss what I read with my husband. I decided to talk to Buddy about my concern over dinner.

I trembled inside. This discussion held the potential for ending my hope to prove there was nothing wrong with me. Besides, there might be conflict, and I hated conflict. I worked up the nerve to say, "While I dusted today, I noticed you don't have any books and bookshelves in your apartment."

He glanced up, and responded, "Yeah?" and continued eating.

"Don't you like to read?"

"No, not really."

He finished dinner with no expression of interest in my question. I didn't know where to go next. After we cleaned the kitchen with no more discussion about books and reading, he flipped on the television. Disappointment surged through me.

His major interest was the TV and we didn't even like the same programs. He could watch the same Western over and over. I had difficulty finding any program so interesting I couldn't stand to miss it. Human interest and educational programming didn't exist at that time. Football occupying his attention every weekend left me feeling lonely. The TV had become like another woman competing for his attention, and she was winning. I had noticed this before, but now it hit me hard.

Crestfallen, I returned to my apartment upstairs and to the current novel capturing my attention. As I read, I fought off admitting to myself how much Buddy's lack of intellectual curiosity bothered me. *Am I a snob?* That night I tossed and turned, unable to fall asleep. Thoughts swarmed through my head. *If I break our engagement, I'll prove Mom and everybody right. Something is wrong with me, and I might never have another chance at marriage. But what will life be like married to someone with interests so different from mine? Arrangements for the church and the reception have been made; the invitations ordered. How can I call it off now?*

A voice inside me spoke clearly, "You're not a good match for each other."

I took note of this unmistakable warning—the first time I had received such an unambiguous message from the still small voice of wisdom within. The next day I tried to give expression to my misgivings. I told Buddy, "I'm having second thoughts about our getting married. I'm not sure we're right for each other."

He responded with an authoritative tone. "If you aren't sure by now, you never will be." He showed no curiosity or concern about my qualms. His "by now" referenced the two or so months we had known each other.

Between my lack of intimate communication skills and my ignorance of the importance of trusting and heeding my inner guidance, I was unable to advocate for myself. I conceded, "I guess you're right."

A month before the wedding, my parents came to visit. The October leaves were ablaze in reds, oranges, and yellows. We decided to take a drive to view the fall finery.

I invited Buddy, "We're going for a ride to see the leaves. Want to go?"

"No, I'm gonna watch the game."

I exhaled a heavy sigh and glared at him. My parents observed as he ignored me. I whirled around and headed for the door, signaling to Mom and Dad to follow. We piled into my car and headed toward country roads, my disappointment permeating the atmosphere.

My mother broke the silence. "You can still call this off."

"That's a decision *I* have to make."

My forceful reply shocked me. Behind what sounded like anger stood guilt for being what I thought was a promiscuous woman. I had stepped outside my "good girl" role and slept with Buddy. I was so confused. To my mother, it wasn't okay to be a prude, but I also felt sure she would disapprove of my having given up my virginity before marriage.

Girls engaging in premarital sex in the 1950s and '60s were considered tramps. The so-called "free love" movement didn't gain momentum until the '70s. As I prepared to marry Buddy in 1966, I still carried a '50s-girl mindset. *No other man will want a tarnished woman. I have to get married. I'm stuck.*

Thanksgiving Day 1966

Years of heartache later, I realized the "wrong" of premarital sex pales in comparison with the "wrong" of betraying your innermost self. Sadly, I possessed little relationship with my depths, my inner voice of wisdom. It was as though I fumbled my way through dense fog.

I couldn't tell my parents why I "had" to marry Buddy. We drove on in silence.

Marriage—
An Unwise Agreement

1966

*The unwavering truth is that when we agree to any demand,
request, or condition that is contrary to our soul's nature,
the cost is that precious life force is drained off our core.*

~Mark Nepo

Unaware I possessed inner wisdom that I needed to heed, I walked down the aisle and said "I do" to another future that was not a good fit for me. Just as I had chosen a college major that didn't suit me, now I chose a mate who wasn't a good match. I didn't know myself or the importance of choosing a path in alignment with my soul—one leading to well-being. I continued trying to make the best of my wrong turns.

After college graduation, I worked at being a conscientious business education teacher. After our honeymoon, I trudged toward the 1960s myth of "happily ever after," as though I could find some way to make straight the crooked paths I had chosen. However, being out of sync with one's heart and soul grates on a person, like the gnashing of gears with missing teeth.

As I look back, I find my hunger for love intensifying at age ten years old. When we moved to my mother's hometown, New Bremen, a small farming community in northwest Ohio, I lost a loving surrogate family and a host of playmates in our previous neighborhood. Worse was the loss of my parents' open expression of affection. Before the move, hugging and kissing seemed natural to Mom and Dad. But now Mom scowled and shrugged Dad off. For the first time, I heard them arguing after my brother and I went to bed. Mom's thin lips took on a sour frown, and her small hazel eyes glared in irritation.

Even though Mom paved the way for Dad's job at Crown Controls, a business established by her former classmate, I imagine she found it hard to move back to the town where she had experienced so much trauma growing up. She thought people there looked on her as the town drunk's daughter. A couple of years after the move, Dad confided his thoughts to me, "I wonder if your mother loves me at all. I almost didn't marry her and sometimes wish I hadn't." I understood and felt sorry for him. Mom seemed displeased with both of us. Fear of Dad's leaving Mom, losing him along with what little protection he provided against her biting criticism, filled me with dread.

Family get-togethers didn't make Mom happy or ease the tension in our house. I observed my mother and her four siblings as the decibels rose, their laughter switching to bickering. I found it confusing when they separated in a huff and then came back together later as though nothing had happened. Instead, they'd laugh and joke and play cards and make an effort to avoid the sudden eruption of festering childhood wounds. Before long the drama started again. They didn't seem to know how to handle their feelings any other way. It jangled my nerves.

They regarded my serious nature as "weird." I couldn't remember a joke's punch line and failed at the competitive card games they loved. Shoved to the sidelines of their merrymaking, I didn't fit into this jolly but contentious tribe. With a heavy heart, I blamed the specter of alcoholism and held to the belief that my family loved each other but didn't know how to express it. I wanted more than anything to be part of a happy family able to show their love for each other. Focusing on how to help them find *a better way* distracted me from my pain.

Church became the place I relied on to meet my relational needs. I was seven years old the first time I experienced the love and acceptance I longed for. Mom took my brother and me to St. Paul's Evangelical and Reformed Church in Sidney, Ohio. Dad stayed home. One morning as we strolled down the red carpeted aisle, I swelled with wonder at the warm glow cast over the sanctuary from the light shining through the stained glass windows. The soft organ music competed with the gathering congregants' whispers and added to the ambience. I watched in fascination as the choir, wearing burgundy robes and white stoles, filed into the loft behind the lectern, pulpit, and altar and took their seats facing the congregation.

When I spotted the older sister of a neighborhood playmate in the choir, I poked Mom's arm and pointed, "Look, Mom, there's

Fred's sister."

Shirley noticed and smiled at me. I scrunched close to Mom and buried my face in her arm. When I peeked out, Shirley wore a bigger grin. Her beauty awed me—her glistening chestnut eyes and ruby lips; her sleek, stylish bob cut below her ears and curled at her temples; her black hair framing her ivory skin; her slender figure. Each week I anticipated the smile she never failed to flash. It spelled love.

One day I arrived home after school to find her waiting for me. Mom said, "Shirley wants to know if you would like to be the flower girl in her wedding."

I must have looked ridiculous standing there speechless, but my heart was so happy I didn't have the words to express my joy.

"Would you like that?" Shirley asked.

I wanted to jump up and down and exclaim, "Yes. Yes. Yes." I wanted to hug her and feel her arms around me. But I avoided disapproval by being quiet and restrained, especially around Mom. Giving no hint at the waves of specialness washing over me, I murmured, "Yes." Inside I rejoiced. *She's choosing me. I must be her favorite.*

When we moved to New Bremen, Mom stopped attending church, using Dad's refusal to go as an excuse. But I could walk to church so I continued. When I was twelve years old, our congregation hired Alice, the parish worker who later recommended I go to college. Young, vivacious, and fun, Alice always had a smile on her face. Every chance we could, my friend Saundra and I climbed the stairs to Alice's three-room apartment on the top floor of the old parsonage across the street from the church. We enjoyed hanging out at her place, and because she lived alone and didn't know many townsfolk yet, she welcomed our company.

I remember most how Alice made me feel. When we spent time alone, she treated me as someone important to her. She listened as though interested in what I thought and how I felt. She didn't seem to consider it "weird" talking about serious topics. She gave me the individual attention I received from no one else. I felt "at home" with Alice and wished she could adopt me so I could live with her.

Thus having these positive experiences with members of my church, I naively believed marrying a religious man would engender the same attention and affection I had experienced with Shirley and Alice. But Buddy's choosing TV over spending quality time with me and showing no interest in connecting with me emotionally only recreated the isolation I had experienced in my childhood home. I hadn't anticipated the effect of his lack of intellectual curiosity, his lack of enthusiasm about anything consequential. My loneliness intensified at not being able to share something vital to my existence–personal and spiritual growth.

Later in life, through my professional training, I met couples committed to an equal partnership in support of each other's growth and healing. They helped me articulate the better way that had been the source of my longing since I was ten years old. This is all so clear to me now, but in 1966, I groped my way through heavy fog, attempting to ameliorate my growing disenchantment by focusing on what was working in our marriage.

Our first year of marriage proceeded without serious conflict and only one minor disruption. We were both frugal with our paychecks, but Buddy liked to control the finances. The first time we sat at the kitchen table to pay our bills, he asked me to account for how I had spent my allowance down to the last penny. I wracked my brain trying to remember how I'd spent the money before it dawned on me that this was nonsense. "I don't have to remember every pack of gum or bag of chips I buy. This is crazy. It's my money to spend as I wish. I don't ask you to account for how you spend your allowance."

Buddy backed down.

Our social life revolved around Buddy's family. My parents weren't interested in socializing with us, my brother lived at a distance, and we had only one couple as friends. Most weekends we visited his parents' or brother's homes in Cincinnati. I loved their tradition of celebrating birthdays. At first, their enjoyment of each other's company raised my hopes for being part of a loving family. However, Buddy's mother's coolness toward me left me on edge when I was around her. She later revealed to me that she feared getting too close to me and eventually losing our relationship as had happened with Buddy's first wife. My sister-in-law's idea of conversation centered on gossiping and criticizing people I didn't know. The guys watched sports on TV. Still, I tried to fit in.

We agreed on the purchase of our first home in Germantown, a small community two miles from where I taught. Buddy's nine-mile commute to work and our drive to church in Middletown seemed doable. Even though I preferred the charm of older homes, we could afford this lovely ranch in a new subdivision attracting young families. We moved Buddy's furniture into our family room and master bedroom. He showed no interest in joining me to choose furnishings for our living room. He didn't care what I selected as long as I stayed within our budget.

I felt valued when Buddy joined me in cleaning the kitchen after dinner, my detested childhood responsibility. I showed consideration for his meat-and-potatoes tastes in meal preparation, even though I enjoyed more adventurous fare. He seemed happy and content as long as we handled daily activities such as doing chores, shopping for groceries, and preparing meals in a way he preferred.

By the time our second year of marriage rolled around, with the milestone of buying and furnishing our first home behind us, I began to grow restless after dinner. We had little to talk about, so most evenings I read while he watched TV. He had no friends or outside activities. We socialized some with Chuck and Linda, my friends who had warned me to beware of him. We moved to Germantown in part because they lived there. We went to movies together on occasion and invited each other to our homes for dinner. Chuck and I worked together, so our spouses attended some school functions with us. But still, they had their own lives, and I couldn't depend on them to be available whenever I felt the need for stimulating conversation.

I decided to break my isolation by joining the Bible study group at church, the milieu that had always valued my serious nature. When some of the group went for pizza afterward, I went with them and made new friends. Most of them were married and talked about getting together to socialize. I wanted Buddy to join me in developing a social network with these friends. He attended worship but showed no interest in other church activities. A conversation about this issue arose on our drive home after services one Sunday. After we arrived home, it escalated into a battle.

I broached the subject in the car. "Gibby said she and Bob are having some friends from church over to their house later for a cookout. She invited us. I'd like to go."

Buddy asked for clarification to make sure he knew whom I was talking about. After I described their features, he remembered meeting them but said nothing more.

I continued, "The Bible study group plans get-togethers. It makes me feel good to be included."

He continued driving and didn't respond to my enthusiasm.

The first thing he did when we walked into the house was flip on the TV. My impatience for a response from him turned to alarm and then anger. "What are you doing?"

"I'm checkin' to see what time the game comes on. It's s'posed to be good. I've been countin' on it all week."

"I'm tired of you watching TV all the time and football every Sunday. I want to go to Gibby and Bob's. Can't you miss one game to do something with me?"

"They're your friends. I'd just be bored. You can go without me."

"It's for couples. I don't want to go alone. Married couples are supposed to do things together."

"So, you could watch the game with me. Then we'd be doin' somethin' together," he mocked.

"I'm not interested in your damn football games."

He turned his back. Nothing I said made any difference. My insides boiled.

"I refuse to be a blob in front of the TV like you. I'm sick of it."

I stormed out, slammed the door, climbed in my car, and headed north toward New Bremen. I rehearsed what to say to my parents. *I've made a big mistake. I need out of this marriage. Please, help me.*

But humiliation and self-doubt won the day. I can see the smirk on Mom's face. I'll prove her right. Something is wrong with me. I can't bear hearing them say I have nothing to complain about. Buddy doesn't beat me, and he makes decent money. Being miserable and lonely isn't a good enough reason to end a marriage.

I felt lost and alone as I reversed my direction and headed back to Dayton. To kill extra time, I grabbed a bite to eat and took in a movie. I dreaded going back to that house—to that life.

The sun dipped below the horizon as I turned the car toward Germantown. When I entered the house, Buddy, holding a plate of chips and a sandwich, passed me on his way to the family room. He threw me a relieved glance, but said nothing, and headed for the couch. The football game's blaring stabbed at my heart like a knife. I headed for the bedroom, picked up my current novel, crawled under the covers, lost myself in someone else's life, and fell asleep before Buddy came to bed.

The next morning we awoke and went through our getting-ready-for-work routine in silence. No discussion about the day before arose; our differences remained unresolved. Once more our dearth of intimate communication skills rendered us impotent in working out our dissimilarities. The atmosphere in our home grew flat and lifeless.

The Worst Kind of Loneliness

1968

You see, the worst kind of loneliness comes to people who are, technically, not alone.

~Dr. Mardy Grothe

Five months into my pregnancy, I walked into the kitchen just as Buddy opened a cupboard door looking for a snack. I felt a rippling sensation in my abdomen and wanted to share the wonder and joy of our baby's movements with him. I reached for his hand and guided it toward my belly. "Come, feel. The baby's kicking."

He recoiled without a word, turned his back, and walked toward the family room. I shriveled inside.

I thought my mother would be pleased to have her first grandchild on the way, so I extended an invitation. "Mom, I'm due the middle of August. Will you come to help out after the baby's born?"

She said, "Well, I don't know. That's golfing season."

Her words, worse than a slap in the face, rendered me mute.

I decided to ask Buddy's mother. She was thrilled because mothers of boys rarely receive such an invitation. She never expected to have this experience. To my relief, her initial coolness toward me began to dissipate.

My baby bed had been passed around the family, and now I wanted my first child to sleep in the crib that had held me as an infant. My mother helped me retrieve it from the cousin who had last used it. Buddy liked that we wouldn't have to buy a new one. He left decisions about furnishing the nursery to me. I complemented the room's jungle animal wallpaper with a giant stuffed lion. Buddy painted a secondhand chest of drawers red, white, and blue, and I selected a matching throw rug. I moved my stereo system in, planning to play classical music because it was believed that would raise a baby's IQ.

Two weeks after my due date, the morning of one of Ohio's hottest, humid August days, my labor finally began. On the way to the hospital, Buddy stopped for gas. While he filled the tank, my feet pushed against the floorboard as I bore down with another contraction. *So much for preparation.*

Once I settled into the bed in my sparsely furnished, stark white hospital room, Buddy slumped into the straight-backed chair nearby and sat stone-faced. The only window faced another hospital wing's brick wall. Long fluorescent bulbs added to the bleakness. I would have welcomed a TV to provide a distraction from the silence between us.

As my contractions grew intense, I cried out. Buddy squirmed in his chair. Laughter and animated conversation emanated from the nurse's station a short distance down the hall. I felt certain the nurses could hear me, but no one responded.

Do they hear women crying out in pain all the time so it's no big deal to them? Guess I shouldn't make a fuss. I would like to know how far along I am ... how much longer this might last. Is the pain going to get worse? How are they going to help me deal with it? I wish I had someone to talk with ... someone who seems to care.

Dr. Hammill arrived late afternoon to check on my progress. He said the six hours I had been in labor was long enough so he was going to induce. An attendant wheeled me into the delivery room while Buddy headed for the fathers' lounge. The anesthesiologist administered a saddle block, and soon I was numb from the waist down.

I told the doctor, "Don't forget. I want to watch." My mother had often relayed how glad she was to be knocked out when my brother and I were born. I didn't want to miss a thing.

Dr. Hammill pointed to a mirror close to the ceiling aimed at the delivery table. I experienced awe as I shared the miracle of birth with that mirror. As my baby emerged from my womb, he gave out a hearty cry. "You have a healthy baby boy," the doctor announced. He looked at the clock, and said, "4:43." The nurses whisked him away to a nearby sink and table.

After dinner, a nurse brought our son to the room where I had been moved. Buddy stood by the bed fidgeting when she handed the baby to me. I had insisted Buddy participate in choosing a name. We searched for one complementing Keith, Buddy's middle name. Douglas Keith sounded good to us.

The nurse left the three of us alone for the first time. I opened Doug's blanket and counted his fingers and toes. Buddy stood there staring at me and his namesake, stiff and wooden. I wished I could read his mind. I hoped he was happy to have a son. Surely he must be feeling the same sense of relief I felt that we had a healthy baby ... my same mix of emotions at being a parent. But after he refused to share in my joy at feeling our baby kick inside my belly, I couldn't risk disappointment again. I kept my happiness, doubts, and fears to myself.

Much later, Buddy did reveal his reactions. He admitted to jealousy and fear the baby would come between us. I frowned and walked away, muttering under my breath, "The TV came between us long ago. You're not the least bit concerned about that."

I did want Buddy's mother's help, but on the way home from the hospital uneasiness about my ability to hold my ground with her weighed on me. I looked forward to taking care of my baby, a pleasure I wanted all for myself. How would I handle it if she took over? But she surprised me when she said, "I'll take care of everything except the baby. If you want me to do something for him, ask and I'll be happy to do it."

My heart warmed toward her. However, that evening while drying myself outside the shower stall, I overheard a conversation she and Buddy were having in the family room. The hair on the back of my neck raised as I heard them planning how to spend my teacher retirement money. *He hasn't said anything to me about this. I haven't given any thought to my retirement account. He obviously has.* Still exhausted and weak, my anger bolstered me. As soon as I could corner him out of earshot of his mother, I said, "I overheard you and your mother talking about my retirement money."

"Yea, we thought it would be a good idea to put it toward ..."

"You were talking about this with your *mother*? Don't you think it would have been better to talk with *me*? It is *my* retirement money after all."

He grinned sheepishly, "Well, I guess so."

"I'm leaving that money right where it is. If I go back to teaching, which I probably will, it will go toward my retirement. If I don't go back to teaching, then *I'll* decide how it should be spent."

He grumbled, "Okay, okay," shrugged, and walked away, a vexed expression on his face.

Somehow I was able to find my voice around finances. I had more confidence in handling money than in expressing my emotional wants and needs. It must have been those accounting classes I struggled through in college.

Buddy's mother helped out for a week before she returned home. The first night on our own, Buddy headed for the family room and flipped on the TV after dinner instead of joining me in cleaning up the kitchen as usual. I felt as though I had been kicked in the gut. My chagrin went deeper than his insensitivity to the fatigue I experienced caring for our baby, our home, and preparing meals—the isolation exhausting me more than a day of teaching. Over time I realized Buddy only valued my work when it came with a paycheck. The father of my baby didn't value child-rearing, the most important job anyone could hold. It appeared that he would not be my partner in parenting any more than he was proving to be my partner in marriage. This small withdrawal of joining me in doing the dishes after dinner foreshadowed how alone I would be in the years to come.

Trust

1968–1972

Trust yourself. You know more than you think you do.

~Benjamin Spock, M.D.

Before Doug's birth, signs were there pointing to the difficulty I would experience as a parent, but I missed their significance. Growing up, I wasn't around babies and toddlers much. The first baby I remember holding cried. After that I tensed up every time I picked up an infant. My experience as a babysitter was limited, and I didn't feel comfortable in that role. I knew how to keep the children in my charge physically safe, but I didn't know how to play with them or how to respond when they acted out. I avoided acting out at home to escape my parents' worst methods of discipline—Mom's biting criticism and slaps to my face; Dad's belt swinging at my behind and legs. I knew it was unacceptable to physically correct children, but once, in exasperation, I gave a child a swat on the behind with my hand. My parents' friends never asked me to babysit for them again.

With little experience and no good role models to guide me, my preparation for parenthood left much to be desired. It didn't take long for my insecurity to show itself. On our first day home from the hospital, I stood next to the bassinet in the family room looking at my contented baby—his sable eyes wide open, his little arms moving back and forth. I restrained my longing, and said to my husband and mother-in-law, "I want to hold him, but I'm afraid I'll spoil him."

My mother-in-law said, "He's your baby. If you want to hold him, hold him."

Having been given permission, I reached down to pick him up. Breathing in his sweet baby powder scent, I smiled with satisfaction when he didn't cry. Moving to my antique platform rocker, I relaxed as Doug settled into my arms, made little grunting sounds, and soon fell fast asleep. I gazed in awe at this little miracle and felt a huge desire to be a good mother rising from deep within. Shuddering at the remembrance of my parents' methods of disciplining my brother and me, I wanted to be a different kind of parent.

Lost in thought and oblivious to Buddy and his mother's conversation as I rocked my infant son, I couldn't imagine ever whipping Doug with a belt or slapping his face. I wanted to grant him the freedom to be a little kid, not the miniature grown-up I had felt forced to be. I longed to give him the understanding and support that had been denied to me, to give explanations so he understood my reasoning when I needed to set limits with him. I wanted him always to see love in my face. Scary images of rebellious, troublemaking teenagers reinforced my belief about the importance of handling parenting "correctly" while he was young. Doug pulled me out of my musings when he let out a little sigh, his chin moved up and down, and his lips made a sucking sound.

At the baby shower thrown before his birth, I had received two books—Benjamin Spock's *Baby and Child Care*, a parent's child-rearing Bible in the late 1960s, and Frances Ilg's, Louise Bates Ames's, and Sidney Baker's *The Geselle Institute's Child Behavior*. Dr. Spock encouraged mothers to trust themselves, saying we know more than we think we do. Just in case he was wrong about me, I decided to adopt Spock, Ilg, and Baker (pediatricians) and Ames (a child psychologist) as my expert guides.

Somehow Buddy's attitude toward parenting changed. I hoped his willingness to be involved would last. He took a turn feeding Doug and found he could manage it. He even changed diapers on occasion. He boasted to family and friends about Doug's latest achievements and bragged about his milestones. When I grew antsy being away from my friends and the intellectual stimulation and connection they provided, he offered to "babysit" so I could continue attending my weekly Bible study. I'm sure that made me easier to live with.

I loved participating in the birthday celebrations for Buddy's niece and nephew and imagined his family doing the same for Doug's first birthday. I went all out in preparing, decorating the family room and his cake in a jungle animal theme. However, when Buddy's brother, Ritchie, and his family arrived, Lena, his brother's wife, announced they needed to leave early. I felt as though a bomb had dropped on my expectations.

Interpreting their behavior as a slight to our son, I looked to Buddy to stand up for Doug ... to tell Ritchie our son deserved the same consideration we showed to his children. But I was the only one upset. Buddy's blasé manner was like throwing water on the fire building inside me.

I fell back into old coping mechanisms. Like a chameleon changing colors to fit into its environment, I obediently went about pleasing people whom in that moment I didn't like. I squeezed the celebration into my in-laws' timeframe and hurried Doug in opening his gifts. He began playing with a new toy when I took it away and handed him another package to open. He protested loudly. I didn't blame him. I blamed them. But in truth, I ruined my son's first birthday. The energy it took to squelch my anger made it impossible to consider a way to meet everybody's needs.

A worse event occurred while I still seethed with resentment about Doug's birthday fiasco. This time it was over how Buddy and I had decided to celebrate Christmas.

Before Doug turned one, we had observed Christmas at Buddy's parents' home. Because my brother lived at a distance, my parents complied with what worked best for us and joined us there. But when Doug reached the age to enjoy the holiday, I wanted us to create traditions for our immediate family. So, shortly before Thanksgiving, I initiated a conversation with Buddy about my concern that Doug be allowed to open and play with his new toys on Christmas Day without interruption. I shared my hope for this to become our tradition. We agreed to be available on any other day to celebrate with family and to open our home on Christmas Day to family who wanted to come be with us. Buddy communicated our plans to his parents.

In early December, we visited Ritchie and Lena's home to celebrate our niece's birthday. After dinner, I joined Lena, her brother and his family, and the children in the basement playroom. I did my best to engage in conversation with these people I barely knew. When a discussion arose about Christmas, I shared the plan Buddy and I had developed so Doug wouldn't be dragged away from his toys. Lena's voice rang out from across the room, "I think you're selfish."

I felt as though a two-ton truck had hit me. Her family grew quiet for a few seconds, and then conversation resumed with no comment on what had just happened. I waited in silence to regain my equilibrium, picked up Doug, and went upstairs to find Buddy. I passed his mother and Lena's sitting at the kitchen table talking. I found Buddy in the living room watching football with his dad and brother. I told him I was ready to leave.

We went to the bedroom to fetch our coats. Lena came in, closed the door, and directed her remarks at me. She said our Christmas plans had so upset Buddy's mother, she was about to have a nervous breakdown. Buddy said nothing. I couldn't get out of there fast enough.

It seemed I had stepped on Christmas traditions developed to accommodate Lena's family after she married Buddy's brother—traditions Buddy went along with but didn't know were set in stone. Ritchie and Lena had alternated spending Christmas Eve and Day with each set of parents. Lena seemed furious about my interference in their already instituted pattern.

On the way home, I told Buddy what had happened in the basement and emphasized our need to talk with his mother. I asked him to take the lead in the conversation. Conflict scared me and I avoided it whenever possible. I couldn't avoid this.

When we called his mother later that evening, Buddy did little more than get the conversation started. I asked my mother-in-law to talk with me when I upset her. It didn't occur to me that was a two-way street. I just wanted to avoid being talked about behind my back as I had witnessed Lena and her mother doing often. I didn't like being their most recent topic. Even though I didn't believe our plan was selfish or out of the ordinary, I took responsibility for "almost causing my mother-in-law to have a nervous breakdown." At that time, I was unaware that it was a common manipulative ploy. My mother-in-law did go on to apologize for wanting the holidays to be done her way.

We, however, complied with Buddy's family's wishes and never developed our own traditions, something I lament to this day. Without Buddy's support, I didn't possess the backbone to stand up to them. From that point forward, to tolerate visits with his family, I brought a book along to hide behind. Once more, I was dubbed as "weird"—the serious, studious one with my nose in a book.

Despite this setback with Buddy's family, I looked for the positive in our relationship at home. When Buddy showed a willingness to learn from Dr. Spock, my hopes for our being partners in parenting increased. Dr. Spock's advice had worked in handling Doug's fears of the dark, his likes and dislikes, so we decided to follow his recommended potty training techniques.

Dr. Spock said around two years old a child begins to give "a meaningful grunt." I had noticed Doug doing that a couple of months before he turned two, so I took him to the bathroom, sat him in his potty chair, and gave him toys to entertain himself. He sat there playing for quite some time before wanting up. I pointed to his poo, praised him, and said, "What a big boy you are." More interested in returning to his toys in the family room, he paid no attention. Dr. Spock said this means a child isn't ready, so we decided to give Doug more time.

During this time, I talked with Buddy about having another child. We agreed Doug needed a little brother or sister. In August, when Doug was two, I stopped taking birth control pills. In October 1970, we learned I was two-months pregnant.

About this time, my mother expressed disgust with me because Doug, a little over two-and-a-half years old, was still wearing diapers. She had bragged about having trained me by the time I was nine months of age. Feeling pressured and doubting my own judgment, I began to coerce Doug. When I sensed he might be ready for a bowel movement, I forced him to sit on his potty chair. He refused and pooped in his diaper instead. I grumbled while cleaning him up, making us both miserable. Finally, I decided to let him be.

A few days later, Doug said to his daddy, "I have to have a stinky." Amazed, I followed them to the bathroom. Buddy and I watched and waited. When Doug said he was done, to our delight he had been successful. We let out a cheer and gave

Doug holding Nicole

him a hug. We each told him, "I'm so happy at what a big boy you are." This time Doug beamed with pride. Buddy and I shared a triumphant parenting moment. A month later, when Doug was two years and eight months, we had crossed this hurdle. That meant we would have only one in diapers when our second child arrived in June.

My mother made it clear she was coming to help out this time. She claimed she had been kidding about it being golfing season when Doug was born. And as it turned out, I received just the help I needed after the birth of each of my children. When we returned home from the hospital after Nicole's birth, my mother proceeded to handle everything without asking what I wanted or needed. I welcomed her take-charge style because this time the doctor ordered physical restrictions and requirements for rest.

Nicole was such an easy baby. She slept through the night by the time she was eight weeks old. She faced her first major challenge at four months when her twisted thigh bone required her to wear hard-soled shoes. Later, a brace was attached to the shoes for twenty hours a day. She didn't let that stop her. She rolled and heaved her legs in whatever direction she wanted. At seven months, the brace was removed during the day and her hard-soled shoes replaced with corrective ones. She walked at nine-and-a-half months.

With Nicole's cheery disposition, Buddy took having a second child in stride. Doug added, "Thank you for my baby sister" to his nightly prayers. Our family felt complete with the addition of this delightful child.

I tried to make friends with other young mothers in our subdivision for adult conversation during ordinary days. I enjoyed comparing notes on potty training and teething but could only do that for so long when I wanted to move on to more substantive topics. We were sending young men to Vietnam to fight and die. The Ohio National Guard shot at unarmed protesting students at Kent State, only three-and-a-half hours from our home. Four of them died, and nine were injured. I wanted to know how other mothers felt about allowing their children to play with toy guns.

My next door neighbor invited me and other mothers in the neighborhood to a Tupperware party at her house. It included the usual "silly" games; one involved naming our favorite television program. Everyone else identified a soap opera. When I offered *Phil Donahue* as mine, they all looked at me as though I had three heads. I didn't fit in.

I pleaded with Buddy to move back to Middletown. I wanted to live closer to my friends in the Bible study group—the friends who provided the stimulation I needed. He eventually capitulated, and when Nicole was one and Doug almost four, we made the move.

Intuition

1972–1974

The only real valuable thing is intuition.

~Albert Einstein

In 1972, we bought a three-story Dutch Colonial with natural woodwork, built-in bookshelves, hardwood floors, and a big front porch on an enchanting tree-lined avenue. I was thrilled with this charming older home. Our street in Middletown, one long block between a busy thoroughfare and an elementary school, overflowed with children of all ages.

At first, the boys Doug's age picked on him, hit and pushed him, grabbed his toys, and ran away. He wasn't used to playing with other kids and didn't know what to do. He ran home crying. I tried to teach him to stand up for himself, but he found a more workable strategy. He followed after older kids who protected him. Soon the taunting stopped. Doug became best friends with Tony, a boy a year younger who lived a few doors down.

Despite his shaky beginning, Doug adjusted well to our move.

When he said grace at dinner, in addition to his continuing prayers of thanks for his baby sister, he added, "Thank you for my new house and new friends." He was adorable, and I delighted in him.

At one year old, Nicole seemed unaffected by our move. I put her playpen on the front porch so she could watch the neighborhood kids playing. I sat on the porch swing and read or worked on projects while keeping a watchful eye on both children. That gave Doug freedom to visit his friends on the street.

At eighteen months, Nicole graduated from hard-soled shoes into regular ones. She took to dancing to her parents' rock and roll records, stamping her feet, and clapping her hands. She grew into a loving child, easily initiating hugs and kisses with family and friends. She was such a pleasure, enchanting everyone, especially her mommy.

When Doug was an infant, Rev. McNamara had invited Buddy and me to attend a weekend retreat designed for southwest Ohio pastors and lay leaders. The invitation surprised me because neither of us had assumed leadership roles. On the ride to Cincinnati, I worried about making a fool of myself, intimidated by being included in a wider group of church leaders. I couldn't anticipate the significant turning point that awaited me.

It didn't take long after the retreat activities started for me to relax and realize that the other participants welcomed my participation. The facilitator divided us into small groups and led us through several trust exercises. Rev. Gay, a lanky, balding, mid-fifties minister I didn't know, and I partnered for one such activity. He sported a mischievous grin during our instructions to sit knee to knee, close our eyes, and express various emotions by using just our hands. When prompted to express anger, I slapped his hands with gusto.

When we opened our eyes and processed the exercise, Rev. Gay's eyes danced. He declared, "I thought you were a wimp, but you have more strength than I imagined. I was wrong about you."

His response gave me the courage to participate fully in other exercises. I fell back into the group's outstretched arms, trusting they would catch me, exhilarated as they lifted me high above their heads. I allowed two clergy wives in another small group to draw me out. I risked revealing the lack of emotional connection in my marriage. Their empathy and acceptance touched me deeply.

Being seen and valued by these admired leaders planted a vision within me. I saw myself facilitating small groups and providing opportunities for others to experience a turning point like the one I was having.

When we moved back to Middletown, Buddy expressed interest in becoming involved in church. To his credit, he made an effort, and my friends became our friends, giving us the social life I longed for. We attended adult Sunday school classes and took a turn providing leadership for one quarter a year. In addition to attending Bible study, I joined the mothers' group where I experienced the substantive conversations with other mothers I valued. I finally had an opportunity to receive small group facilitator training. Buddy served on the finance committee. Talking about our activities provided some stimulation but failed to close the emotional abyss between us. Buddy didn't seem to notice what was missing or care as long as our daily living activities and his sexual needs were met to his satisfaction.

I relaxed into mothering, unaware of the years of trials ahead. I faced my first real challenge when Doug was four. I taught him to ask for help when he needed to cross the street to play with friends. However, if I was in the house when he was ready to come back home, he wouldn't wait. Interpreting his behavior as defiance, I grounded him to the house. His behavior didn't change. I enlisted Buddy's help, and we called a family meeting to explain our concerns. I told Doug that if I was in the house I would check regularly to see when he was ready to come home and Doug agreed to wait for my help. But despite all this discussion, he wouldn't cooperate with our plan.

One night I ran to Dillman's grocery for milk. The store, located on a busy thoroughfare, stood across the alley behind our house about a half block away. Doug and I were shocked to see each other there. He said, "Hi, Mommy. Are you mad?" He was with two preteen girls, but he hadn't asked permission to leave the neighborhood.

I brought him home with me. We called another family meeting and decided to ground him to his room. The next evening, after dark, I discovered him missing. He wasn't in his room, and I couldn't find him anywhere in the house. My heart pounded as I raced outside and headed in the direction of the noise two doors away. Our neighbors' front porch was filled with kids playing ping-pong. I spotted Doug in their midst clapping his hands and cheering them. I lost my cool, ordered him off the porch, grabbed his arm, and marched him home. I spanked him so hard I broke a yardstick on his behind.

Despite the yardstick's softwood, I was shocked at myself for losing control. Memories of my father's belt flashed through my mind. After I tucked Doug in bed and calmed myself, I pulled out Ilg's, Ames', and Baker's child behavior book and was relieved to read that Doug's behavior was normal. The authors noted that four year olds thrive on defying parental commands, often bellowing, "You make me so MAD." Doug added a refrain: "Mommy's a meanie. Mommy's a meanie." Relaxing again, I resolved to remain unruffled during the next episode.

Doug began attending preschool three days a week, giving him an experience all his own away from Mommy. Tony, his best buddy, attended two days. Doug resisted going on the day Tony was absent. I explained, "You're bigger than Tony. He's too little to go three days a week. You'll be having a lot more fun."

I approached another mother at the school, and we arranged play dates for Doug and her son, expanding his friendships outside our neighborhood. He now looked forward to attending, even on the day Tony wasn't there. This successful resolution boosted my parenting confidence.

However, as Doug's fifth birthday approached, I grew uneasy about changes in his behavior. When denied something he wanted, he grew belligerent and disgruntled. His lips pursed and his eyebrows formed hoods over his glaring eyes. He crossed his arms and jerked them from chin level to chest. Sometimes he threw toys at me or hit me. Even worse, he moped and complained in a continuous low drone like a nonstop electric motor. He followed me around calling, "Mom, Mom, Mom," in a rhythmic, guttural, discontented whine. He rejected my attempts to soothe him or interest him in toys or other activities. At these times, I escaped to the bathroom, relieved the door muffled the sound.

At gatherings with church friends, I received sideways glances when Doug's droning began; one woman, in particular, sighed and rolled her eyes just like my mother. I found it difficult to carry on conversations when Doug was around. He interrupted with his "Mom, Mom, Mom" chant. I stiffened and gritted my teeth. My eyes pleaded with him to stop and with others to help. *What can I do? Nothing I try at home makes a difference. I need help. Will someone please tell me what to do? I don't know where to turn.*

I turned first to Doug's preschool teacher with concern about his readiness for kindergarten. His August 31 birthday made him among the youngest in his class. She described him as a beautiful child and a natural conversationalist. She said he enjoyed math equipment, and she seemed impressed that he had begun subtracting already. She thought he would do fine in kindergarten. His preschool teacher didn't seem to recognize any behavioral issues with Doug.

I wanted a formal evaluation to help clear up the disconnection between his behavior at home and at school. I worried about how our home environment might be contributing to his problematic behavior. My mother's intuition told me something was different about him as compared to other children. Years later, I learned Dr. Spock was right about mothers knowing more than we think we do.

During a visit to the home of my sister-in-law's parents, Mrs. Shock pulled me aside and said, "Doug's a special child. He needs to be treated sensitively."

"Would you be willing to share that with Buddy?"

She took a step back, her eyes widened, and she clutched her chest with both hands. "Oh, no, I couldn't do that. Maybe I could talk to Ritchie, and Ritchie could talk to him."

In retrospect, if I had been open, Mrs. Shock, the mother of a severely intellectually disabled son, might have said something helpful. However, I wasn't comfortable sharing confidences with her because I didn't want her talking about my son and me behind our backs as I had witnessed her and Lena doing. Besides, I needed specifics, not generalities, like "special" and "sensitively." I wanted help, and I particularly needed Buddy's help because parenting a "special" child alone was too much to handle. She couldn't help me if she wasn't willing to talk with him.

As his children outgrew the cute toddler stage, Buddy's impatience with them increased, the novelty of parenting wearing off. He provided little respite for me when he arrived home after work. Typically, he spanked their bottoms with his hand or a yardstick and huffed and puffed while threatening dire consequences whenever their antics disrupted his television viewing. His lips tightened and his eyes bulged before narrowing into a menacing glare. Friends described him as lying in wait for the kids to do something wrong, his arms crossed over his belly. He pounced at the first provocation. He deferred to me when they came to him asking permission to do anything, saying, "Go ask your mother."

I convinced Buddy to join me in taking a Systematic Training for Effective Parenting class, but we were unable to work together to implement their system. I relinquished hope for us being partners in parenting. Buddy was as difficult for me to deal with as Doug was becoming.

My mother-in-law tried to help. She, too, had assumed the major responsibility for parenting her sons. She shared the different styles she had used to parent Buddy and Ritchie. Ritchie responded to requests with no questions asked. In contrast, Buddy interpreted requests as demands and didn't like being told what to do. She learned to make his requests extra polite. Her technique didn't work with Doug—nor did giving him extra attention or taking away privileges. Buddy was not present during his mother's discussion with me, and, as far as I know, she never attempted to coach him.

I couldn't turn to my parents because they had made it clear: "We raised ours, now you raise yours." I didn't want to use their methods anyway. They handled whining with "Quit your crying or I'll give you something to cry about." Physical punishment followed.

None of my friends needed to address behavioral problems this severe with their children. My initial "be reasonable" strategy didn't work. My child-rearing books had ceased to help. I was at a loss.

Today, parents receive guidance from pediatricians who do routine well-child checks, paying special attention to developmental milestones. Parents are encouraged to ask questions about any concerns. In the late 1960s and early 1970s, I consulted books written by pediatricians but gave no thought to taking my children to see one. If they practiced in our area, I was unaware of them. I followed my parents' example and what I saw as the normal pattern at that time. I took my children to our family doctor for vaccinations and illnesses. Dr. Hammill didn't address behavior problems.

On one visit we remained in the waiting room to make sure Doug didn't have an allergic reaction to his shot before heading home. On this hot, humid summer day, the waiting room steamed with body heat despite the air conditioning. The seats were full, so we sat on the stairs facing a window wall. The sun beat in through the glass. Despite the sweltering heat, the kids ran up and down the stairs. I resisted the temptation to leave early and pleaded with them to sit still. I tried to interest them in a book, but that didn't work, so I screamed, "Sit down or you'll be grounded to your rooms when we get home." Magazines dropped into laps and all heads turned toward us. The doctor's office door flew open, and the receptionist appeared with two lollipops. Her sugary "peace offering" only added to my children's antsy behavior and to my frustration and embarrassment. It never occurred to me to talk with Dr. Hammill about Doug's behavior changes.

Despite my uneasiness, I enrolled Doug in kindergarten. During the year-end, parent-teacher conference, his teacher pointed out a problem to me, expressing surprise that Doug tested high normal in reading readiness. That didn't surprise me because he had shown interest in learning new words when I read to him after tucking him in bed for the night. She said, "He's easily distracted by other children. He doesn't listen to directions and often doesn't know how to do the work assigned."

I asked, "Could that be a sign of immaturity? Does he need to repeat kindergarten to give him more time to mature?"

She didn't seem to have an opinion about what caused this behavior, and she didn't recommend he repeat kindergarten.

Making choices alone that could have a huge effect on Doug's future weighed on me. I yearned for someone to rely on to help me think through situations and how to respond to my concerns. I attempted to reach the school psychologist to request formal testing. I hoped he would provide the guidance I needed. I didn't know where else to turn. He didn't return my call.

Feeling totally alone in dealing with Doug's challenges, I knew I couldn't handle having a third child. For fear of compromising my health, I wanted to discontinue using birth control pills. I initiated a conversation with Buddy about other options, hoping he would consider a vasectomy. He avoided the subject—his typical reaction when he was uncomfortable about something. So I made an appointment to seek a tubal ligation.

My gynecologist indicated that my prolapsed uterus would begin causing problems sooner or later. He said, "You might as well have it out now."

"Okay. How soon can we schedule it?"

"Don't you want to go home and talk it over with your husband first?"

"He doesn't care what I do as long as I'm the one who does it."

I had the surgery in June of 1974.

I ached for Doug and the disapproval he faced from others. It troubled me more that I had come to view him as a problem needing fixing. The pure love I had hoped to transmit was now laced with frustration, fear, and worry. My parenting confidence plummeted. I tried to make sense of what was happening, sometimes blaming Doug's behavior changes on my mothering or our parenting. Other times I fell back on my intuitive knowing that there was something different about him. Lacking confidence in my judgment and unable to find the guidance I needed, I enrolled Doug in first grade. I hoped and prayed he would outgrow his troublesome behavior.

Sustenance

1975–1977

> *We humans require the animating sustenance of our fellows. We have to know that an echoing and enthusiastic resonance to our unique existence is available somewhere in this vast and ravaged world. We cannot make that happen, but we can be open to it and welcome it.*
>
> ~David Richo

As in my childhood, I was sustained by the echoing resonance I found with people at church. To my amazement, a larger experience of church than I ever imagined possible presented itself. But at first, I resisted.

Church was the one place where Buddy and I found common ground. During a major conflict in the congregation, we joined with other progressives advocating for Rev. McNamara, our pastor, and Ruby, our director of Christian education (DCE). However, they both found it necessary to resign.

My friends and I attempted to continue the Bible study that had been so important to us, but it wasn't the same without Rev. McNamara's direction. We hoped our new pastor would take up where Rev. McNamara left off, but he was unwilling to do that. And so I proposed leading a group of us around my dining room table. I couldn't offer Rev. McNamara's in-depth critical interpretation of Biblical passages, but I could provide guidance using Serendipity resources, which combine Bible study with personal sharing about how we applied the scriptures to our lives. I welcomed the opportunity to use the training I had received in facilitating small groups.

After we had met for several weeks, Phyllis, our church's new DCE, asked to observe the group. A tall, stately woman in her late fifties, Phyllis's presence made an impression. Soft white curls framed her face. Her dark, deep-set eyes regarded others intently as she listened to discover the values that guided their life choices. When she was delighted, a huge smile lit up her face. When troubled, her thick eyebrows furrowed and her generous lips tightened. I hoped she wouldn't find any reason to furrow her brows or tighten her lips while observing our group.

Some group members balked at personal sharing and expressed a preference for Rev. McNamara's intellectual approach. Despite their discomfort, I made space for heartfelt sharing in alignment with Serendipity's approach. Phyllis asked to stay to process the evening after the rest of the group left. When I turned around after seeing the last participant out the door, a huge smile lit her face. Her words thrilled me. "Wow, I'm surprised at the depth of sharing tonight. The group went very well. I'm impressed with the strength of your leadership. You have gifts as a small-group leader."

A few weeks later, Phyllis gave me a suggestion similar to the one Alice, my beloved parish worker, made fourteen years earlier regarding a career in the church. She said, "I think you should consider going back to school to become a DCE." She also recommended I read *Call to Commitment*, a book about a church that structures itself around small groups.

I had done some substitute teaching and given thought to resuming my career. But I didn't look forward to teaching typing and shorthand again. What I enjoyed was the stimulating interaction involved in facilitating small groups. I had learned through my volunteer work at church that I had more talent working with adults. For that reason, I doubted my effectiveness as a DCE responsible for training others to teach children and teens. I also questioned whether I could manage going back to college for three or four years to obtain another bachelor's degree while my children were so young. Doug was six and Nicole, three years old.

Yet, here was an opportunity to grow and become a better person. Perhaps my studies would lead me to a more effective way to deal with Doug's challenges. That would certainly have a positive effect on our whole family. And maybe it would be good for my children to witness their mother using her God-given gifts to fulfill her potential. Besides, I had allowed this suggestion to pass me by in the past and had chosen a career ill-suited for me. I didn't want to make that mistake again. So I began exploring options for continuing my education.

I talked more with Phyllis and wrote to Ruby, our former DCE, as I explored workable alternatives in my situation. Phyllis began to mentor me, and I accepted her invitation to join a group she organized for several DCEs in the area. "We'll use *Eighth Day of Creation* by Elizabeth O'Conner, the same woman who wrote *Call to Commitment*," she explained. "We'll focus on discerning our spiritual gifts and call to ministry."

The letter from Ruby arrived, giving me another viewpoint. She said my bachelor's degree and four years of teaching experience made me an asset to the field. "Frankly, I think you're more advanced than college-level work. If you're serious about going into the profession, a seminary education will be to your advantage. I recommend you talk with Harriet Miller at the seminary in Dayton. She's excellent in the field of Christian education and can give you further guidance."

Ruby's suggestion shocked me. Seminaries train parish pastors, and I didn't see myself in league with pastors called to serve churches. Going to seminary to become a DCE seemed a bit extreme to me, even though United Theological Seminary's Dayton location would be a more doable commute than other options I had researched.

In the *Eighth Day* group, we set about identifying our spiritual gifts. I shared what Phyllis named as my gift and my love for facilitating small groups. I also told them about the turning point I experienced years before at a retreat and my desire to offer these opportunities to other adults. The group encouraged me to trust this desire as a Divine leading. They saw my qualms about serving as a DCE training teachers of children and teens as more evidence of my call to retreat and small group ministry. I felt an inner peace with the clarity emerging from this process of discernment.

After another group member experienced a call to ordained ministry and applied for a Master of Divinity degree at United, the group encouraged me to apply as well. I continued to resist this path, but several people in and out of our group said, "Go to United and talk with Harriet Miller." I thought I might as well visit the school. I called and made an appointment.

My hands felt cold and trembled on the steering wheel despite the heat that radiant June day in 1975 as I drove from Middletown to Dayton and up Salem Avenue to the seminary grounds. I noted that it took me less than forty minutes to arrive.

The charming campus sat amid stately 1920s and 1930s homes in a declining neighborhood. A wooded area stood behind the five buildings surrounding a one-way oval drive. Two dorms, Fout and Robert's Halls, flanked the chapel, the administration building, and the library. Dr. Miller's office was in Fout Hall. A plump white-haired woman wearing polyester slacks and a tunic top emerged from behind a desk stacked high with papers and books. I chuckled at the sign on the wall reading, "A clean desk is a sign of an empty mind."

Dr. Miller's warm welcome put me at ease. She said, "Call me Harriet. We're on a first-name basis here." After asking what had brought me, she described the school's uniqueness among United Methodist seminaries. When she told me about UTS's emphasis on community building through small groups, my skin tingled. This seemed one more sign that UTS was the right school for me. When we finished our conversation, she gave me a tour, introducing me to the president, the dean of students, and several professors as we made our rounds. They all smiled and seemed genuinely interested in what brought me to UTS. I searched their faces but perceived no disapproving signal toward me as a woman or toward my call to a retreat and small group ministry. I soaked up the safety, warmth, and nurturing that radiated within this small campus. Enrolling seemed less intimidating after my visit.

On my drive home, my mind buzzed about taking this momentous step I was now seriously contemplating. Because I had found college challenging, I wondered about my ability to do graduate work and handle school full-time. *Even if I'm smart enough, Doug just finished a difficult year in first grade, and Nicole will still be in preschool. United's intensive term in September requires attendance several hours daily. How will I arrange childcare? Trading hours in the sitters' club doesn't seem feasible. What will Buddy say?*

I shared my dilemma with another mother in the babysitting club that had been formed by mothers on our street and surrounding neighborhoods. Her son attended Nicole's preschool, and they lived closer to Doug's elementary school than we did. She offered for Doug and Nicole to come to her house after school during September. This might work because the schedule would permit me to pick them up before Buddy arrived home from work.

I explained to Buddy why United seemed the best option for continuing my education. I told him I would start by taking one course a quarter to determine whether I could handle graduate work and whether Doug and Nicole could adjust to their mother being in school. When I told him about our neighbor's offer to help during September's intensive term, he offered no objections.

I enrolled in United's fall quarter in 1975. For my thirty-third birthday on July 15, Phyllis gave me a butterfly pin and a card reading, "Now you can fly."

After assessing the course offerings, I registered for a class taught by Harriet Miller, *Woman, Man, and the Sexual Revolution*. I kept quiet about my reason for choosing this class. I suspected it would spell out in black and white the answer to a question haunting me—*Am I inadequate as a woman?* With the emotional and intellectual distance in my marriage and my son being difficult for me to parent, I feared I was lacking in some essential attribute. *Perhaps Doug isn't*

the only "different" one in our family. I was compelled to face the truth.

The third week, our class viewed documentaries about growing up male and female in the 1950s and 1960s produced by local filmmakers Julia Reichert and Jim Klein. Harriet showed *Growing Up Female* first. I couldn't understand the point the film made and why Harriet had included it in our syllabus. It looked like normal life for girls to me—learning how to apply make-up, style hair, and dress fashionably. *Maybe that guidance counselor telling those girls to attend to their future husband's every little need is a bit over the top.*

A male classmate broke the hush that descended on the room and remained several minutes after the lights turned back on. Ken's voice sounded incredulous. "You get so many messages you're not okay just as you are."

Oh my gosh. Could this be the reason I feel so inadequate as a woman?

The next week we wrote our names on the board and told about their origins. I related my name's origin, something I had told many times and found humorous. "I was named Linda Alice to appease my great aunt Alice who wanted me to be a boy to carry on the Marshall name." Instead of the laughter I expected, the whole class groaned in unison.

Oh my gosh. I've never seen this before. My name was chosen as a result of boys being more highly valued than girls. This is mind-blowing.

A few women in my class had been part of the women's consciousness-raising movement. I had not. As I became educated about it, I learned the women's movement encouraged women to stop operating on automatic pilot, blindly following the path our families and culture had laid for us. Leaders in the movement advocated for women to expand our awareness of many possibilities for our lives. Then when we make a choice, it would be a conscious choice, one easier to live with.

In this context, my classmates shared their experience of starting families, saying, "I would have liked to have made a conscious choice instead of just doing what was expected of me."

This class was an awakening for me. It showed me the source of the fog I groped through—making unconscious choices that were out of alignment with what was best for me and with my natural abilities. When I majored in business education, I didn't see myself as capable of making another choice. When I married Buddy, I did so because the only other option I saw, becoming an "old maid," meant choosing the negative and prevailing view of single women. I couldn't entertain my mother's suggestion about calling the wedding off because I thought that meant succumbing to the cultural shame inflicted on women engaging in premarital sex. In this class, I faced a disturbing reality: I had chosen to marry without considering options better suited for me and to become a parent despite my lack of nurturing qualities with children. I had not made conscious choices.

On another day, Harriet divided us into small groups to envision a different future. My group imagined choosing names reflecting our essence—our true selves—the way Native Americans do. We collaborated on naming each other. After relaying the story about the butterfly pin Phyllis gave me, the name *Emerging Butterfly* surfaced.

"That's a perfect name for you," my classmates enthused. The butterfly became my favorite symbol for resurrection and transformation—and after graduation, the symbol for my retreat ministry titled *Emergings*.

As the year progressed, our family seemed to adjust well. Most days I arrived home before my children's school dismissed. When I needed to use the babysitting club, Doug and Nicole enjoyed playing with the children in the sitter's home. Buddy voiced no objection to my studying in the evenings after the children went to bed or occasionally elsewhere as I babysat others' children to repay the hours I had used. We continued our already established pattern of going our separate ways after dinner. He had the freedom to watch TV in peace.

Amazingly, what I needed to attend school fell into place as though Divinely orchestrated. However, when it came to my marriage and my son's troublesome behavior and school challenges—when my family life seemed too difficult to bear—my prayers seemed to go unanswered. Today I can see how my childhood sense of being wrong and defective contaminated my relationship with The Divine and suffocated my true self deep within. I had not yet grown to the point where I could trust that a loving presence was seeing me through my "dark night of the soul" experiences. It took years for me to awaken to this great spiritual truth and for it to become a reality in my life.

Intuition Confirmed

1976–1978

Intuition is a knowing, a sensing that is beyond the conscious understanding, a gut feeling.

~Abella Arthur

My first contact with Dr. Bennett, the school psychologist, occurred when he spoke at a PTA meeting. He listed physical, emotional, and social signs used to determine a child's readiness for school. A second grader, Doug was only beginning to exhibit some of these readiness signals. Others he didn't display at all.

He couldn't skip. He found buttoning his clothes difficult and had just mastered tying his shoelaces. Using scissors, pencils, and crayons frustrated him, so he hated writing and didn't like coloring as most children do. He continued paying more attention to his classmates than his teacher and missed directions. He resisted sharing and taking turns. He preferred playing with younger girls he could boss around and sometimes seemed to resent his sister. Even though his preschool teacher had seen him as a natural conversationalist, he now seemed unable to express his wants and needs in any way other than his electric-motor drone, "Mom, Mom, Mom."

After hearing Dr. Bennett's list, my hands shook, and I choked back tears. As the meeting adjourned, the noise in the room unnerved me. The realization Doug didn't seem ready for kindergarten, let alone second grade, overwhelmed me. I chastised myself for not trusting my intuition. I had sent him to school before he was ready.

In a daze, I couldn't summon the strength to work my way through the crowd to confront Dr. Bennett, thus postponing my efforts to effectively advocate for my child. It seemed less threatening to talk to him privately. So I tried repeatedly to reach him by phone, but he was either out of the office or in conference. Despite my telling his secretary how important it was for me to talk with him, for two more years, he neglected to return my calls. Teachers' complaints about Doug's lack of productivity and disruptive behavior in the classroom escalated. *What does it take for a school psychologist to respond to a plea for help?*

Church friends recommended a private children's diagnostic center in Hamilton, a neighboring community about fifteen miles away. In November, I scheduled an appointment—two months into Doug's fourth-grade year and my second full-time year at seminary.

Buddy and I each received a nine-page questionnaire. I have no idea what he put on his form. He grudgingly filled it out and probably answered the questions as briefly as possible. I, on the other hand, went on at length, as truthful as possible, about how I understood Doug's difficulties and the reasons behind them. I attributed his deteriorating friendships with boys his own age to not having athletic ability, making him an easy target for bullying. I described his ambivalent relationship with Nicole. Sometimes his bossy behavior turned mean, and he shouted at her, threw a toy, and marched away pouting because she didn't yield to his demands. Other times, they played together amicably.

I expressed my frustrations regarding Buddy's and my intractable marital problems and being overwhelmed with shouldering ninety-five percent of the parenting responsibility. I described my inadequacy as a mother, my guilt and fears, and my difficulty finding satisfaction in my roles as wife and mother. I speculated on the possibility Doug might resent my attending graduate school. Disclosing all this embarrassed me, but I was willing to do it in order to help my son.

Guilt tortured me. *Is Doug not receiving what he requires at home? Are we neglecting him? Is that why he acts so needy? Is his behavior the result of the tension between his dad and me? Do I give in too easily and allow him to manipulate me?* The books I had relied on when he was younger didn't address the kinds of behavior and school problems Doug currently presented.

Buddy and I were each required to meet individually with the agency psychologist. Buddy didn't seem bothered by his session, and I no longer remember what he said about it. But if the psychologist said anything positive in my individual session, I blanked it out. The half-hour drive back home blurred as I turned over and over in my mind his words, "You're an angry woman."

Woman, Man, and the Sexual Revolution, my first seminary class, had enlightened me about cultural biases against women, portraying negatively those of us dissatisfied with traditional roles, often blaming children's problems on mothers. Despite this awareness, I found the psychologist's accusation frightening. My son's life was at stake. All the way home I agonized, *Are Doug's problems my fault? Is that what the psychologist is inferring?*

Full of doubt and shame, I withdrew from my friends as I tried to decipher how to change myself into a satisfactory mother. They sought me out, encouraging me to tell them what was going on. At first, I withheld my thoughts and fears, but their genuine concern melted my resistance. I relayed the psychologist's accusation. "I know I get angry sometimes, but I've never thought of myself as an 'angry woman.' I don't know what to do. I'm scared I'll harm Doug more."

Their consistent message soothed my distress. "We don't see you as an angry woman. Remember, it's always the mother who gets blamed. The stress your family is under would make anybody angry. You're doing the best you can. Be gentle with yourself. Wait to see what the testing shows, what they're going to recommend. You'll have a clearer picture then."

My parents had forbidden the expression of anger in our household and had been uncomfortable with the show of any strong feelings. They had typically responded with "Stop your crying or I'll give you something to cry about." I didn't know how to express anger or any painful feelings appropriately. I replicated what I learned from my mother. Anger leaked out sideways in the form of resentment and disappointment. I couldn't admit how much like her I had become. I knew there had to be *a better way,* but I still had no clear picture of what that might be.

When the diagnostic testing agency interviewed Doug's teachers, they said, "We've about had it with him. He's disobedient. He forgets to bring his books and pencils to school. He refuses to do any written work. He doesn't complete his assignments. We can't keep him in his seat. He's always bothering other kids."

The agency assisted Doug's teachers and us to collaborate on instituting a trial behavior modification program. We posted a school behavior chart on the refrigerator at home, and Doug earned stars for completing assignments and for good behavior. We gave and took away privileges based on the stars he earned. At last the help we received seemed to work. His teachers saw a huge improvement, our first hopeful sign.

In April, five months after we had begun the diagnostic process and two months before Doug's fourth-grade year ended, the agency called a meeting to give us the test results and recommendations. Buddy and I were outnumbered by the eight professionals present. After five years of trying to get Doug some professional help, I was finally meeting with not one, but two school psychologists! In addition to Doug's two teachers, Mrs. Milgrim and Mr. Sonner, four people represented the agency, including the psychologist who accused me of being an "angry woman." A social worker charged with helping us after the meeting to implement the recommendations and an education specialist were also present. The prescription coordinator conducted the meeting.

Although the room was far from cold, I shivered at the sight of them all and goose bumps erupted on my arms. I pressed my lips together to keep my teeth from chattering. I braced myself in case they blamed me for all Doug's problems.

The education specialist began: "Doug tests at grade level in all subjects. He scores extremely well verbally and on vocabulary development and formation. That pulls his IQ into the above average range." This good news calmed my shivering body and chattering teeth. Whatever his problem, it didn't appear to have anything to do with lack of intelligence.

I fidgeted as the psychologist prepared to give his report: "Doug's afraid of failing. He thinks if he doesn't do the work, he won't have to face failing. He puts himself down a lot." He paused before giving the most troubling news. "The evaluation also points to some underlying aggressive and hostile components to his personality."

Doug isn't yet ten years old and tests as aggressive and hostile? His behavior drives us all crazy, but aggressive and hostile? I don't want those labels attached to him any more than I want to be branded an angry woman.

I found what I heard disturbing, but I did as my friends suggested. I waited to hear all the results and recommendations, focusing on how to help my son. I prayed whatever was wrong could be fixed.

The prescription coordinator's report gave the results of Doug's perceptual motor evaluation: "He has slight to severe difficulty on all sections of the sensory integration test. That explains several things about his behavior, including his short attention span and his nervous energy." He turned toward Doug's teachers. "It's his nervous energy that makes it difficult for him to remain in his seat. It also makes it difficult for him to remember to bring his homework and supplies to school."

That I understand. I've known for a long time there's something dif-

ferent about him. It's not because he's a bad kid. There's a reason why he acts like he does. I hope we can fix whatever is wrong.

The prescription coordinator went on to describe Doug's deficits. The long list sounded ominous: eye-hand fine coordination, shape awareness/discrimination, spatial relations/visualization, figure ground, bilateral integration, and motor planning. I didn't understand the meanings of these terms or what it must be like for Doug to have all these limitations.

At last, we're getting some answers, and it looks like we might get some help, too.

Mrs. Milgrim, Doug's gray-haired petite teacher, sat ramrod stiff and remained silent throughout the conference, her thin lips pursed and downturned. Mr. Sonner, his thirty-something teacher, leaned in as though listening intently. Before the agency professionals gave their recommendations, Mr. Sonner noted how much better Doug had been doing since we instituted the behavior modification contract. Doug had been completing his assignments, so the agency recommended weekly tutoring to help him catch up where he was behind.

That's doable. Why didn't I think to find a tutor?

The social worker encouraged the teachers to consider the quality of Doug's work rather than the quantity. "Find where he's succeeding. Then give him compliments."

The school psychologist seemed to be on board. "We can withhold his grades until the final grading period. That will give him time to make up the work he's missed." Turning to the teachers, he went on, "You could let Doug do his spelling tests verbally since he has so much trouble with writing. Then his grade could reflect only the words he can verbally spell correctly."

The social worker added, "And a tape recorder could be used to help him practice his spelling words."

Wow. We have a whole team working to help Doug succeed. There's hope.

The prescription coordinator turned to Buddy and me: "It will also be important to engage Doug in occupational therapy on a weekly basis to help with his perceptual motor training."

Okay, we can do that ... a tutor and an occupational therapist. There's a way we can help him. This is great.

He continued, "I need to go over the recommendations from Doug's psychiatric evaluation." He directed his attention to Doug's teachers and the school psychologists: "Dr. Peterson is concerned about the school's plan to retain Doug in the fourth grade. He believes this could cause him severe emotional damage and make his school problems even worse. Because the behavior modification contract is working so well, Dr. Peterson believes it should continue until Doug's teachers and parents agree it's no longer necessary."

He looked at Buddy and me: "Dr. Peterson also thinks Doug needs to be involved in a group activity where he can develop supportive relationships with male adults—something like Cub Scouts. And he highly recommends Doug receive depth counseling or play therapy. That will give information about his personality, about what's driving his behavior. He also recommends counseling for the whole family."

I had already convinced Buddy to see a marital therapist with me, hoping counseling would be the key to helping us improve our relationship. So as I listened to this recommendation, I thought: *We can include the kids in our counseling. Sounds like there's hope ... help for Doug ... a way to fix his problems. Whew. What a relief. If only we had learned this years ago. We could have spared Doug and his teachers all this trouble.*

Mrs. Milgrim broke her silence: "In my opinion, all he needs is a sense of responsibility and self-discipline. He doesn't need extra help from me, and he doesn't need a tutor." Staring daggers at Buddy and me, she continued, "The behavior modification contract is working well. All these other recommendations would take too much effort. I don't have time to give him all this individual attention. If he can't keep up, then he should be held back."

Please ... we'll hire a tutor ... an occupational therapist ... buy a tape recorder ... see he receives therapy. Please, Mrs. Milgrim. Please help us. All you need to do is give him a chance. Please, somebody, make her see the importance of following these recommendations. We're willing to do our part.

I looked to Dr. Bennett, hoping he would intervene. He didn't. The school personnel maintained a united front behind her. If they disagreed, they remained silent about it. They supported the plan already in place to retain Doug in Mrs. Milgrim's fourth-grade class. I supposed they deferred to her because she was a tenured teacher close to retirement. I doubt they had experience dealing with limitations like Doug's. I left the meeting believing Doug had a fixable learning problem or one we and his teachers could address. I despaired about the school's refusal to work with his deficits but determined I would follow all the recommendations made by the diagnostic center. I would do everything I could to help my son.

We continued the behavior modification plan. I found the recommended therapists. Doug received weekly occupational therapy for a year and then another year of monthly follow-up appointments. We supplemented his play therapy by occasionally including him and Nicole in our marital therapy sessions. Buddy didn't follow through with the one task I asked of him—involving Doug in Cub Scouts.

Just as the psychiatrist predicted, Doug's school problems became increasingly severe. Having Mrs. Milgrim a second year had to be grueling for him. This meeting with the agency and Doug's teachers took place twelve years prior to the passing of the 1990 Americans with Disabilities Act, requiring Individualized Education Plans for students with learning disabilities. In 1978, our only recourse was learning to cope.

At home, Doug couldn't entertain himself or tolerate being alone. Nothing soothed him. He clung to me, his body in constant motion. So much was expected of me, and yet nothing I did seemed to make a difference. I blamed myself, his father, our marriage, the school.

While writing this memoir, I conducted research on the Internet and learned that "sensory integration" was a new field in 1978. The field of neuroscience was in its infancy. The professionals at the diagnostic center did their best to explain Doug's disorder to us, but they didn't fully understand it themselves. Even if they had been able to help us comprehend what it was like inside Doug's skin, no resources existed to help us live with the effects on a daily basis.

The Internet articles I found helped me understand the terms used so many years ago ... to link Doug's acting out behavior to his brain's "traffic jam," preventing it from doing its job—processing sensory information from his eyes, ears, nose, tongue, and skin. No wonder he droned and whined. Nothing made sense to him.

And nothing made sense to me either. Where had my lovable son gone—the one who endeared himself to me when he expressed gratitude for his baby sister, his new home, and his friends ... who cheered me up on a difficult day with, "I like you, Mommy. You're cute." ... who made me laugh when he said, "You're a good cooker, Mommy," and then, mimicking a coffee commercial, added, "It tastes so good you hate to put it down" ... who amused me when he told me he forgot to brush his molars ten times as the dentist had instructed and brushed them eleven times instead?

I'm losing my precious son and don't know how to get him back.

Call

1976–1980

A call need not offer a definite sense of vocation or direction ... calls that come from the deepest places of ourselves ... are more like awakenings. They call us to attention.

~David Spangler

The ten years I spent at Dayton's United Theological Seminary, four as a student and six as a field education supervisor, had a profound effect on my life. I had not anticipated learning to walk a little taller in the world as a result of my experiences there.

I blossomed while studying subjects aligned with my interests and natural aptitudes. Professors praised the clear and concise writing in my academic papers as well as the depth of my thinking. I learned I was smart, my ideas held value, and I could, indeed, handle graduate work. After my first year part-time, I enrolled full-time for the next two years.

During my full-time years (1976—1978), I participated in a core group. The faculty assigned twelve students as different from each other as possible to the same group. A professor and field education supervisor co-facilitated. Our agenda involved learning to get along with each other, giving us practice to work effectively with parishioners when serving parishes. Because of my enthusiasm for small groups, I loved this aspect of the curriculum. A bonus I hadn't expected included receiving life-changing support.

When I articulated concerns about the disparaging attitude of the church hierarchy toward women seeking ordination, I expected the silence, resistance, or disapproval I received from my family when I expressed myself. Instead, my group leaders welcomed my candor as an opportunity to describe their efforts to address gender bias in the church. They valued my opinions and emotions. I mattered to them.

To be taken seriously in this small circle of leaders and peers stunned me at first. But gradually I learned I could trust the support of many others in and outside of core group. I built a dependable support system that taught me to trust my instincts, beliefs, and gifts. My courage and my voice grew stronger, not just as a student, but as a woman and a worthwhile human being. Thankfully I was gaining in wisdom and strength for the long road of challenges ahead in my marriage and with my children. I needed self-confidence and a strong voice to match it.

A major way I learned to trust my instincts occurred as I fulfilled my field education requirement by working in a social service agency. I volunteered at Middletown's Planned Parenthood Clinic as an intake coordinator responsible for gathering patient information. A one-time encounter with a client expanded my ministry's trajectory.

When I called this client's name at the entrance to the waiting room, a chunky woman with scraggly brown hair in her late thirties or early forties, a few years older than I, responded. She wore a tan rain jacket over a wrinkled print housedress, white socks, and black canvas shoes. A deep sadness pervaded her countenance.

I escorted her to my tiny, one-window, wood-paneled office. Fluorescent lights brightened the dark and dingy space. She placed her coat on the chair inside the door and sat in the chair I indicated next to my desk. She propped her left arm on the desk and leaned forward as though exhausted. Her other arm rested in her lap.

I opened the file folder and arranged my paperwork, asking, "What brought you to the clinic today?" Her tears flowed as she poured out her story. I ignored official procedure and shoved the tissue box toward her.

She told me about her husband beating her regularly. At one point, she and her three children ran away. She met a man she thought loved her and became pregnant. When he learned she was expecting a child, he disappeared. With no skills and no way to support her children, she saw no choice but to return to her husband. Fearing he would kill her if he knew about the other man and her pregnancy, she took the only step she could. She had an abortion. Now, she believed her paralyzed right arm was God's punishment for her sin.

Her story moved me deeply. I knew unhappiness in a marriage, even though I was not physically beaten. In my own neediness, I had been attracted to another man and, even though I hadn't acted on it in the way she had, I empathized with her submitting to what she thought was love, perhaps her first such experience. I didn't believe God would punish her for this. An overwhelming urge to soothe and comfort her arose within me.

When she stopped, I said, "I don't know if you're aware, but I'm a seminary student."

She sat back in her chair and looked straight at me for the first time.

"I don't think God's judging you or punishing you. I think God understands you made the best decision you could under the circumstances."

She continued to stare at me.

"And it's possible your arm is paralyzed because you feel so guilty."

She sobbed. I touched her arm and handed her tissues. Several minutes later, after she regained her composure, I gathered the information the doctor needed.

When we finished, she thanked me, and I escorted her back to the waiting room and headed for the clinic director's office. I told her this woman's story, emphasizing her guilt and paralysis. Later, the director came back and thanked me. "I talked to her after she saw the doctor, and she told me you helped her a lot."

When I presented this case to my core group for supervision, I doubted my actions. "I've never spoken for God before, and I don't know whether that was appropriate."

Doris, an Episcopal priest and my field education supervisor, wrote on my evaluation, "Linda has good instincts. She just doesn't always trust them."

I don't know how this woman fared or whether her paralysis subsided, but I will never forget her profound effect on my life. I had been used as an agent of grace. My marital unhappiness made it possible for me to empathize with this troubled woman and extend Christ-like compassion. I possessed a gift for creating a safe atmosphere where people feel free to share their vulnerability. Now, realizing I could trust the instincts that led me to give her spiritual guidance, I decided to explore adding pastoral counseling to my small group and retreat ministry.

Students in the Master of Divinity degree program at seminary face the ordination question. Whenever someone asked me whether I planned to be ordained, I answered, "No, I don't feel called to serve a parish as their pastor."

In my third year (1977–1978), Harold, the professor leading my core group, offered a thought-provoking observation: "If you were ordained, you could serve the sacraments at retreats. You wouldn't have to call in an ordained minister to do it."

I decided to take a sacramental theology class to explore the idea of ordination. After the third class, I told Buddy as we prepared for bed, "I don't think I need to be ordained. Church history is full of dissension about the differences between sacraments and ordinances. I'm leaning toward ordinances, and you don't have to be ordained to serve those."

After I fell asleep, I experienced a vivid dream that took place in the social room of a church. Several men sat up front, side-by-side at two long tables facing rows of mostly empty metal folding chairs. One man looked like Robert Moss, our denomination's second president. He had died at fifty-four of cancer. I had never met him but had admired the stands he took on controversial social-justice issues.

I sat in the back row next to three or four men I didn't recognize. The man looking like President Moss stood, pointed his finger at me, and demanded, "You're supposed to be ordained, and don't you forget it."

I awoke with a start. *Oh, my gosh. Maybe I need to consider ordination more seriously.*

I opened to the possibility, believing it unwise to ignore this vivid inner guidance. I didn't want to make another mistake by not heeding what seemed like direction from a higher source. And so, during my fourth year at United, I investigated the requirements for ordination in the United Church of Christ and entered what our denomination calls the "student in care" process, a procedure used by church leaders to determine our fitness for pastoral ministry. Potential ordinands are examined psychologically and theologically.

I recognized the possibility for being rejected as many women had experienced. To soften this potential blow, I adopted the attitude, "If it's meant to be, it will be. If not, that's fine with me." When I learned entrance into the pastoral counseling field required serving a church in a pastoral role for at least four years, my dream made sense and seeking ordination took on greater significance.

During my final year as a student at United (1978-1979), I attended part-time while Doug repeated Mrs. Milgrim's fourth-grade class. That made it easier to monitor

Doug and Nicole check out their mother's diploma — 1979

his behavior modification contract and coordinate his occupational therapy and counseling.

I found the months after graduation difficult. Leaving behind my solid support system was like walking out of a lush flowering garden to return full-time to the parched arid desert of my marriage. A project at Buddy's work required him to work long hours during the week and on weekends. During that summer, I continued to chauffeur my daughter to her piano lessons and to take Doug and Nicole to the library. To add to their fun, I enrolled them in swimming lessons and day camp at the downtown YMCA. While they attended day camp or played with neighborhood friends, I prepared for my October oral examination before the Department of Church and Ministry, the last "student in care" step, and worked on developing my retreat ministry. Kathryn, a seminary friend who lived nearby, and I designed a retreat to co-facilitate in the fall.

I tried not to let the long and difficult ordination process bother me, but, try as I might to retain the attitude, "If it's meant to be, it will be," the potential for refusal by my denomination's leaders lingered in the back of my mind. Rejection and the withdrawal of being valued and supported by people in the church would feel as if someone I love had died. The thought produced legions of grief. *How can I move forward without their approval?*

In September, Doug entered fifth grade and Nicole entered third. My job at the seminary required my presence two mornings a week. In addition to our stipend, field education supervisors could take classes without charge. I enrolled in as many pastoral counseling courses as my schedule permitted.

In October, after a difficult exam, the department approved my ordination contingent upon being called by a local church to serve in a pastoral role. My anxieties increased as I passed one hurdle and faced the next. Finding a congregation willing to call me would be difficult enough. Finding one in the area that wouldn't disrupt the children's schooling or Buddy's work only complicated the situation more. Buddy stated he wouldn't leave his job. Even if he had been willing, salaries for women serving the church remained among the lowest in any profession, making it impossible for me to support our family. I resented all the barriers I faced while my male peers breezed through their process with family support while receiving enthusiastic welcomes from congregations.

While I worked with church officials to find a congregation willing to call me, I grew depressed. Without a call to serve a church, I worried about how I would find purposeful work where I could make use of my gifts and could see myself making a difference as well as support me and my children financially? Despite being unable to determine how I could support myself and our children—a retreat and small group ministry wouldn't provide much—I talked with Buddy about divorce. "Maybe it would be best for all of us."

He said, "If you divorce me, I don't ever want to see you or the kids again."

I stared at him in disbelief. He glared at me. I left the room, wringing my hands and shaking my head. As I returned to my desk in the dining room, tears stung my eyes. I muttered to myself, "I probably wouldn't be able to handle single parenting anyway. Doug is a challenge for the two of us. I know I need out, but how can I manage it? It scares me to death. I'm stuck."

In January, with no progress in finding a church placement, I dipped into despair, seeing no viable way out of my untenable situation. The progress I had made strengthening my self-confidence while a student eroded in the absence of regular contact with my support system. My temper grew short with Doug and Nicole. For no good reason, I yelled too loud or swatted their behinds too hard when they were just being children. Then I chastised myself even more for being a bad mother.

My emotional roller coaster took its toll on our family. A church friend confronted me, telling me Nicole confessed to her that she couldn't wait to grow up and move out. Bernice also pointed out how I allowed Doug to manipulate me. When I explained my failed efforts to avoid this, she told me to look him straight in the eye, explain why I'm setting a limit, ask if he understands, and then say, "I don't want to hear another word about it." I tried it twice the next week, and it worked.

Nicole hid her feelings at home. She presented a cheerful façade, showing enthusiasm for her responsibilities at school and excitement about playing with her neighborhood friends. I didn't know the significance at the time, but today I realize her stress came out through her feet. She developed eczema.

Despite my earlier feelings of being stuck and fears of being a single parent, I consulted a divorce attorney for information about how divorce works. I sought out divorced women friends or friends with divorced parents asking about the effects on children. They calmed my fears and assured me Doug and Nicole would eventually accept the situation and might be relieved to live with less tension. One day I felt sure I could handle divorce, and the next I scared myself out of it.

It may have been Buddy's nervousness about the possibility of a second divorce that caused him to approach me in early February. He asked what I needed for us to continue living together. He probably regretted asking. I presented him with a long list stating my need for open communication, for using conflict resolution techniques when we experienced an impasse, and for monthly evaluations of our progress. I wanted weekly family meetings to plan fun activities and equitable distribution of household chores. I insisted we each spend individual time with Doug and Nicole. I asked for his support to accept a call from a church, even one at a distance. I emphasized that if our arrangement didn't work, I wanted to be prepared to separate in June. Buddy agreed to give my requests a try.

We implemented our plan. I engaged Doug and Nicole in developing a list of ways they could cooperate to get along instead of resorting to fighting. I no longer remember what Buddy did, but I took Doug to the high school basketball games he enjoyed and spent time with Nicole before bed. We read to each other, cuddled, and discussed topics she found interesting or had questions about. I cherished these times with her and felt at my best as a mother—imparting wisdom and connecting in a loving manner.

The atmosphere at home seemed to improve, although our family fun nights provided challenges. Doug fidgeted throughout an ice show we attended, complained about the hard arena seats, and balked at their distance from the skaters. Buddy donned a scowl and crossed his arms over his chest. Such fun.

Two weeks after we instituted family meetings, I received a part-time position description from a Kettering church, a Dayton suburb. It looked a promising possibility.

I couldn't help but notice how Buddy's cooperation declined as soon as it looked as though I had found a church placement. He wanted to crack down on Doug for avoiding the jobs he had agreed to do. I wouldn't consent, so he sat in the family meeting looking like a block of concrete, refusing to participate.

Later he approached me wondering if I agreed with him about our working better together as parents. I asked for examples. He had none. The only improvement I had noticed involved increased participation in attending to household chores. I reinforced the need for the conflict resolution techniques I had originally requested. He admitted to resistance learning them.

The Kettering congregation wanted an associate pastor responsible for directing its volunteer ministry program, a position suited to my interests and skills. While the remuneration would not make it possible to separate from Buddy, it would make handling Doug's school challenges easier. We wouldn't be required to move because I could commute. Having weighed the pros and cons, I took the next step and filled out the application.

Toward mid-March, Kettering church representatives interviewed me twice. Interviews made me nervous, but I was sure of my competence in fulfilling the position requirements. I confidently answered their questions, and they responded positively.

In April, I received the church's call. From the pool of applicants, they chose me. At last, my career seemed on track, and the door opened to my ordination.

Many of those present on Mother's Day, May 11, 1980, had mixed feelings about my being ordained. Buddy feigned support in public, but his behavior at home demonstrated what he admitted many years later—he gave up on our marriage when I entered seminary. Our children, too young to understand what ordination meant, showed interest and pride. However, they must have recognized how my studies and work stole time and attention from them. My extended family didn't understand my path and didn't know how to converse about it, but my parents drove up from Florida, and my brother flew in from California for the ceremony. Buddy's family didn't believe women should be ordained, but, probably to avoid conflict, accepted my invitation. Many ordained clergy who were resistant to ordaining women fulfilled their duty to be there.

Fortunately, many people present did support me, my ministry, and calling. I wanted them closest to me in the circle for the laying on of hands, the rite where ordained clergy recognize the call and authorize the ordinand to perform the duties associated with the ordained ministry. I invited my most ardent supporters to form a circle around me, named the contribution each had made to make this day possible, and expressed gratitude. Then I invited the ordained clergy to join them. Two significant women stood in that circle—Alice, who first encouraged me to consider a church career, and Phyllis, who mentored me, helped me uncover my gifts and calling, and set me on a path I could never have imagined.

Guerilla Warfare

1980–1983

Raising kids is part joy and part guerilla warfare.

~Ed Asner

A woman in the congregation invited me to a book study session dealing with M. Scott Peck's *The Road Less Traveled*. Several women parishioners organized the study and met in each other's homes. The first line in Peck's book, "Life is difficult,"[2] validated my experience and softened my self-judgment. His definition of love, "the willingness to extend yourself for the purpose of nurturing your own and another person's spiritual growth," gave words to the better way I longed for in my marriage and family relationships. Beyond the desire for the closeness of a best friend, I yearned for my husband and me to support each other's individual growth while we developed an equal partnership serving a higher purpose.

Through the years, I had dragged Buddy to five different therapists. Because I was still focused on my needs not being met, I brought my disappointments and complaints to our sessions in the hope that the therapists would focus on Buddy's need to change. That was the only way I could see for our relationship to work...for us to learn to love each other. Instead, the therapists seemed to see me as looking down my nose at Buddy. They, of course, knew that each of us had to take responsibility for what we contributed to our marriage not working. In my ignorance, I made it easy for Buddy to maintain his "nice guy married to a shrew" image.

We moved from one therapist to another in search of elusive harmony and happiness. To avoid a second divorce, Buddy went along for the ride.

But, after twelve years of marriage and so little success in our counseling, I lost hope of our ever achieving the kind of partnership I longed for. Engaging Buddy's passive-aggressive procrastination and stubbornness with my own immature pleas for his attention grew less appealing. I found fulfillment outside our home and lived my life around him. He seemed relieved to have me off his back. Our children suffered.

I had served the church for six months when Doug entered middle school in September 1980. His sixth-grade teacher called. He knew nothing about Doug's elementary school experience and the testing and recommendations made three years earlier. He voiced the same complaints about Doug's distracting behavior, and he wanted me to do something about it. The behavior modification plan had stopped working long ago, so I didn't know what he expected me to do. He gave no specific recommendations. When I asked how he handled Doug's distractions, he said, "I spank him."

"You spank him? Every day?"

"Yes, I don't know what else to do."

Oh my God, here we go again.

I poured out my despair to Jack, the senior pastor with whom I served. He told me about a private school specializing in learning disabilities and behavior challenges located ten minutes from the church. I investigated and enrolled Doug in January 1981. It was a triumphant day when I marched into the principal's office with my head held high and withdrew Doug from Middletown Public Schools.

The half-hour commute to Doug's school made our life frenzied. On the three or four days I worked at the seminary or church, transporting him posed no problem. Sometimes a neighbor attending school in Dayton helped out. However, on the one or two days a week I staffed evening meetings at church, Nicole, a fourth grader, came home to an empty house and waited for her dad to arrive home—not a situation I was comfortable with. Then they drove to Kettering, we all ate dinner at a restaurant, and the three of them returned home. I arrived later after my meeting ended. I talked to Buddy about moving so I could be available to the children after school.

After acclimating himself to the possibility of another move, Buddy broached the subject of divorce. He said, "Let's go ahead and move to Kettering and get you and the kids settled. Then if you still want a divorce, I'll move back to Middletown and rent an apartment."

It took over a year to sell our house. Easygoing Nicole voiced no objections. She treated our search for a home as an adventure. She made friends at church and envisioned developing new friends in a similar idyllic neighborhood full of playmates like the one she had known since she was one year old. She thought life would go on as normal.

We found a remodeled ranch on a quiet suburban street where all the houses looked pretty much the same. The extension on the dining room, kitchen, and garage made the one we bought much larger than it appeared from the street.

I was sold on the finished basement. With the family room, Doug's bedroom, and his bath down there, visitors wouldn't be exposed to the mess Buddy and the kids made. This also gave me some distance from Doug's clinging. The extra bedroom upstairs could serve as my office. I preferred an older home's charm, but this one seemed ideal for our needs. Most importantly, this move made it possible for me to be present when Doug and Nicole arrived home after school.

By the time we moved, Doug was in his second year at the private school and Nicole, in the middle of her fifth-grade year.

My parent-teacher conferences with Doug's private-school instructor grew increasingly upsetting. Our meetings degenerated into something like gossip sessions. He dumped his complaints about Doug's behavior on me, acting as though I obviously understood. He gave no indication that he possessed special expertise in handling children with learning disabilities and behavior challenges and offered no suggestions on how to deal with Doug at home.

I came to the opinion that this time period would someday be looked upon as the dark ages in education. I believed children like Doug had a different learning style—one no one knew how to work with. Rather than take the time to discover how to teach them effectively, educators dismissed these children with pejorative terms like undisciplined, disobedient, disruptive, irresponsible, and learning disabled. I felt powerless in the face of this overwhelming obstacle.

I failed Doug by not being assertive enough with his teacher. I couldn't face the private school turning into another nightmare. I couldn't avoid it any longer, however, when I learned the teacher had left Doug alone in his classroom while he taught a class in a different part of the building. To make sure Doug stayed in his seat working on assignments, the teacher handcuffed him to his desk. I felt drained. All our efforts to help Doug had failed. Clearly, another change needed to be made.

When Doug said he wanted to go back to public school, I spent the summer searching for resources to give him the best chance at succeeding. I took him for neurological testing, but an EEG and CAT scan revealed nothing. Right brain learning was a hot topic. I thought that maybe this applied to Doug, so I found a bio-integrative specialist and took him across the state for testing. A learning disabilities teacher from our church accompanied us, and I hired her to tutor Doug twice a week using methods recommended for right brain learners.

We enrolled Doug in Kettering Public Schools for his eighth-grade year, 1982–1983. Their special education services responded immediately to my concerns. By November, he had been given tests to determine the best placement for him in their system. When the guidance counselor described Doug as "extremely cooperative, considerate, and pleasant during the testing," I hoped this meant my precious little boy was returning.

At our meeting with the guidance counselor, he said, "Doug was easily able to name the activities that interest him. He's making friends. He's quite verbal. His only area of resistance was in drawing a person and writing. He seems to have some weakness in his left hand ... his dominant hand. He was emphatic that he doesn't like to read and write." Doug joined the computer club and served as the basketball team's statistician. Witnessing his excitement raised my hopes. He seemed like a normal kid again.

The testing revealed Doug's sensory integration deficits and also evidence of previous occupational therapy. The special education department recommended more OT to strengthen his weak areas—outside the school system so he wouldn't be singled out among his classmates. Doug functioned at a seventh-grade level, but the school didn't want to damage his self-concept by placing him only one year ahead of his sister. Instead, the special education department proposed using alternative learning methods. Grateful for their sensitivity to Doug's emotional needs, I held my breath, hoping his teachers would cooperate.

The guidance counselor thought the weakness in Doug's left hand made it difficult for him to grasp a pencil and might contribute to his struggle transferring his ideas to paper. He recommended using fine tip felt markers and an electric typewriter. He wanted Doug to continue using a tape recorder to practice spelling. I was willing to do whatever they proposed and more if it kept the positive momentum rolling.

The guidance counselor explained how they proposed to work with Doug's teacher. "We'll recommend his teacher put fewer math problems on a page. That way, he won't feel so overwhelmed. Miss George has done this sort of thing before, so it won't be a problem. We'll also recommend she place his desk close to hers so she can more easily assess his ability level and make assignments accordingly. She'll also be able to see if he needs extra help. And we'll do what we can to help him develop good peer relationships."

This seemed like a dream come true. We had found a supportive school system at last. However, when it came time for my first parent-teacher conference, I braced myself. I suffered pounding tension headaches every time I entered a school building, even if just to watch one of my children perform in a program.

Miss George greeted me warmly at the door to her classroom and invited me in with a smile. We sat next to each other in student desks, friendlier I noted than if she had positioned herself behind her desk. She was young and soft spoken with dark curly hair and a kind face. She said, "Doug's making good progress in his studies. He's pleasant and cooperative in the classroom."

I burst into tears.

Miss George leaned toward me, a puzzled look on her face.

I dug in my pocket for a tissue, wiped my eyes, and explained while choking back sobs, "This is the first time I've heard anything good about my son from a teacher in years."

Doug in his band uniform.

After our conference, Miss George sent home "Happy News Telegrams" and lengthy notes about improvements in Doug's behavior and work. She often wrote, "I'm very pleased with him, and you should be, too."

Meister Eckhart, the medieval theologian, philosopher, and mystic, said, "If the only prayer you say is 'thank you,' it is enough." I had much to be thankful for during this time and began to relax. *Perhaps we've turned a corner and my precious son is returning to us as a normal kid. Perhaps our lives will be better now.*

Struggle

1982–1983

Strength, both physical and spiritual, is the product of struggle.

~Napoleon Hill

Most people in our new suburban Kettering neighborhood were the age of Doug and Nicole's grandparents. No children lived on our street. I prayed for someone to befriend them at school. When Doug came home with Jon, an exceptional boy his age who lived on the next block, I jumped for joy inside. Lacking experience as the new kid, Nicole had never faced the challenge of making new friends at school. At ten, she found it more difficult than she imagined. Jon included her in the fun when he visited our home, but his friendship wasn't enough. Nicole didn't find friends to bring home, but I had no idea how much this affected her.

On a Friday afternoon while she was in sixth grade, almost a year after we moved, I sat on the living room floor surrounded by poster paper and magic markers working on a church project. Straining to rise when the phone rang, I hurried to answer it. The man on the other end introduced himself as Nicole's guidance counselor. He said, "We have some concerns about Nicole. Her teacher just told me another student reported to her that she's talking about killing herself."

It was as though the world stopped spinning. However, I responded calmly, "Thank you for letting me know."

I gasped as I hung up the receiver and reached for the phone book. My whole body shook while I fumbled to find the section on counselors. *No! No! No! screamed inside my head. Doug's the one who receives all the attention. All this has been too much for her.* Dr. Darington, a child psychiatrist's name, caught my eye. I called her number and scheduled the first available appointment.

My heart was in my throat when Nicole came through our front door after school. I watched her head for her room as usual. She deposited her book bag and proceeded to the kitchen for a snack. I followed waiting, but she acted as though nothing was different. I asked, "Is there anything you need to tell me?"

She looked at me puzzled.

I told her about her guidance counselor's call. "He said you told a friend at school you feel like killing yourself."

She said, "I was just kidding."

I put my arms around her, pulled her close, and said, "Nicole, that isn't something to kid about. I'm really concerned about you. This move and all Doug's problems ... he gets all the attention ... I can understand if it has been hard for you."

She pulled away and said, "It's no big deal, Mom. Don't worry. I'm fine."

"I'm sorry, but I can't believe you'd say you wanted to kill yourself if you're fine. I've made an appointment for you to see a counselor next week."

"Oh, Mom. You're making a big deal out of nothing."

"Nicole, threatening to kill yourself isn't 'nothing.' I'm not taking any chances."

Full of fear, shame, and guilt after the guidance counselor's call, I felt like an actor playing a role—trying to be the confident mother I was not—putting myself under a microscope, judging myself harshly, blaming my children's problems on my mistakes and inadequacies.

I wanted Doug and Nicole to talk through their feelings with me, thinking that would help resolve their difficulties. Of course, they resisted. They needed me to be their mother, not their therapist. Besides, at that time I lacked active listening skills. I remember only one occasion when Doug was a teenager that I accidentally demonstrated proficiency in empathetic listening.

Distraught and crying when he came home after school, Doug headed for the recliner in the living room. Nicole and I followed him and sat on the couch across from him, waiting for his sobs to wane so he could tell us what was going on. He told us about being bullied and humiliated by younger boys on the way home. Nicole and I listened quietly as he choked out his pain, one hand covering his eyes. When he finished his story, I said, "Children can be so cruel."

Doug's hand moved away from his eyes, and he looked at me with a startled expression, saying, "Really?" It was more of a question than a statement. It was as though he couldn't believe what he heard. For once, I had validated his reality instead of identifying him as the problem.

In my Imago Relationship Therapy training many years later, I learned this listening method is a loving action we all need extended to us, especially when we're in pain. I remember that experience with Doug vividly because it was such an anomaly. I couldn't help but notice how my uncharacteristic response made a huge difference to him. I wish I had done it more often.

For many years, I mothered my children by identifying their challenges and looking for help to resolve them. I possessed skill at tracking down potential resources. It was the best way I knew to handle problems like those they demonstrated. I believed if my parents had found outside resources for me instead of ignoring my childhood and adolescent struggles, I would have made healthier choices and created a more satisfying life. I felt most competent as a parent when I did this for my children. I fooled myself into thinking that was a sufficient way to demonstrate my love. Instead, I gave them a painful message. Nicole had said it best during a family therapy session, "I feel like I'm growing up wrong."

Now I see how much they needed my nurturing touch, my presence, my empathetic listening, and my encouraging words. To my children's detriment, I was not demonstrative in these ways. I wish I could have done it differently.

The weekend after Nicole's guidance counselor called, I watched her like a hawk, afraid to address the issue directly again. I saw nothing out of the ordinary. I chastised myself for taking advantage of her easygoing nature and overlooking her need for the attention all children possess. I reinforced my efforts to spend time with her after school, asking about her day and telling her I loved her as often as possible. At bedtime, we cuddled as I read her stories. I tucked her in with a kiss and an "I love you." I tried to make evident her preciousness to me. I wanted so much for her.

After we moved to Kettering, Nicole continued her piano lessons with our church organist. She expressed a desire to learn to play the organ. I encouraged her dreams. I enrolled her in a dance school and a soccer league and hoped she would make friends to bring home and hang out with. She didn't. We cheered her on at her recitals, programs, and games. When she wanted to redecorate her room for a school project, I enrolled her father's assistance. She chose lavender, and he helped her paint. I took her shopping for a new bedspread and curtains. None of this, of course, came soon enough or made up for all the neglect she had experienced.

The Tuesday after the guidance counselor's call, a call from Nicole's principal surprised me. "We'd like to talk with you. Can you come in tomorrow afternoon at three?"

He ushered me into his office and motioned for me to take a seat on the couch. He joined Nicole's teacher and guidance counselor sitting in chairs across from me.

The principal began, his forehead wrinkled and his voice strident, "We've called you in because we're concerned about your daughter. We consider it a serious situation when a child talks about suicide."

The guidance counselor added, "When I called you, you hardly had any response. It didn't seem like you considered this serious.

What's going on?"

"I assure you, I took what you said very seriously. As soon as we hung up, I called a child psychiatrist. We have an appointment on Saturday."

Her teacher continued, "I talked with Nicole last week, and she told me a story about her father throwing her brother against a stair railing. She sounded scared of him."

Before I could respond, the principal barked, "Is that how your husband disciplines his children? What's going on in your home?"

I started to defend Buddy. "He does get physical sometimes. He's been working on it." Heat rose in my tense body. *I'm the one being confronted again. I'm sick of it. I refuse to be caught in the middle this time.*

I declared, "I am NOT going home to talk to my husband about this. He needs to hear it from you. It won't have any effect if I tell him. I want you to call him in."

They stiffened and hesitated, looking back and forth as though stunned. After a moment, the principal said, "Okay." They checked their schedules, and we settled on a day and time.

"He'll be here. I'll see to it."

When Buddy arrived home after work, I said, "The principal at Nicole's school wants to talk with us on Friday at four. You'll need to take off work early. They're concerned about her threat to kill herself."

I gloated for two days, visualizing them blasting Buddy as they had me ... Buddy having to experience confrontations like I had endured over and over ... Buddy being given advice as I had been. *Maybe they'll get through to him and he will change. I hope.*

Four chairs formed a half circle opposite the couch. They added a school psychologist to the mix. As Buddy and I settled on the sofa, I was primed for the attack, smug in the face of the blast about to come.

They began, their voices halting, soft and gentle, asking, "Would you be surprised if we told you …?"

Over and over, they implored, "Would you be surprised if we told you …?"

"… your daughter talked to us about you?"

"… she told us about you throwing your son against a stair railing?"

"… she sounded scared of you?"

I searched their faces, trying to figure out what was going on.

Buddy looked puzzled at first. He admitted to throwing Doug against the stair railing once as though it was no big deal and denied Nicole's fear.

My stomach clenched.

They asked him, "Would you be willing to learn more effective ways of disciplining your children?"

He looked at me and back at them saying, "Well, we've already taken a parenting class."

"We would encourage you to think about taking another one. Additional support can be helpful. We can help you find one if you change your mind."

Instead of protecting my child and speaking up for myself, I sighed in defeat, lowered my head, and sank back into the couch. *Why will no one confront him? Why does everyone coddle him? Are they afraid of him? Will there be no end to this?*

The school psychologist asked for permission to do psychological testing.

I said, "I don't think it's necessary. Our appointment with the child psychiatrist is tomorrow."

He thought testing would give them a clearer picture of how to help Nicole at school, so I conceded. I didn't want to deny her help.

A woman small of stature, Dr. Darington wore a cobalt blue suit, and despite her dark upswept hair, carried the sweet countenance of a grandmother. I liked her immediately and hoped I was right to put my trust in her. She took several weeks to complete our family interviews and her assessment. In the meantime, the school psychologist requested an appointment to go over Nicole's test results. He said, "Your daughter has severe emotional problems."

If he said anything more, I can't remember. His words "severe emotional problems" clanged in my head like a bell that wouldn't cease tolling. The deafening noise made me want to scream, "Stop! Stop! Stop! I can't take anymore."

My heart broke into a thousand pieces. I clenched my fists and dug fingernails into my palms to fight off tears. What has happened to my happy, upbeat, loving baby girl? How can I deal with two children having severe problems? I don't think I can handle losing the one bright spot in our family.

I prayed, "Please, God, don't let it be true. Don't let both my children be scarred for life." As we awaited Dr. Darington's assessment, I continued praying, "Please don't let there be bad news about Nicole. Please give us some ray of hope."

I wanted to understand what was happening to my children but dreaded what Dr. Darington would say. No human being had given me the understanding, guidance, and hope I needed. At this point, I wanted to hear from God—God with skin on and with an unmistakable voice. I wanted God to explain to me why my children had so many problems and what I could do differently to help them. I wanted guidance from the highest source possible—guidance I knew I could trust.

Buddy and I arrived early at Dr. Darington's. We parked ourselves on opposite ends of the sofa in her waiting room. Buddy sat stone-faced chewing his fingernails. My heart thumped as I flipped through magazines. The calm I sought eluded me. I threw the magazine on the end table, crossed my legs, and leaned back. My foot pumped wildly up and down. Waiting a few minutes seemed an eternity.

The door to Dr. Darington's office opened. She smiled and invited us inside. *She's smiling. She doesn't look upset ... like she's ready to lay bad news on us. I hope that's a good sign.*

We took our seats on her loveseat. Buddy sank back into the soft pillows and crossed his legs. I sat on the edge, leaned forward, and readied myself for another blow. Dr. Darington sat in her swivel desk chair facing us. She continued smiling and said in the soft voice of an angel, "Nicole is such a delightful child."

I continued looking at her—waiting for her to lower the boom.

"She's very shy," said the doctor.

Her words didn't compute. I said, "The school psychologist says she has severe emotional problems."

Her voice grew emphatic. "No, she does *not* have severe emotional problems. She's shy."

I paused and tried to process her words. "Are you sure? Is there any way you could be mistaken? Could you have missed something?"

"I've done a thorough assessment."

"I'm sure you have. I'm not questioning that. I'm just wondering if there's any way Nicole could have fooled you."

Again, Dr. Darington smiled. "I've worked with lots of children. I know when they're trying to pull one over on me. That's not Nicole. She was a little reticent at first to open up—she *is* shy after all, but I have a way of building trust with children. She was eventually quite verbal and relaxed during our sessions."

"But she said she felt like killing herself."

"Well, your family is under a lot of stress. The move here has been especially hard for her. With her shyness, it's been hard for her to make new friends and handle new situations. The isolation has taken a toll on her, and your son's situation seems to have been difficult for all of you."

"Yes, it has. I was so scared after what the school psychologist said. I didn't realize all this was affecting her so much." I looked at Buddy. "Did you?"

He shook his head.

I leaned back on the couch, the tension in my arms and legs oozing out. I still couldn't quite believe what I heard. "If I understand you correctly, you're saying Nicole threatened suicide because her shyness has made it difficult for her to make friends at school and because of the stress in our family. Am I hearing you right?"

Dr. Darington nodded.

"Where would she have picked up such an idea? Committing suicide is a drastic step to take."

"She doesn't remember where she heard about suicide or why she thought to say she was going to do it. She may have heard the idea from a television program, read about it, or overheard an adult conversation. She wasn't planning to act on it and didn't anticipate the reaction she got."

I asked, "Okay, what do you recommend?"

Dr. Darington saw no need for psychiatric treatment. She advised us to continue our family counseling and increase Nicole's involvement in activities with other kids.

As we left her office, I looked up with my hand on my heart and murmured a prayer of thanksgiving. Dr. Darington seemed so sure. Still, I found it hard to trust such good news. When I asked around about her, I learned Dr. Darington had a stellar reputation. Those reports bolstered my confidence in her assessment. I trusted her more than the school psychologist. We could work with shyness and stress. I held onto a tentative hope Doug's improvement and Nicole's positive outcome pointed to answers to my prayers.

However, shame about our family tortured me with doubts about my worthiness as a spiritual leader and potential pastoral counselor. *How can I make a difference for others when I don't make a difference in my own family? How will I be able to counsel others when my family life is such a mess?*

Growing in my ability to love as I am loved by The Divine, to express gratitude for the presence of a power greater than myself in the midst of the struggle hasn't come easily for me. Looking back, I see how my doubts and questions pointed to my deep desire to move forward and how my experiences with my children gave me opportunities to grow emotionally and mature spiritually. I see now that the painful events yet to come were preparing me to embrace a rare experience—that of witnessing grace in the midst of darkness.

Darkness Descends

1983–1984

> *In order to complete our amazing life journey successfully, it is vital that we turn each and every dark tear into a pearl of wisdom, and find the blessing in every curse.*
>
> ~Anthon St. Maarten

Doug's tutor called: "I'm wasting your money working with Doug. He just isn't interested in doing the work."

I implored, "Oh, please don't give up on him. The school system has been so helpful. For the first time in a long time, we have hope for him."

"I'm sorry, but Doug's becoming very uncooperative. I haven't been able to help him for a while now. I'm not willing to continue when I see no positive results."

Doug's sabotage was the tip of the iceberg.

I arrived home after work a little late. It shouldn't have been a big deal. Doug was fourteen and Nicole, eleven. But Nicole needed extra attention, and Doug's school work needed monitoring, so most days I made it a point to arrive home before they did.

I pulled into our attached garage and heard screams coming from the house as I stepped out of my car. I raced inside and down the stairs to our basement family room. My heart pounded as I took in the scene before me. Nicole kneeled sobbing, her pants pulled part way down. Doug, a few feet away, wore an innocent grin.

I glanced around and clenched my fists to calm the trembling taking me over. I asked, "What's going on?"

They tossed blame back and forth.

I sent them to their rooms and ran up and down the stairs, from her room to his, trying to figure this out. I couldn't get a straight answer. Clothes, toy cars, school books, and papers littered Doug's room. I told him to straighten it up. He moved in slow motion, so I grabbed some clothes and hurled them into his laundry basket. I held on to the side of his bed for balance and leaned down to pick up papers. Under his bed I noticed magazines.

"What are those?"

He didn't answer.

"Pull them out."

He hesitated.

"Pull them out," I demanded.

I watched in horror as he removed a large stash of sexually explicit adult magazines.

"Where did you get those?"

He hemmed and hawed and then admitted to stealing them from the neighborhood drugstore.

I felt sick to my stomach just as I had eight years earlier. The memory was still vivid. Doug, Nicole, and I were heading home after running errands. As usual, they were horsing around in the back seat. Without warning, they settled down, and the mood changed. They told me about a "bank scene" and appeared to be feeling guilty.

I didn't understand, so I told them, "Show me when we get home."

They led me to the master bedroom and to sexually explicit adult magazines in their father's nightstand drawer. They opened one magazine to reveal a picture of a Wild West bank robbery—the characters scantily clad in little more than ten-gallon hats, holsters, and six shooters. Doug and Nicole admitted to having acted out this scene.

Doug in elementary school.

"Were we bad, Mommy?" my six-year-old son asked.

I wanted to spare them guilt for something not their fault. "No, you weren't bad. But you shouldn't be pretending to be the people in those pictures. Daddy's books are for grown-ups. You're too young to understand what they're about."

I steamed as I awaited Buddy's arrival home after work. When confronted, he acted like a bad little boy who had been caught rather than a father concerned about the effect on his children. I glared at him. "Get that crap out of our home or get out yourself."

He agreed to clear it out, but gradually magazines, books, and videos reappeared. Buddy and I pretended not to notice his violating my ultimatum. Doug's school challenges and my studies overwhelmed me, and so I neglected to protect my children. Now, eight years later, my failure smacked me in the face.

And worse, now Doug had turned into a thief and a liar. His earlier guilt gone, he lied about the reason for his sister's screams and seemed indifferent to her terror at having him rub his penis against her bottom. He seemed unaware his behavior was not only wrong but abusive. This time I raged at him, hoping to inflict guilt. *Can't he see what a hard time his sister has had adjusting to this move—a move we made for his benefit? I have to stop him. I can't let him hurt my baby.* Despite my positive motivations, I see now how once more I emotionally neglected Nicole, thinking if I protected her by controlling her brother's behavior, I would be demonstrating my love for her. She needed so much more from me.

I paced the floor wringing my hands. I blamed these types of publications for contributing to my parents' confusing messages about sex and to my marriage's sexual wasteland. Now they were poisoning my children.

As an adolescent, I found sex perplexing. Mom avoided giving me information about menstruation, childbirth, and intercourse until she couldn't sidestep the issue anymore. Then she did so with great discomfort, giving me pamphlets to explain the details.

She told me about menstruation one summer when I wasn't feeling well, linking it to illness. She told me about childbirth when younger playmates noticed my confusion and told me to ask her. One playmate's mother apologized. When I couldn't understand why a high school senior "had to get married," my teenage friends sent me to my mother.

"Don't you know where babies come from ... how babies are made?" they said. "Ask your mother."

The night I asked her, she put off answering me, telling me she'd explain in the morning. Then, while brushing my teeth in the bathroom next to their bedroom, I noticed a tone of dread when I overheard her say to Dad, "Guess what Linda asked me tonight." *What's wrong? What's so bad about me knowing? Everybody else seems to know.*

My embarrassment about being the last to know led me to try to answer Doug's questions in a straightforward manner. After Nicole's birth, he wanted to know where babies came from. I told him, "A special place inside Mommy."

I responded to his curiosity about how the baby got out of my body by sitting with him, showing him pictures, and answering his questions.

When he wanted to know if his baby sister had a penis, I explained, "Boys have penises. Girls have vaginas. Girls go in, and boys go out."

I didn't want him to feel embarrassed as I had when my friends had access to this information way before I did. However, my good intentions backfired on me.

Despite her discomfort giving me reliable information, Mom seemed to delight in her reputation for telling off-color jokes. Dad displayed Marilyn Monroe's nude picture in various locations. One time he placed her picture on a stand in the hallway upstairs where any guest using our bathroom was sure to see it. Sometimes it competed with their wedding picture for space on their bedroom dresser.

As my own body blossomed into puberty, I experienced throbbing in my vagina but didn't know what it meant. When a distant cousin about my age visited, she asked if I had experienced this while admitting she had. I denied it. My mother's embarrassment talking about sex in any other way than through off-color jokes led me to avoid the topic.

While I was in college, Dad left several *Playboy* magazines on the coffee table when he knew a male friend and I were due for a visit. I tried to hide my uneasiness from my friend and appear sophisticated. I wanted to be comfortable with my sexuality but had no healthy role models to guide me.

Somehow, in this bewildering milieu, I sensed sex was meant to be something sacred and beautiful between two people with a deep emotional connection. I have no idea where this impression came from. I had no exposure to such thinking. In my seventies, while reworking this memoir, Episcopal priest, mystic, and author Cynthia Bourgeault, gave me what I like to call "a sanity check." In her book, *The Meaning of Mary Magdalene*, she writes about transforming the raw force of sexual desire into a sacred channel of conscious love. However, my youthful ignorance and discomfort left me vulnerable.

When I met Buddy, I hadn't explored my body. I hadn't heard about foreplay and its importance for women. The only impression I had regarding the term "orgasm" had something to do with how good sex was supposed to feel. I didn't know it was possible to give myself this pleasure or of its importance in preparing me to guide my future husband. Like many 1950s girls, I thought the guy knew what to do. Because Buddy had been married, I was sure he must know.

I wasn't prepared when he revealed one evening during our courtship, "There were sexual problems in my marriage. I'm not even sure I can have sex again."

It might have been enlightening if I had asked a few questions. What were your problems? How did you deal with them? What makes you think you can't have sex again? If that's what you think, why have we been getting hot and heavy with each other? What are you trying to prove to yourself? But I didn't ask. Instead, I set about demonstrating to him he would be okay with me. He has to be. If he's not, I'll wind up an old maid.

I invited him to my place for lunch and greeted him at the door wearing a sheer gauze duster over my underwear and slip. His face lit up, and he gave me a big bear hug, lifting me off the floor. I slid down his body and felt his hard penis. I took that as proof that he would be all right with me.

Our necking and petting escalated. I didn't stop his roving hands. Pleasure rose in my tense body, guilt quashing climactic ecstasy. When he worried I wouldn't like touching him, I acquiesced, hoping he wouldn't want to go further. Of course, he did. In a swirl of confusion and mixed emotions, I gave up my virginity.

As it turned out, Buddy had little more sexual knowledge than I. He didn't know about the length of time it takes many women to reach orgasm, and neither did I. After a short period of gruff foreplay, he asked, "Have you come? Have you come?"

I took that as a signal he was about to, and I needed to hurry. I thought my lack of enjoyment meant there was something wrong with me. So I faked it just to be done with it. He rolled over, turned his back, and fell asleep within minutes. I stared at the ceiling waiting for his energy to depart—waiting to come back to myself.

After cleaning up in the bathroom, I climbed back into bed and put my loneliness to sleep for the night. I was too embarrassed to ask anyone if this is how it's supposed to be. Then I overheard my mother-in-law tell a family friend, "You have to give your husband what he wants if you want to keep him from straying."

Enduring sex to keep a husband from wandering sounded strange, but it seemed the prevailing attitude. So I did my duty—at least at first I did. Much later in our marriage, a therapist accused me of trying to control Buddy by withholding sex. Thinking there was something wrong with me and in the dark about how women experience pleasure, I lacked the awareness and skills to adequately communicate to the therapist my torment at being approached almost every night for sex devoid of an emotional connection or physical satisfaction.

Then, while I was in seminary, I had an experience of pleasure like never before. Eight classmates with similar theological orientations and political leanings formed a group. We all enjoyed hanging out between classes in the lounge and during lunch in the cafeteria. We engaged in spirited conversations about our experiences as students and our philosophies of life. Men on campus treated me as someone interesting to them. They took what I said seriously. The life force surged through me. I found myself attracted to a man in our group and went a little crazy.

I sat next to Andrew one day as we gathered on couches and overstuffed chairs in the lounge. The punch line to a story caused us all to roar laughing. I reached over and squeezed Andrew's knee. He stopped laughing, turned toward me with a stunned expression, and smiled. It does not reflect well on us that before long we crossed a forbidden line and sought ways to be alone together. The sexual tension between us pulsated, but we were both married.

Andrew made it clear he loved his wife and would never leave her. Leaving our spouses for each other hadn't entered my mind. I was just innocently enjoying the male attention I craved. Those feel-good chemicals knocked my brain off-line.

One day after lunch about fifteen classmates, including our group, arranged cafeteria chairs into a large oval between the tables. Andrew and I sat next to each other, but a two-foot gap separated our chairs. A vigorous debate ensued. Andrew leaned forward, his back toward me, arguing his theological or political perspective with a guy across the circle.

Without warning, waves of sexual energy coursed through my body, catching me off guard. I had never experienced such heightened pleasure and felt closer to an orgasm than ever in my life. *This feels wonderful, but does anybody else notice what's happening? What could have triggered it in this unlikely setting?*

Later I realized the trigger related to how I felt at the seminary. I belonged in this place with these people. They accepted and valued me for who I was. This vibrant man found me attractive. My body awakened and I experienced the joy of full aliveness. At thirty-three years old, I was in love with life for the first time.

Satisfied with the point he made, Andrew leaned back in his chair and turned toward me as though looking for affirmation. My face felt so hot, I must have been blushing. His smile turned to puzzlement as he studied me for a moment. A knowing grin spread across his face. He apparently sensed the energy. To my relief, no one else seemed to notice.

When I came to my senses, I realized the improper nature of our "affair of the heart" and was grateful for the restraint we exercised. Not about to succumb to the sexual tension between us, we remained friends until his graduation, a year before mine. Our tryst lasted only a few months. I admired Andrew's wife and carried guilt for many years for having intruded into her marriage.

I gained understanding and compassion for myself years later after reading an online quote attributed to Daniel Wile, author of *Couples Therapy: A Non-traditional Approach*. It said, "It's not that someone's acting crazy. It's just that they're suffering from emotional malnutrition. Withholding love, affection, and care will drive someone to do things they would not normally do." [3]

Yes, my emotional malnutrition had led to an inappropriate attachment to another man. However, it had also served as the backdrop for my ability to empathize with my Planned Parenthood client. It had led to a call to use my gifts as a pastoral counselor. A positive outcome emerged.

But now, after hearing Nicole's screams and finding Doug's stolen magazines, questions swirled in my mind. *Does Doug's behavior come from being exposed to his father's magazines? Is he acting out what we aren't dealing with? Are we such bad parents? Are our sins being visited on our children? Is this God's punishment? How can I be effective as an ordained minister? Do I deserve to be an ordained minister?*

Tired to the bone of Buddy's passivity and irresponsibility, I stopped expecting him to help me deal with our children's challenges. I saw him as a big part of the problem. Ashamed for not protecting our children from his magazines and videos, I could not afford to be a wimp again. When Buddy arrived home after work, I did the only thing I knew to do. I took charge, trying to bring some order from this chaos. I bellowed out the full story of how I found the magazines and barked commands. "Figure out how much they cost. Take Doug to the drug store, and work out a plan with the manager for Doug to reimburse them for every penny he owes. And you supervise to make sure he does."

I continued, "I'm calling a counselor in the morning to schedule the first appointment available. Whatever they recommend, we'll do. And we can't leave the kids alone. I don't know for how long. We'll see what the counselor says, but I can guarantee it'll be for a long time. So be prepared."

Buddy stared at me impassively with no hint of concern or heartbreak or anguish. If he held any guilt or shame for our family's mess, he hid it. He assumed no responsibility, showed no understanding of my distress, offered no consolation, and suggested no alternative course of action. He did what I told him to do.

I revealed my controlling behavior to the counselor when I scheduled an individual appointment. He asked why I came alone. I don't remember my exact answer, but I remember thinking his question strange. *Isn't it obvious we can't leave the kids alone? We haven't figured out who will stay with them. This is serious. We need help fast. I'm the one who has to take charge. No one else will. Haven't I made that clear?*

Our counselor scheduled an appointment to assess us as a family. He recommended marital therapy supplemented with individual therapy for Buddy and me. Our children were not to be left alone for a year, and we were charged with finding healthy outlets for Doug to take his mind off acting out sexual fantasies. Joan, a close friend from Middletown, agreed to stay with Doug and Nicole while their father and I attended counseling sessions. She was like a sister to me and an aunt to our children. She had known them since they were infants, had taught them in Sunday school, and cared about them deeply. I arranged my schedule and redoubled my efforts to make sure I arrived home before school dismissed.

A parishioner sought my counsel about her unhappy marriage. I felt honored to receive her trust, but questioned my ability to minister to her or others with our family on the verge of collapse. I covered my pain and hid our shameful circumstances as best I could. But I felt ripped apart, like a fraud living a double life. I hated the incongruity between my home life and my professional life. It needed addressing, and I felt ready to face the challenge. I felt ready to make a change. And a big change was what was called for.

PART II - AWAKENING

It is in facing your conflicts, criticisms, and contradictions that you grow up. You will remain largely unconscious as a human being until issues come into your life that you cannot fix or control and something challenges you at your present level of development, forcing you to expand and deepen. It is in the struggle with our shadow self, with failure, or with wounding, that we break into higher levels of consciousness.

~Richard Rohr

*Yesterday I was clever, so I wanted to change the world.
Today I am wise, so I am changing myself.*

~Rumi

Finding a Better Way

1983–1984

There's always a better way.

~Thomas Edison

In 1978, a seminary classmate returned from a conference with a grainy tape recording of Anne Wilson Schaef's keynote address based on her forthcoming book, *Women's Reality*. I joined a dozen or so women seminarians gathered on the lush green lawn around the tape recorder, leaning forward to catch every word Schaef spoke about the three value systems she had identified that operate in our culture.

First, she described the values and behaviors of the "white male system" that are prized in our patriarchal society—seeing oneself as innately superior, performing competitively and aggressively to win and gain power over others, and maintaining the status quo once one has accumulated power. Her description validated the experience some of us encountered while seeking ordination within the church's patriarchal, hierarchical system. We nodded our heads in recognition.

Schaef went on to describe the way women react in this dominant system in order to survive. Seeing ourselves as innately inferior, we compete with and are aggressive with each other while behaving passively with our supposed superiors. She labeled this pattern of behavior the "reactive female system." Knowing smiles and chuckles ensued as each of us identified with one or more of our ineffective reactions to the cruel rejection we had experienced by church authorities.

Schaef then invited her audience to embrace an alternative system of values and behaviors that she called an "emerging female system." Because it focuses on equal relationships, people in this system are forthright in expressing their wants, needs, and opinions while at the same time considering those of others. They share power and cooperate with others in the service of a common goal. Mesmerized, we looked at each other around the circle with wonder in our eyes. We yearned for the respect this alternative bestows on actions taken for the greater good, regardless of who makes the contribution.

Five years later, in 1983, Schaef's name jumped off the flier I pulled from my mailbox. When I read the description of her upcoming weekend intensive workshop two hours from my home, I sensed Divine guidance leading me to the help I needed for the big change I sought. According to the flier, the workshop would help participants work through denied, suppressed, or distorted past or present feelings so they might experience healing and spiritual growth.

Receiving this flier didn't seem a coincidence. Presented with what seemed a perfect environment to address the widening gap between my personal and professional life, I lifted a silent prayer: *Thank you, thank you, thank you.* I made the necessary arrangements and registered.

In April 1983, at Hartford City's John XXIII Retreat Center, twenty-five women sat in a circle on Back Jack floor chairs and huge pillows in the basement meeting room. Schaef outlined the weekend and invited us to introduce ourselves and share what brought us to the workshop.

The women who recruited Schaef to Hartford City started us off by sharing intimate details about their personal and professional lives. Tears and laughter accompanied their stories, and feedback followed each narrative. Accustomed to preplanning the retreats I facilitated to the nth degree, I watched warily as Schaef sat across the circle knitting. *I've never seen anyone do this before. How can she facilitate while she's knitting?* No one else seemed concerned.

By the end of the session, I had relaxed. *Strange. I find her knitting comforting. It's as though hypervigilance isn't necessary here. It's a safe space to go with the flow. Nothing is going to happen we can't handle. Very interesting.*

Schaef's feedback included references to addictive and codependent attitudes and behavior. Because of my awareness that my grandfather's drinking had inflicted scars on my mother and her siblings, her feedback about addiction piqued my curiosity. I also wanted to learn about codependence, a new term.

I sat back, observing how others interacted with the workshop structure before I summoned the courage to share anything about myself. I mentioned my grandfather's alcoholism and the scars I noticed in my mother, aunts, and uncle. Several women related to having grown up in an alcoholic family or had parents who did. Someone mentioned Claudia Black's book about adult children of alcoholics, *It Will Never Happen to Me*. I made a mental note to read it when I returned home, thinking it might help me understand my mother.

Then Schaef invited me to go deeper—to share what was going on in my life. I no longer remember the specifics of what I revealed or the feedback I received. I do remember I was not ready to expose the details about my unhappy marriage and problem children. I was relieved no one pushed me for more.

As I listened to others' feedback and heard more about addiction and codependence, a few pieces of my life's puzzle began to fit together. The link between my mother's scars and the pain in my marriage and mothering was one puzzle piece I wanted to explore further. I felt hopeful because if codependent and addictive behavior was the problem in my family, it could be changed. Healing was possible.

During lunch, women already involved in Schaef's work—two as therapists and one as a nun—told me their experiences at intensive workshops similar to this one but longer in duration. They talked about the development of Schaef's thinking, which she planned to describe fully in the book she was currently working on, *When Society Becomes an Addict*. She now views the patriarchal, hicrarchical system as addictive and endemic in American culture, numbing and deadening our spirit and sometimes our bodies every bit as much as alcohol and drugs do. In the book, she renames the "emerging female system," referring to it as a "living process system."

They also told me about Schaef's training program, Living in Process, which would begin in September. All three had enrolled because of their enthusiasm for the training's spiritual foundation and their desire to live and work in a life-affirming manner. The two therapists intended to create a private practice adhering to these values. Attracted to the spiritual dimension, the nun hoped to make a difference in her community and order.

These women and their intentions inspired me. Living in Process seemed to give shape to *the better way* I had searched for since childhood. I sensed it would bring my personal and professional life into alignment and restore my integrity. When the weekend intensive came to a close, I was convinced I must register for this training program.

While driving home, I tried to figure out how to make taking this step possible. It wouldn't be easy, but I had five months to work on it. In addition to the four week-long training sessions, each trainee must serve as a staff member for three or four intensive workshops to hone facilitation skills. By September we would be a year-and-a-half down the road from our family's last crisis, but I couldn't fathom leaving Doug and Nicole alone together yet. We had no family who could help. Joan, our friend who stayed with them during our counseling sessions, worked during after-school hours. At fifteen and twelve, they were too old for a babysitter. The only person I had to rely on was Buddy.

He agreed to take a vacation week for the first training in September but couldn't guarantee his availability for future sessions. Citing demands at work, he said he would do what he could. I was anxious about this but decided to go ahead and apply, trusting I would figure out childcare when the time came.

Our first training session was held in Estes Park, Colorado, near Schaef's home. Anne, as she preferred to be called, began by creating an environment in alignment with the values and behaviors of the Living in Process system. She encouraged us to be open and honest about our thoughts and feelings. Coming from dysfunctional and addictive families, we were accustomed to protecting ourselves by repressing our feelings and hiding our true thoughts. Honest expression took courage even though we had been given permission.

Unnerved, at first I felt as though I had been dropped into an alien world. With time I came to experience this directness as more trustworthy than the indirect, confusing messages I had learned to give and receive in the family I grew up in and had unknowingly perpetuated with Buddy, Doug, and Nicole.

During the training and at intensive workshops, we sat in a circle and shared our stories. When strong feelings emerged, we were encouraged to allow them expression. An experienced facilitator sat with us and coached us to stay with our undulating feelings until they subsided naturally. We called this a "deep process." Other participants helped the facilitator by creating a nest of pillows that they shifted in harmony with our body movements to allow for the safe discharge of emotions. During a deep process, sobbing, angry pounding, or gales of laughter intermingled with thrashing and moments of quiet respite. Afterward, we often looked brighter, sounded clearer, and sometimes expressed profound wisdom.

Twelve-step meetings and principles were incorporated into all the sessions. Each trainee was to identify her or his addictive process and give Anne and each other permission to call us on our "stuff." I identified my addiction as codependence. Since childhood, I had wanted to fix my mother's family by helping them heal their scars. That led to my attempts to fix our family by changing Buddy and our children. I thought I couldn't get my needs met any other way.

Anne called my complaints about Buddy "a deeply ingrained addictive way to deaden the painful feelings" I had carried since childhood—my fear, guilt, and shame. She was clear that my recovery's focus needed to be on changing my own thinking and behavior, not Buddy's or anyone else's.

We found it impossible to hide our unhealthy thinking and behavior from Anne. She was unrelenting at spotting and naming it. I found it shocking to have my codependence called out—my manipulative attempts to control everyone and everything around me, arrogantly thinking I knew how things were supposed to be. It felt like being under a microscope.

Anne insisted on our need to attend meetings and work the twelve-step program at home between training sessions and workshops. Without this reinforcement, we could not move beyond our painful, survival-oriented existence. We were encouraged to turn our will and our life over to a power greater than ourselves. Doing so promised to lead to fullness of life—very different from the chaos our addictive minds created. Choosing to live fully and thrive would take consistent fortification.

During the intensive workshops held throughout the year around the country, trainees participated in staff meetings. We were expected to share what we observed about group dynamics and the attendees' addictive processes. Anne would then give her perceptions and the reasons for her interventions, teaching us to strengthen our observation and facilitation skills.

During my first two or three staff meetings as a trainee, I kept quiet. I didn't trust my intuition and feared I was damaged beyond repair. I thought that if Anne discovered this, she would kick me out of the training. However, I noticed others gave feedback I would have given if I had possessed the courage. My insights were usually accurate. I noticed those who spoke also received confrontations about their "stuff." Anne threatened no one with expulsion. My confidence grew and my voice strengthened.

The Living in Process training was the closest thing to *the better way* I had found after searching for so long. It was a spiritual approach with concrete steps and practical suggestions. It held the promise that I would be able to see more clearly my part in contributing to the pain in our family and make needed changes that could lead to healing for all of us. I wanted that more than anything, especially for Doug's and Nicole's sakes.

In November 1983, after weeks wrestling with the decision, I resigned from my position at the church, withdrawing from work giving me a huge sense of purpose. Jack, the Senior Pastor, had resigned to accept another position. I didn't see how I could handle increased responsibilities during the interim before a new pastor was found. There was no way I could even entertain the thought of giving up the Living in Process training. Besides, how could I minister to others given our family's situation?

Resigning made my professional life as unstable as my personal life. Even though I would continue receiving a stipend for my work at the seminary, I tossed and turned at night worrying about how Buddy would react to my not contributing as much to the family income. Would he try to control me? If he did, how would I handle that?

The end of January 1984, four years after I began, my service to the church came to an end. I set a priority to devote my extra time to my recovery.

Linda behind the pulpit.

Changing

1984–1987

*Incredible change happens in your life
when you decide to take control of what you do have power over
instead of craving control over what you don't.*

~Steve Maraboli

Changing proved more difficult than I imagined. I found it challenging to replace "they need to change" with "I need to change." I came home from my first training session sounding strong as I declared, "I've learned that some of my behaviors keep me miserable. I'm going to figure out what I'm doing, and I'm going to change myself."

First, I decided to change the way I acted when I was angry. I knew I needed to stop mumbling and grumbling resentments under my breath or worse, holding them inside until they burst forth in slamming cupboard doors and yelling "Damn, shit, hell." I attempted to communicate my thoughts and feelings directly, but being open and honest took all the courage and skill I could muster.

I started off well by confronting Buddy about his attitude toward parenting. "I feel angry when I need you to care for our children while I'm at training and you use work as an excuse. I'm frustrated you give me all the responsibility for making sure the kids are taken care of. You're their father. I need you to take equal responsibility for finding someone to stay with them if you can't. I need you to see yourself as a father and not a babysitter."

"You're being unreasonable. We're not that different from other people."

"When you tell me I'm unreasonable about something so important to me, I feel hopeless."

I felt proud of myself for speaking up, but then I started to slip back into my codependence. I did the best I could with my limited awareness and skill.

I told Buddy that I intended "to trust my process and live." When he said he didn't know what I meant, I told him about my tape of a talk Anne had given on the subject. "If you want to know what I mean, you could listen to it."

That is when I started to slip. I hoped Buddy would listen and experience an epiphany. I began to pay more attention to his behavior than to my own. Under my self-centered wish for him to meet my needs was my fervent wish for healing for our family.

Sometime during the next few days, he did listen to my tape of Anne's talk and even decided to read a paper she had written on creative intimacy. He said, "I see how I'm not doing it ... how watching TV and drinking pop and eating snacks at night helps me stuff my feelings."

Pleased that he responded better than I expected, I began to watch him. I noticed him cutting down on pop and snacks, but not his TV viewing. What I didn't notice was my steely-eyed focus on him.

I felt proud of myself for speaking up, so I raised an even scarier issue. Because he had come to some awareness of how he avoids intimacy, I shared my honest feelings about sex. "I feel used when you approach me for sex after paying no attention to me all day. I can't give in anymore."

"Okay, I'll probably be mad at the time, but I'll have it all figured out by morning."

I continued watching to see if he would change his intimacy-avoiding behavior. My codependence had a tight grip on me.

To my relief, Buddy did respond to my concerns about childcare for the December training. It was now two years after our crisis, and we had achieved success involving Doug and Nicole in activities interesting to them. We left them alone for short periods. Buddy arranged to leave work early, arriving home shortly after they did, assuming the responsibility I had requested.

At first, my process of changing was slow and laborious. I would take two steps forward followed by one step backward into old coping behaviors before proceeding forward again. Keeping the focus on changing myself needed consistent fortification. Fortunately, Anne had built reinforcement into the training program.

Anne divided the fifteen 1983–84 trainees into regional groups and encouraged us to meet one weekend a month to share our progress and give each other "tough love," naming any addictive behavior or attitude we spotted. The women in my group hailed from New York, Georgia, and Indiana. This group became a learning laboratory for authentic relationships. The eight of us held each other accountable for our decision to root out and replace our survival attitudes and behaviors with life-enhancing ones. We supported each other's personal and spiritual growth, which filled a deep need for me. It reinforced my belief that I had been led to this path.

However, shame held me back from divulging the extent of our family dysfunction. My group's honest and loving feedback about what I did reveal expanded my trust and gave me the courage to share our family's deplorable circumstances. I also admitted to my jealousies and insecurities with the members of our group, naming a major addictive process of mine—comparing myself with others and seeing them as smarter, prettier, more well-liked, well-balanced, or savvy.

Instead of the judgment and rejection I expected, my candor opened the door for frank confessions about our insecurities with each other. Amazed that I wasn't the only one carrying these feelings, I saw how isolated my self-loathing left me and how liberating being vulnerable could be.

Their feedback and that of others in our whole training group about my growing and healing increased my hope about being on the trail of the better way I had longed for my entire life. They all strengthened me to continue moving forward.

However, I resisted attending local twelve-step meetings. I worried about seeing someone I knew and didn't want anyone in the Dayton area knowing the truth about our family. I much preferred depending on my training allies. But I suspected Anne would question my commitment if I hadn't given meetings a try before our March training.

In late February 1984, I forced myself to attend my first local twelve-step meeting for family members of alcoholics, even though the thought of it brought on diarrhea and stomach cramps. I didn't see anyone I knew and made it through the entire meeting. I appreciated their recommendation to newcomers: "Listen to see what we're all about. If you don't like what we have to offer, we'll refund your misery."

The meeting topic focused on the first step of the program—*We admitted we were powerless over alcohol—that our lives had become unmanageable.* While listening to how the group members addressed this step in their lives, I recalled my first visceral reaction to hearing the Serenity Prayer—*God, grant me the serenity to accept the things I cannot change, the courage to change the things I can, and the wisdom to know the difference.* I didn't want to accept there was anything I couldn't change.

I was well aware that my life was unmanageable, but the words "powerless" and "things I cannot change" vexed me. If I couldn't control Doug's acting out behavior, I was sure he would go wild, worse than he had already. Letting go seemed like weakness and irresponsibility to me.

Before attending my second meeting the next week, I decided to give "admitting I'm powerless" a try—letting go like some said they did. *What do I have to lose? Nothing I've tried so far has worked. It's only for a week.* I was surprised at how much less tension I carried after being relieved of the necessity to keep everybody under control.

At my second meeting, I shared, "It's weird. I tried to be in control because I felt powerless. And now, admitting I'm powerless, I feel more powerful." The other attendees smiled and nodded knowingly.

Despite my positive beginning, I wasn't sure I belonged. Others talked about their alcoholic or drug-addicted family member. I had no such stories. I attended meetings sporadically; by May, I had quit altogether.

My forty-second birthday fell on a Sunday in July. The phone rang and Penny, a member of my regional group, called to wish me a happy birthday.

Noticing the tone in my voice, she said, "You sound pissy."

"I am." I relayed the details of my miserable week. "Doug and I just fought over chores. Buddy has been on vacation all week. He hasn't showered, and he smells awful. His hair is greasy, and he is running around the house barefoot. His t-shirt is too small and his belly hangs out over his pants. On top of that, he growls at me because I don't want to have sex with him."

I had no way of knowing then that Buddy's poor hygiene provided a clue to a family puzzle we would not solve for another fifteen years.

Penny asked, "Have you been to a meeting?"

"No. Well, I've been to a few, but it's been awhile. I don't know if I belong there. I've never lived with an active alcoholic."

"Could you relate to the people there at all?"

"Oh, yeah, I act as crazy as they do."

"Did you feel better afterward?"

"Well, yes, it seemed to help, but I feel out of place."

"Sounds like you're trying to handle everything yourself. That keeps you in your shit, you know. Get to a meeting."

And so I did. That evening I attended a "lead" meeting, during which someone recounts what life was like before meetings and what life is like now. The person scheduled to give her lead didn't show, so someone suggested we form a circle and share what was going on with us.

When it came to my turn, I burst into tears. I told them why I had been avoiding meetings and about Penny's telephone call. They welcomed me, saying, "It's clear you're in pain, so you must belong here."

I had just been graced with a swift kick in the rear—Penny serving as an agent of The Divine. It seemed no coincidence the person scheduled to lead failed to show. If she had, I would have remained silent through the meeting and gone home untouched by the extravagant welcome the group extended and I needed.

I started attending at least three meetings a week. The family hardly noticed my absence. I was away less than two hours and always returned in a better mood.

Because anonymity is observed at twelve-step meetings, no one knew I was an ordained minister. I liked it that way. It helped me hide my embarrassment at the difficulty I had trusting the wisdom and guidance of a power greater than myself. I couldn't reconcile my intellectual understanding of a compassionate spiritual presence with my one-damn-thing-after-another episodes with my children.

The depth of my difficulty revealed itself at a meeting focusing on the third step—*We made a decision to turn our will and our lives over to the care of God as we understood God*. I was stunned by the sudden spasm of sobs that burst forth when it came my turn to share. All I could squeak out was, "I don't believe God cares about me." My prayers for my family seemed to go unanswered. I interpreted what seemed to be God's silence as judgment and lack of care. I couldn't make sense of how I could have been called to be an ordained minister while being judged for my personal life.

Years later, I realized that the God I experienced when I was in pain bore a striking resemblance to my mother—critical and disapproving. As a result, I turned God's judgment in on myself and created a toxic cycle of self-reproach and suffering. All this tortuous thinking contaminated my relationship with God. Bringing my intellectual image into my everyday life at an emotional level was what ultimately transformed my relationship with The Divine and provided the key to lasting change.

The practical tools offered in the twelve-step program brought this transformation about more than church and theological studies. As Richard Rohr, a Franciscan priest and mystic, avows, "The twelve-step program represents the best of American spirituality, offering a very practical way of living the Gospel." [4]

In the training and twelve-step program, others described how they practiced self-care without trying to control others' inappropriate behavior. I decided to give it a try. It provided the greatest contribution to the positive changes occurring in all my relationships.

I held resentment about "having" to cajole Doug and Nicole into cleaning their messy and grit-laden rooms. In my new behavior, I let go of persuading them except on rare occasions. I avoided going near Doug's room in the basement. I closed Nicole's bedroom door or passed by without looking.

I didn't mind doing their laundry, but I resented "having" to wash, dry, fold, and hang the clean clothes Doug and Nicole threw on the floor and walked on all week. One day I summoned them to the laundry room. "I'm going to show you how to do your own laundry."

I taught them how to use the washer and dryer and declared, "As long as you don't abuse my laundry room, you're welcome to use it. If you abuse it, there's a Laundromat down the street." To my surprise, they took responsibility and never needed to resort to the Laundromat. *Why didn't I do this sooner?*

Buddy and the kids snacked after school and in the evenings. I resented "having" to clean their mess before I could prepare dinner. One day I announced, "If the kitchen is a mess when it comes time to make dinner, I'm going out to eat. You'll find hot dogs and tater tots in the freezer. You can make your own dinner."

After a few nights, they missed my cooking, and Buddy resented spending extra money to eat out, so they all decided cleaning up was a better option. I let go of my perfectionism and accepted a messier kitchen than I preferred—a reasonable compromise.

Setting boundaries and having the backbone to make them stick became crucial because by the age of seventeen, Doug had turned into a master manipulator, and I had allowed myself to become putty in his hands. Whenever he didn't get what he wanted, he wore me down with, "Why? Why? Why?" Caught in the trap of explaining every "why," I often yielded in exasperation.

One weekend he asked for the car to take friends to a concert, a privilege he hadn't earned. I stood firm saying, "No" and "No discussion."

He could tell his efforts would not change my mind. He screamed at me, "You're changing. I hate you."

I noted this as a sign of progress.

I went on to set a boundary with my mother. When she criticized my daughter as she had me, I confronted her unacceptable behavior: "We won't come to Florida for Christmas if this is how you're going to treat my daughter."

As a result, for two years my parents rarely initiated contact. During this time, my mother, who I doubt would ever consider seeking therapy or attending a twelve-step meeting, found a way to change her behavior. From that point forward, with few exceptions, she treated both my daughter and me with respect.

Despite my family's initial discomfort and hatred of my boundary-setting, they grew to respect me. Many years later, Doug demonstrated his awareness of how he had manipulated me. He and Nicole approached me, smiling mischievously. Doug handed me a cartoon from the Sunday funnies. It depicted a mother caught in the "Why?" trap with her son. After his mom gave in, the son walked away saying to his friend, "I find it takes eighteen 'whys' to get a 'yes.' How about you?" We laughed together, and I tucked the cartoon in a scrapbook for safekeeping.

During this time, I met area addiction professionals who invited me to a nearby addiction treatment center to observe their family therapy program. Their invitation changed my professional path.

I found the center's education program on family roles and codependence familiar but had not witnessed a therapist assisting a family in a group format. One family was asked to sit in the center of a huge circle surrounded by other families and observers. Those of us observing learned from this family's healing work. When they finished, we gave supportive feedback, sharing how we identified with them and what we learned about ourselves. I so admired these families' vulnerability and courage—their honest, raw expression of love and pain. It moved me to tears.

I knew in my soul I was meant to work with families caught in the pain of addiction. As unlikely as it seemed, I sensed a call to serve as a healer of relationships. This time, I did not ignore my inner guidance. Trusting my life's process, I chose this new path instead of the one leading to pastoral counseling.

In October 1985, that treatment center hired me as an outpatient addiction family therapist. I continued attending Living in Process regional gatherings and at least one intensive workshop a year for six years. My experience growing up in a family scarred by addiction gave me perspective laced with compassion and empathy. My Living in Process training and recovery gave me essential skills. And then, in 1987, while I served as a healing agent for others, our family hit bottom. Thankfully, this time I was better prepared to handle it.

Shattered

1987

Life does not accommodate you; it shatters you.

~Florida Scott-Maxwell

Doug and I tussled. He was determined to participate in Senior Skip Day by staying home from school; I was just as determined he go. With Ds and Fs, he hadn't earned the right to participate in senior shenanigans. I locked him out of the house when Nicole and I left. Driving to work, I counted the days until graduation on May 15, 1987. We hadn't received any word that he wouldn't graduate so despite his low grades, I was sure they planned to give him his diploma.

I didn't think to lock the windows. He jimmied a screen off a kitchen window, opened it, and climbed in. When I arrived home, I walked into a mess in the kitchen. When I discovered he had stayed home watching TV all day, I went berserk.

I knew it wouldn't do any good, but I stomped and yelled and screamed and threw my hands in the air. Doug would turn nineteen in August, had been legally an adult for almost nine months, but acted worse than a two year old. *What is to become of him? When will he grow up and take responsibility for his life?* Doug took refuge in his basement bedroom. Nicole cowered in her room upstairs.

I plopped on the living room couch, exhausted from my rampage. Seeking calm, I took several deep breaths and prayed the Serenity Prayer to what seemed an absent God. Nothing was working. My powerlessness over Doug grated on me. I felt suffocated and near a breaking point. I didn't know how much longer I could stand his living with us.

The storm subsided. Nicole inched toward me, saying, "Mom, I have to tell you something you don't want to hear, but I can't take it any longer. You have to promise me some things first. Promise me Doug will never hurt me again—ever. Promise not to get too angry. If you promise me these two things, I'll tell you. Please don't tell Doug or Dad." Her slumped shoulders radiated heaviness. Her sorrowful eyes searched mine.

She needs me to be sane and strong. I must regain control of myself. "Okay, I won't let Doug hurt you, and I promise to stay calm. I can't promise I won't tell your dad."

She handed me a folded note addressed to her teacher. "I almost gave this to Mrs. Hellman today."

The note read, "A friend of mine told me her eighteen-year-old brother has made her have sex with him. Do you know a way to help her with this problem? Help."

The shock was like a bomb exploding and scattering shrapnel. Clutching the note with an iron grip, my hands fell into my lap. My throat constricted and held back a wail. *I must remain calm for Nicole. I have to handle this well.*

I lifted my head to Nicole standing before me, her face ashen. Her moist eyes stared at me; her chin trembled. I reached for her hand and pulled her down on the couch beside me. I drew her close, and put my arm around her shoulder, saying "I'm sorry. I'm so, so sorry. Don't worry. Doug won't hurt you again. I'll see to that. I'll take care of this."

Her head rested on my shoulder. We sat entwined until she wriggled away and returned to her room.

I pressed my lips together hard and let the gravity of our situation sink into my bones. *This is bad, really bad. I don't think we can go any lower than this. I can't imagine anything worse. Incest has to be a bottom.*

Sick to my stomach, I considered my responsibility for this situation. Despite all we had done the past four years, the situation only grew worse. My thoughts tumbled out pell-mell as I bombarded myself with blame. *We shouldn't have left them alone together again. It's as though an evil force lurks in our home. Those damn magazines, books, and videos. I've been too weak to protect my children from them. I should have left Buddy years ago. How will I ever live with myself? I've screwed up so much. I have to do better now. I have to be strong.*

I muttered a prayer: "God, are you as disgusted with us as I am? I hope this is a bottom. Please help me handle this well." I was praying to an external deity, but it was the Divine force within that strengthened me to handle this crisis in *a better way* than any I had handled before.

I took a deep breath and gathered my resolve. I wouldn't be like those mothers I had heard about in my training who couldn't face the pain and refused to believe their daughters. I knew the importance of trusting Nicole's word and giving her my total support. That was my intention. I began sorting out the steps we needed to take to ensure her safety.

When Buddy arrived home, he expected dinner on the table. Instead, he found me still sitting on the living room couch holding Nicole's note. I handed it to him. As he read it, his face turned red and his eyes narrowed. Before he could do or say anything, I said, "We have to handle this well for Nicole. We have to be calm. She's scared of our anger."

He stood there looking at me frozen in place, the note dangling from his fingers.

I continued my composed resolve. "Doug has to move out tonight. I want you to find a place for him to live."

Buddy located the newspaper and checked the classifieds. He found an ad for a room, called, and rented it. We went downstairs to Doug's bedroom. Buddy told Doug to pack a suitcase. I said, "We know what you've done to Nicole. You're moving out tonight. You can't live here anymore."

At first, he smirked as though he didn't believe we would follow through.

Buddy fetched a suitcase, and I filled a bread wrapper with toiletries and a plastic grocery bag with fruit and snacks.

Doug's voice rose as he pleaded ignorance, "What did I do? I didn't do anything to Nicole."

Buddy sorted through clothes strewn all over the room and tossed his choices on Doug's bed. I appeared and placed the plastic bags on the bed next to them. When neither of us responded to Doug's denials, they tumbled out faster and faster as he tried to convince us to change our mind. Buddy told him to help pack. I leaned against the doorjamb, my arms crossed, and watched.

Doug's voice slowed and grew shaky, "Where am I going?"

Buddy started packing the suitcase and said, "I found you a room downtown."

"What about school?"

"Looks like you won't be going back to school," I said.

Doug gathered a few items he wanted—comic books, toy cars, a notebook, his tape recorder, and tapes—and put them in his backpack.

Buddy closed the suitcase and said, "Let's go."

I trudged up the staircase behind them and watched them climb into the car, back out of the garage, and drive off. Numb and drained of energy, I tried to maintain a sense of normalcy for Nicole's sake. She had heard what went on and if she felt angry about the actions we took, she didn't say so. She seemed relieved I had made good on my promise to prevent Doug from hurting her again.

I went to the kitchen to prepare dinner but walked around in a haze, my mind unable to identify ingredients, organize a menu, or locate cooking utensils. I shook my head to clear the smog and managed to throw something together. It was after dark when Buddy returned. We sat down to eat, our mood solemn as we tried to come to terms with our new reality.

The room Buddy rented was located in a questionable part of town and was more of a flophouse than a rooming house—not a place I ever imagined a child of mine would live. When Doug made a collect call after dark from a pay phone across the street, he pleaded to come home. Another tenant had propositioned him for sex.

I blurted out, "Now you know how your sister felt in her own home."

Doug said nothing.

Shocked by my coldness, I shivered as goose bumps broke out on my arms. Softening my tone, I told him, "Go back to your room and lock the door."

Three weeks earlier, I had started counseling in an agency that specialized in treating sexual abuse survivors and offenders. I wanted to deal with a memory that had surfaced during my Living in Process training of possible abuse by a neighbor when I was seven years old.

On the drive to my appointment the next week, I trembled. I intended to disclose the incest to my counselor and knew she was required to report it to Children's Services. I hated the thought of their involvement in our lives but knew our son needed to answer to authorities beyond his parents.

My revelation set the course in motion. At the end of the week, our family arrived at the agency for scheduled interviews. Buddy transported Doug. Nicole came with me. When we arrived, Buddy was told to remain in the waiting room. No one was permitted to give Doug support during his interview. I dreaded hearing the details of Nicole's abuse but insisted on staying with her. As Nicole's interview concluded, Doug's investigator and Buddy entered the room.

The officer informed us that Doug continued to deny his guilt. He asked Buddy, "Are you willing to press charges?" Buddy looked dazed and didn't answer.

"If you'd heard what I heard, you wouldn't hesitate," I said. Still, Buddy wavered.

So I turned to the officer and said, "I'll press charges."

Nicole followed my lead. "So will I."

I never dreamed when Doug yelled his hatred at no longer being able to manipulate me, it would come to this. When they clicked handcuffs on his wrists and hauled him off to jail, I bowed my head and turned away. The back of my throat hurt as I held back tears. I dug my fingernails into my palms to stop myself from weeping.

As Nicole and I walked to the car, I apologized to her again and said, "I'm proud of the way you handled the interview. You were so mature." We fell silent as though neither of us knew what to say about this gargantuan change in our family.

Images of my son behind bars tortured me. *Will he be safe? God, please protect him. I can't do it anymore. How will our family ever recover from this?*

Clashing

1987

The clash of ideas is the sound of freedom.

~ Lady Bird Johnson

During the weekend Doug spent in jail, Buddy and I met with Sheryl, my counselor at the sexual abuse agency, to find an option after his release. None of us wanted him to go back to the flophouse. Sheryl suggested Doug live with Buddy's parents.

"Wouldn't that be rescuing him?" I asked.

"Probably," she admitted.

This was the first of many clashes to come with mental health professionals, a field I no longer trusted. I now viewed our family through the framework of addiction, convinced addiction was the evil force lurking in our home.

I considered the evidence for my codependent behavior. I issued ultimatums and didn't follow through with them. I avoided conflict by giving into Buddy's bids for sex after he had ignored me all day. I allowed Doug to manipulate me. I tried to fix and change everyone.

I wore myself out trying to control the sick behavior in our family. I tallied the evidence for Buddy's and Doug's sexual addiction. Buddy broke his promise to remove his sexually explicit materials from our home, even after our son stole magazines and tried to molest his sister. He seemed unable to do without these materials. He failed to verbalize any responsibility for our family dynamics, show remorse, or make serious efforts to change his behavior. And now Doug's molestation had progressed to assault.

Today I know that not all sex offenders are addicts, but at the time, with so little understanding about the origin of his and his father's behavior, sexual addiction helped me make sense of our family. No cure existed for addiction, but miracles occurred for those who embraced recovery. Viewing our problem as addiction gave me hope.

All our family's heartache during so many years motivated me to embrace the recovery I had been introduced to through my Living in Process training, and I had benefitted. I continued to work the twelve-step program to change my impaired thinking and behavior; as a result, I had made progress. I had experienced no such improvement during our thirteen years of couples and family therapy. So I pinned all my hopes for our family's healing on the framework used in the addictions field.

I had witnessed rapid turnarounds in many of my twelve-step friends and our treatment center's clients. Enablers' chaos and stress decreased when they stopped rescuing. The addict was often motivated to seek recovery when their consequences became painful enough. I wanted recovery for Doug. I hoped he would choose it, but that couldn't be my focus. Otherwise, I would be back into trying to control him. Codependent enablers walk a slippery slope, and none of us do it perfectly.

I felt tremendous shame about Doug being in jail and guilt for refusing to facilitate his release. However, my recovery depended on finding healthy ways to deal with my suffering and that involved garnering the courage not to step in and try to protect him from his pain. I saw giving Doug "tough love" as our only hope. I was disappointed Sheryl recommended rescuing him. It would have helped to have her backing.

After Sheryl, Buddy, and I had brainstormed several alternatives, hospitalization seemed the best. I agreed to do research and found a reputable Cincinnati psychiatric hospital about an hour away and near Buddy's parents' home. Within days after his release from jail, we admitted Doug. He missed his high school graduation, but during the three months he spent hospitalized throughout the summer of 1987, he earned his diploma in its education program.

For weeks, Doug refused to admit he had sexually abused his sister. During our family therapy session about three weeks after his admission, he attempted to guilt me. We sat on opposite sides of the table facing each other when he said, "You're not supporting me. Dad is. He comes here twice a week. You only come once."

I slammed my hands on the table. Lisa, the social worker sitting next to me, jumped. I yelled, "I supported you by finding the best hospital in the area, and I'm supporting you this minute. I'm here for family therapy. I don't need to come to education sessions. I teach them. Your dad is the one who needs them."

Shocked by my outburst, I turned toward Lisa, "Was that okay?"

Her eyes widened as though surprised by my question. She nodded and said, "Yes."

Toward the end of the session, Lisa relayed the staff's concern about Doug's pending court appearance and his having no representation. Despite being overwhelmed and exhausted by all the demands on our family, I agreed to call a public defender. I narrowed my eyes and looked at Doug. "This is one more way I'll be giving you support."

After he returned to his unit, Lisa prepared us for what Doug's psychiatrist would say in the conference scheduled at the end of the week. She gave sketchy information about Doug being out of touch with reality, living in a fantasy world, and not being capable of responsibility for himself ... perhaps being born with an inability to cope.

Lisa went on to tell us about the staff's concern about our not meeting Doug's nurturing needs. They wanted us to take him out on weekend passes and give him love and support. I gave her a puzzled look and asked, "How do we give love and nurturing when he has hurt us so much and continues to lie about it?"

On the ride home, my mind whirled. *What is love in this situation? How do we arrange weekend passes when he and his sister are to have no contact until her counselor says she's ready? How will he ever experience the consequences of his behavior?*

The next day I called the public defender's office. They gave me scant information, so I called the arresting police officer. He gave me a scary bigger picture. Our daughter would need to testify against her brother in court. That meant Buddy and I would be in the middle—adversaries against our son in support of our daughter in a court of law. Terrifying courtroom scenes played out in my head, tearing me up inside.

I called the prosecutor's office to find out how all this works. The woman who answered the phone and I conferred for more than an hour. She referred me to their Victim Witness Department, a service providing crisis intervention, support, and information. They help victims or witnesses to crimes understand their rights and responsibilities so they can make intelligent decisions that are in their best interests. The prosecutor's office seemed the place to turn for answers.

The next day I couldn't stop crying. I called Sheryl to ask what her agency recommends about contact between offenders and family. Sheryl was on vacation, so Nicole's counselor spoke to me. "I suspect the doctor won't indicate any long-term effects on Doug if you refuse to take him out on passes. He may have other problems he needs to deal with before he can honestly face being a sex offender—like an alcoholic needs to get sober before handling family problems." That explanation made sense to me.

She continued, "Ask them about his treatment plan and goals and what criteria they use to assess the effectiveness."

I couldn't see how their treatment plans and goals would help me as his mother understand how to handle his behavior, so I consulted a Living in Process colleague who worked in an Indianapolis center that used an addiction model to treat sex offenders. The questions she recommended seem more helpful: "Find out about their philosophy dealing with and breaking through his denial system."

The inability to face the truth, a central feature of any addiction, is massive for sex offenders.

"Ask them how they plan to engage Doug in his own recovery and how they deal with his manipulative behavior."

Bolstered by this conversation, I believed I would receive the guidance I needed if the hospital staff explained how they manage Doug's manipulative behavior. I also hoped the psychiatrist would shed light on what the psychologist said about ten-year-old Doug's hostile and aggressive personality. I didn't want to believe it then, but with his sex offender status, I now worried it was true. If one of the professionals we worked with would have confirmed that addiction was our problem, I would have hope for recovery. But if Doug was diagnosed as a sociopath, I foresaw a lifetime of pain before me.

At our meeting, the psychiatrist surprised me when he began by asking how we were doing. Apparently, Nicole's counselor had called to tell the hospital staff about my meltdown. I interpreted his question as kindness and concern, and my eyes welled with tears. I shared my fear of going to trial. His response hit me like a ton of bricks. "Are you afraid of the public exposure?"

What does that mean? Doesn't he understand the trauma associated with testifying in court against a family member ... how agonizing for all of us? What must he think of me with a remark like that? No, I don't want public exposure, but I'm more concerned about the trauma to our family.

When I relayed my fear about Doug being a sociopath, he talked about motorcycle gangs with chains. He seemed blasé about Doug's sexual offense as though he had committed no crime. Then he referred to our refusal to take Doug out on a pass as punishment. "He'll just retreat further into his fantasy world. He's already angry you don't like him and feels abandoned. So even if he did confess, it would be to escape being further abandoned. Under those circumstances, it wouldn't be genuine."

I was so confused and disoriented, I didn't ask how they were trying to break through Doug's denial system and manage his manipulative behavior. The focus appeared to be on our behavior or perhaps on mine—shades of what I had heard nine years previously—"You're an angry woman."

Nicole received counseling, but still the focus was more on Doug's situation than on her healing. The sexual abuse agency tried to figure out the best way to work with our family. They switched Sheryl, my counselor, to Buddy for his individual sessions. She would also work with us as a couple and provide our family therapy. I received a new therapist. My sexual abuse counseling was put on hold as she and I dealt with my part in our family dynamics and my pain about my children's incest.

One day in the middle of my individual session, the therapy room door opened. Startled, I turned to see Nicole and her counselor entering. Her counselor said, "Nicole has some things she needs to say to you."

I straightened my spine, leaned forward, and gave Nicole an inquiring look. I wanted to give her permission to let me have it if she needed to. Her counselor had been encouraging her to confront me. I figured I had it coming. After all, I hadn't protected her. If she needed to express anger, I braced myself to handle it. Nicole said, "You won't let me talk about the shit going on in our family."

"You could call and talk with Joan about anything you want."

"You won't let me talk to anybody else."

"Okay. Maybe I've given you that impression. This whole situation is embarrassing to me. But, if you need to, you have my permission to talk with anybody you want, about anything you want."

"I don't have anybody I want to talk to."

She and her counselor walked out.

I turned and looked at my counselor. "What in the world am I to make of that? Nicole has taken no initiative to call Joan even though she's aware she can. I'm trying to change my overly responsible and controlling behavior. Am I responsible to make the call for her?"

"She is sending you mixed messages. How could you help her build a support system for herself?"

"Is that my responsibility? She's sixteen. I've made sure she's involved in several activities where she could make friends. She has a couple of school friends."

"I don't think she's capable of doing this on her own."

Stunned and lightheaded, no words came. My mind swirled with questions. *What are you saying? Do I have two children who are not capable? What does that mean?*

At our next family session with Doug, I attempted to stand firm about the issue of weekend passes. Doug slumped in his seat and mumbled, "You like Nicole better than me. You always do stuff for her, but you won't do anything for me."

After the session, I summoned the courage to seek the social worker's guidance. "I'm confused. And I feel guilty. The doctor doesn't think Doug is capable of taking responsibility for himself. I'm having a hard time figuring out what I'm responsible for and what I'm not."

Lisa responded, "This isn't intended to be a guilt-inflicting process. We know you care about Doug and are struggling with mixed feelings toward him. There's no clear cut answer to explain Doug's problems."

I wished the hospital staff understood my reluctance to take Doug out on passes. *They think I'm punishing him. They can't see the love behind my refusal to take him out. Am I right to allow him to experience the consequences of his behavior? Maybe I should feel sorry for him ... give him a break. Being kicked out of his home, taken to a flophouse and jail, and now locked up in a psychiatric hospital has to be traumatic. What am I to do?*

I called Lisa the next day and told her I would take him out for a few hours the next weekend.

"What changed your mind?"

I rubbed my forehead with my fingers. "I don't know. I guess I feel guilty ... or maybe I feel sorry for him."

I sank into my chair, shoulders slumped. My face contorted as I held back tears. *What kind of life awaits him if he doesn't change his behavior? Aren't I responsible for doing what I can to see he has a decent life? I want that for him.*

Lisa said, "It's a complicated issue, and you'll just have to keep working on it."

Complicated didn't begin to describe our dilemma. To my eyes, the doctor hurled blame at me. I grew defensive and couldn't understand the sketchy information the staff provided about Doug's fantasy world and inability to cope and assume responsibility. In retrospect, they gave us a clue to his aberrant behavior, but no one would understand its meaning for another twelve years. All I could do during this confusing time was figure out my response to his behavior and this situation.

Weeks later, in another family therapy session with Doug, I asked Lisa, "I'm trying to figure out how to relate to my son. I don't know what is going on with him so the only way I know how to relate to him is by the impact his behavior has on me. Am I on the right track?"

"Yes, you are."

A few weeks later, when she observed me struggling with confusion and uncertainty, she reaffirmed that it was appropriate for me to use the effect of Doug's behavior on me as a barometer in deciding how to respond. "All you have to go on is how his behavior impacts you."

I hung onto her words because they made sense to me. I depended on her guidance to help me figure out how to respond to Doug.

A short time later, the prosecuting attorney called and gave guidance of her own: "I'm trying to get you out of the middle. I want you to stop calling our office with questions your son should ask. He needs to take responsibility to get the information himself."

She didn't understand the complexity of our situation. She didn't know the hospital staff deemed Doug incapable of taking responsibility ... that I had not been able to secure a public defender ... that I could see no other option except to run interference for him. She interpreted my behavior as rescuing and wasn't shy about directing me to stop.

For his pass, I took Doug to visit his grandparents. His grandmother had always experienced a special bond with Doug since she helped care for him after his birth nineteen years earlier. She asked to spend some time alone with him. Buddy's dad and I went to look at their garden. When we returned to the house, to my relief, Doug admitted to abusing his sister. His confession saved our family from the added anguish of having to go to trial.

Living Forward

1987–1988

> *Life can only be understood backwards;*
> *but it must be lived forwards.*
>
> ~Søren Kierkegaard

In my second year as an addiction family therapist, Doug's hospitalization and our family's counseling appointments sometimes affected my attendance at work. I worried about how my colleagues would respond. Our close-knit staff gave me support. They filled in for me, handling my individual appointments, and facilitating my groups when I needed coverage.

I couldn't hide the shameful circumstances in our family from them, and I didn't need to. They gave me emotional support as well. Almost two months into our crisis, Kathy and Carla came into my office and closed the door. "Do you have a minute?" They handed me a picture taken at a recent staff party.

Kathy said, "We want you to look at this picture. We're worried about you. You're losing weight and look tired all the time. You're not going to be good for anybody in your family if you're not taking care of yourself. You know that."

Carla added, "It doesn't look to us like you're taking good care of yourself. We want what's best for you."

My tears began to flow. I knew they were right, and I loved them for their honesty and compassion. They waited while I regained my composure. "I don't know how to practice self-care in the midst of everything that's going on."

I had lived for so many years with shame and fear of judgment about our family that it meant the world to me to be shown care and concern during this worst time in my life. They helped lighten the heavy burden I carried.

We took Doug to Buddy's parents' home after his release from the hospital on Monday, September 7, 1987. We were awaiting word about his acceptance into a halfway house. He hadn't changed much. He walked into his grandparents' guest bedroom, dumped the contents of his suitcase on the floor, and created a mess. Buddy ordered him to straighten it up. He yelled, "Don't tell me what to do. I don't live with you anymore."

I heaved a huge sigh. *Will there ever be an end to this?*

Later in the week, we learned the halfway house had delayed Doug's entrance for at least a month. In the meantime, we reunited as a family at Buddy's brother's house where we celebrated Buddy's and his mother's birthdays. I couldn't relax as I observed Doug and Nicole together again after a three-month separation. They talked about musicians and soap operas and actors, as though nothing traumatic had ever happened between them. My tension only increased when Buddy's mother informed us Doug couldn't stay at their house any longer. She said Buddy's dad was jealous and wanted her to cater only to him. We needed to make other arrangements for Doug by the end of the week.

We found a motel renting rooms on a monthly basis south of town and decided to house Doug there until he entered the halfway house. Its kitchenette saved us money. We bought him groceries and told him he could do his own cooking. I no longer remember the reason, but the admission to the halfway house never materialized. Instead, we rented a furnished apartment and gave him three months to find a job and meet his own expenses.

The court ordered Doug into the treatment program for sex offenders at the agency where Buddy, Nicole, and I received counseling. They also mandated community service, but Doug skipped out on it. I bristled and complained to our therapist. "He should be grateful they didn't send him back to jail. His probation officer should enforce his service. Will he ever have consequences severe enough to deter him from more trouble?"

Sheryl advised me to stay out of it.

The Bureau of Vocational Rehabilitation (BVR) accepted Doug as a client. They also sent him to two different professionals for testing—a risk assessment with a therapist specializing in working with sex offenders and a psychological test with a psychologist. I was relieved to learn that he didn't fit the profile of an adult sex offender. But my relief turned to dread when I was told that the psychological test indicated that Doug had an antisocial personality disorder.

Now Doug joined Buddy, Nicole, and me for family therapy at the sexual abuse agency. I was amazed at my children's perceptions.

Doug said, "Dad plays games. He learns the rules and then does just enough to get by."

Nicole nodded. "He's stubborn."

Buddy chuckled and admitted they were right about him.

Sheryl looked at me and said, "You carry all the expectations and hopes for the family. That's not good for you or for them."

I decided to remain quiet during our next session—a further letting-go step. Perhaps Buddy would lead the way and mention something our family needed to work on. He didn't.

Sheryl confronted him. As far as I know, this was the only time any counselor challenged him. "What is your responsibility in the relationship with your wife and children? What do you contribute to the pain in your family? You must have some responsibility here."

Buddy's face reddened and puffed. He blustered, "I don't know what you're talking about." Spit flew across the room. "I do what I'm supposed to do. I bring in the money. I let her do what she wants. And I do more than most men do. I babysit the kids while she is gone doing her thing. I even cook. I do a lot of the cooking."

I shook my head. *How much pain does our family have to experience before you admit to your part?*

When Anne Wilson Schaef traveled to our area for a consulting job, I sought her advice. She told me she had trained with the developers of the psychological tests Doug received at the hospital. She offered to review his tests if he granted her permission.

Doug agreed. Four months after his discharge, January 1988, against hospital wishes, he signed releases of information to Anne.

She and I began corresponding. I wrote extensive details in long letters, hoping to receive her wisdom and insight. In March, three months later, I received her letter. She gave her interpretation of Doug's tests along with feedback about how my letters portrayed my relationship with Nicole.

Anne interpreted Doug's features as reflective of a nine- or ten-year-old child. His inability to distinguish between different emotions left him with no idea how to channel or work with them. She said it must be frightening for him and contributed to his severe lack of impulse control. She could see why he had so many problems in school. She identified something organic going on and recommended we consult a pediatric neurologist.

Anne made several suggestions and encouraged me not to handle it all on my own. She told me about a new Living in Process trainee, a Dayton occupational therapist. "Let Barbara help you with some of this."

Anne also confronted me about enabling Nicole's learned helplessness. She pointed out that I seemed to have no problem refraining from enabling Doug, but, because I viewed Nicole as a helpless victim, I didn't support her to take back her power. I trusted and respected Anne and appreciated her straightforwardness, though her feedback jarred me. It seemed I had gone overboard in my intention to give Nicole my total support.

Anne's feedback gave me something specific to work on. I hated the thought that I had passed my own learned helplessness to my daughter. I didn't want one more disempowering moment for Nicole or me. I wanted this chain of dysfunction broken.

In May 1988, Anne planned to facilitate a weekend intensive workshop in Brown County, Indiana. I insisted Nicole attend with me, even though she made it clear she didn't like the idea. I hoped both of us would take a giant step beyond our learned helplessness.

Anne thought it important for Doug to meet her and experience for himself her interest in helping him. Buddy agreed to bring him to the workshop on Sunday afternoon.

Doug warmed to Anne and the other attendees and participated more during his short visit than Nicole did the whole weekend. Buddy could have joined the group, but instead he sat at a picnic table a short distance away fidgeting and chewing his fingernails. When he glanced at us, his eyes were cold and hard.

After Buddy and Doug left, the group expressed their regret that Doug didn't stay. I explained that I couldn't take the risk because he and Nicole would have to be watched every minute to make sure Doug had no opportunity to isolate Nicole from the rest of the group. They all grew quiet and thoughtful as they grasped the complexity of our situation. I searched each face for signs of disapproval but found nothing but compassion. Tears moistened my eyes as the sadness and heartbreak I had been repressing was released in the presence of their empathy.

With Barbara's help, we found an Indianapolis pediatric neurologist and scheduled an appointment for August 10, twenty-one days before Doug's twentieth birthday. Barbara accompanied us to the visit.

Dr. Hale, a jovial balding man in his 60s, joked with Doug during the examination. When he discovered cramping in Doug's hands and stiffness in his tongue, Dr. Hale's eyes opened wide, he chuckled and danced around as though celebrating something. I didn't know what to make of his manner. He called it "myotonia." I was aware that Nicole experienced the same phenomenon only to a lesser degree.

He made an initial diagnosis of organic encephalopathy myotonia but gave no explanation I could understand as to the meaning of encephalopathy or what could be done about it. To me, he gave vague responses to my questions. Later, when I searched the dictionary, I couldn't find either term. In 1988, there was no surfing the Internet for information. Hand cramping and tongue stiffness seemed minor and didn't address my reason for bringing Doug to Dr. Hale. I was desperate for help and annoyed that he didn't address how to curb Doug's deviant behavior.

Dr. Hale requested Doug's hospital and sexual abuse treatment records as well as the results of BVR's psychological tests before he made a definitive diagnosis. Doug signed the necessary releases of information. We left the appointment as much in the dark as before but with a slight hope that after reading Doug's records, Dr. Hale would explain more thoroughly and be able to help us.

Meanwhile, Doug sabotaged every opportunity coming his way. He skipped BVR training sessions, and they dropped him from the program. He called me at work one day and complained that his phone had been disconnected.

"People who don't work don't have phones," I responded calmly.

A client sitting in our waiting room overheard my conversation. She, too, struggled with an out-of-control child. As she walked into my office, she handed me the book she carried, *Mother I Have Some-*

thing to Tell You. "It has helped me a lot. You might want to pick up a copy."

I purchased it within the week. This book chronicles the stages traditional, stay-at-home mothers go through when their children's behavior is "unexpected ... unacceptable ... so aberrant in their eyes that it went beyond the bounds of predictable teenage rebellion." This behavior forced these mothers, who sacrificed their own wants and needs to their children's, to find lives outside their mothering role. Despite not being a traditional mother, I took solace in those pages and carried these mothers' stories with me as I navigated my own child having committed the worst act I could imagine. However, I felt alone in my shame. I didn't find a story of sibling incest. I feared my child's behavior related to my having pursued wants and needs of my own.

Doug stopped attending his sexual offenders' therapy group in favor of watching Monday Night Football. They kicked him out of treatment.

Nicole continued to resist her counseling, insisting she was over her anger with me. "I'm just disappointed you didn't notice and stop Doug sooner."

Heavy-hearted, I reflected on her words and the signs I had missed. Despite the steps we had taken to solve this problem, my teenage children couldn't be left alone at the house. If only I had known it wasn't safe, I wouldn't have let down my guard. That I did is something I will regret the rest of my life.

Nicole's counselor used art therapy to surface her anger. Instead, Nicole directed her frustration toward her counselor "for trying to make me angry at you and Doug." She thought coloring for an hour cost way too much money. She asked our permission to quit.

Not long after, I walked into the family room and found Buddy and Nicole watching a TV program. On the screen, a woman sucked another woman's breast while a man looked on. I screamed and yelled. Buddy and Nicole bolted off the couch and scurried around the room like someone fired a gun. They stopped and looked at me as though I was crazy.

It didn't make sense to continue with counseling. We all dropped out.

We applied for social security disability for Doug, but the application was denied. We still hadn't received Dr. Hale's definitive diagnosis. We engaged his help with the appeals process. In the process of writing this memoir, I reviewed my correspondence with Dr. Hale. I wrote, "Doug's psychiatrist at the hospital says he was born with an inability to cope. If true, then he must be eligible for disability." Despite my confusion, I must have possessed some level of awareness of my son's brain abnormality. I just didn't know how to deal with it.

Social Security denied Doug's appeal. At the time, I understood the government message to mean that he was capable of holding a job. Later, I learned most people need an attorney to navigate the Social Security system as most are denied at least three times before approval is granted. Not understanding how the system worked, we stopped appealing too soon.

At this point, weary from the heavy weight I carried alone, I lost all hope of understanding my son and receiving help. I lived in fear of what would happen next. No aid seemed to exist that would help

Doug get his life on track.

As the Kierkegaard quote in this chapter's opening reflects, at that time I lived my life forward. Looking backward as I write, without the chaos involved while living the nightmare, I understand so much more. The professionals we worked with did their best in their area of expertise, but vital information had yet to be discovered. So we trudged forward another eleven years doing the best we could until a clearer picture emerged that solved the puzzle.

Facing Reality

1988–1989

*All human unhappiness comes from not
facing reality squarely, exactly as it is.*

~Buddha

Some of my more obstinate codependent characteristics clung to me like leeches. I continued to hang onto an emotionally sterile marriage, hoping Buddy would change. Even though I had grown in expressing my wants and needs directly, I often backed down at Buddy's hangdog expression, feeling sorry for him and guilty for even bringing the subject up. Intellectually, I knew I wasn't to blame for his feelings, but life seemed easier when I avoided conflict. With my victim mentality, I continued looking for something outside myself to make me happy, stave off depression, and bolster my self-worth.

Some families I worked with in our treatment center made remarkable progress in healing their relationships. The same was true for some of my twelve-step friends who sought treatment at an esteemed center in Arizona. That facility offered a twenty-eight day treatment for codependence that included a week-long family program. Envying these families, I sent for information

Their literature said the family program could be life changing. Each family member would have the opportunity to look at his or her own issues, learn healthy relationship skills, and heal together. Buddy and Doug would have the opportunity to work on what I viewed as their sexual addiction in one of the best treatment centers in the country. I applied for admission and convinced Buddy, Doug, and Nicole to join me for the family program. I wasn't ready to give up on us yet.

As family week approached, I grew increasingly anxious about how to make sure the family therapist addressed what I saw as our most severe problem—Buddy and Doug's sexual addiction. We only had this one week, and I had a lot riding on it. When our family moved to the middle of the circle to do our work, I wasted no time revealing my suspicion that Buddy used sex addictively. I studied the therapist to see how he would tackle this issue. When he seemed to ignore it, I grew desperate and frantic. *Please hear me. Please help us.*

The next day, I squirmed watching the family therapist, upset he wasn't addressing our family's sexual issues. *I have to say something. I have to make him understand. We can't leave here without this being addressed.* The first chance I got, I told the therapist, "Our children have found Buddy's pornography hidden all over our house. They found videos in our basement ceiling tiles."

Once more I scrutinized the therapist, waiting for him to confront Buddy. He didn't. *Oh my God, do I have to name my greatest fear?* I took a deep breath and blurted it out. "I'm afraid Buddy sexually abused Nicole."

Buddy and Nicole flinched as though a bomb had dropped. Nicole said, "No, Mom, that never happened."

The family therapist looked at me. "You haven't dealt with your own sexual abuse issues. You're projecting them onto your family."

I wished a sinkhole would open under my chair and swallow me. I couldn't make eye contact with anyone. *Are our problems really all my fault?*

When the session ended, I fled and found an isolated space behind a nearby building. A staff person I didn't know approached and asked if I was okay. I told him I needed some time alone to think. He moved back a distance but continued watching me. I leaned against the building, trying to focus my mind and make sense of what seemed a disaster.

I coached myself: Okay, stop focusing on what your family does or doesn't do. You're the one in treatment. Keep the focus on your codependence ... on your own issues.

Confused and full of shame during my last week of treatment following family week, I was subdued. My therapist and group seemed to think working on my own sexual abuse issues would turn things around for our family. Doubting that was true, I didn't know how to respond. I was grateful the plane was nearly empty on the ride home. Having a whole row to myself gave me time alone to think and formulate a plan for how to relate to Buddy now. My throat constricted at the thought of resuming a sexual relationship with him. I couldn't see how I could do that without violating myself. No clear picture emerged. However, a statement made in one of the educational sessions played again and again in my mind. "It's very difficult to live with someone whose values are different from yours."

The treatment center referred me to Lynda, a local counselor with a thriving practice among the recovering community. Unbeknownst to me, she and the Arizona family therapist had worked together sometime in the past. When I described our family week, she said, "He did a power trip on you."

"A power trip? Are you sure?"

"We worked together for several years. You're not the only one who has experienced this."

I couldn't respond for several minutes as I took in what she said, tears gathering in the corners of my eyes. She waited.

Finally I said, "I heard someone say something in one of our education sessions that I can't get out of my mind." After telling her what I had heard about the effect of differing values on a relationship, I said, "I wonder if having different values might explain why Buddy and I have so much difficulty living together."

Lynda responded, "I'd encourage you to trust yourself about that."

Finally, I faced my reality squarely. I had become a person I didn't like or respect. I had allowed my fears to turn me into a controlling woman. Buddy, Doug, and Nicole had a right to refuse my values, dreams, and needs. I had no right to coerce them into adopting mine. It was not their job to make me happy.

I faced my fear of never being loved for who I am, of never being part of a family committed to growing and working out differences with honesty and affection—*the better way* of my childhood longing.

At long last, I accepted that Buddy and I possessed irreconcilable approaches to life. Neither of us would or should change our values. We would never be good for each other. The wise voice within had spoken this truth at the beginning of our relationship, "You are not a good match for each other." I regretted not listening.

And now the voice screamed, "Don't do this to yourself anymore." This time I listened, though it was clear I had waited far too long to heed its guidance. After almost twenty-three years, I was at last empowered to release the marriage.

Three months after my return from Arizona, in October 1988, I told Buddy I wanted a divorce. He reneged on his promise made years before to move out and find an apartment in Middletown. He also showed no intention of carrying through on his threat never to see any of us again. He agreed it would be best for Nicole if I served as her custodial parent, but he refused to move out, and I couldn't afford the higher rents in our suburb close to her school. He made it difficult for her to live with me. I wanted to choke him.

We tried living separately in the house, at least until Nicole graduated high school. It was wishful thinking that would work. I faced an agonizing decision. I didn't want to leave Nicole. I felt it important to monitor her relationship with a girlfriend who had been incarcerated for participating in a robbery. She was also starting to date a guy who had a reputation for using drugs. I didn't trust Buddy to handle these situations wisely. But I couldn't tolerate living with him either.

In November, I consulted an attorney, and he advised me to move out before I filed for divorce. I wasn't sure how I could afford to do that. Despite this obstacle, I told Buddy if he wasn't going to leave, I needed to.

A couple of weeks later, a friend called and told me she was getting married in January and moving to a nearby community. I asked about the two-story, three-bedroom house she rented. Because it was located in the city, the fee was reasonable, and I would be able to afford it. I contacted the landlady who agreed to rent it to me when it became available in February. That meant I would be moving four months before Nicole's high school graduation.

The day after Christmas, Doug was arrested and taken to the county workhouse because of his probation violations—dropping out of treatment and being fired by BVR. Buddy and I visited him once. I resented going, but couldn't bring myself not to.

I held on to a small hope Nicole would choose to move with me. When she saw the distance from her school, she thought it best to stay with her dad. I didn't want to inflict guilt, so I hid my pain, hoping she would join me after graduation. I had finally mustered the courage to follow through with separating from Buddy and couldn't postpone my departure any longer. Despite his agreement about what was best for Nicole, by not leaving he made it impossible for her to live with me.

In the process of packing, I gathered my documents from our file cabinet in the basement. For the first time, I looked at the divorce decree from Buddy's first marriage. Early in our relationship, I believed his complaints about how his previous wife took advantage of him. I had felt sorry for him and tried to avoid doing anything to trigger his pain—not easy because I had never met her and had no idea what his triggers might be. When I read through the papers, I discovered his gross exaggeration, giving me a picture of what to expect during our divorce process.

Daunted

1989

> *The best thing about endings is knowing that just ahead is the daunting task to start over.*
>
> ~Jodi Picoult

On a Friday evening in February, with the help of five friends, I began moving out. We loaded clothes, linens, towels, boxes, and whatever else fit into our cars and vans. Buddy stayed at his parents for the weekend. The mood seemed festive as we created a caravan to my new place. Nicole joined the fun.

The resplendent sun brightened the next morning when the moving truck arrived to collect the rest of my belongings. When Nicole and I drove away from the Kettering house for the last time that afternoon, I burst into tears. My tears surprised and puzzled me because I hadn't let go of the celebratory mood of the night before.

It took most of Saturday to haul boxes from my car into my new dwelling. By late afternoon, Nicole and I had worked up an appetite and were bushed, hot and sweaty. I had neglected to make plans for dinner. As we carted in another load, Rachel, a neighbor, came by to welcome us to the neighborhood. She invited us to dinner at her house. I looked at Nicole. She smiled, so I responded, "What a wonderful invitation. We'd love to. Thank you so much."

A single parent with two teenage daughters, Rachel lived two doors down. Her invitation felt like a good omen. I hoped a friendlier neighborhood with girls near her age living close would make Nicole more comfortable moving in with me. When we arrived at Rachel's cozy home, the aroma of roast chicken and mashed potatoes greeted us. Dinner wasn't ready, so Rachel told us to make ourselves at home. I sank into her plush sofa and felt exhaustion in every fiber of my being. After a delicious dinner, Nicole and I went back to my home, flopped on the couch, and went to bed early.

Nicole spent the weekend with me helping me unpack and get organized. When I thanked her for finding a good spot for one of my belongings, she repeated a refrain she often used, "Mom, what would you do without me?"

I dreaded having to take her back home on Sunday evening. I hoped that after spending the weekend with me, my home would feel like her home, too. I know now how unrealistic that was, but it was a wish I clung to.

We were both quiet during the drive. She hated it when I talked about feelings, so I kept mine to myself. I didn't want to say anything to upset her. I wished she would see that the drive wasn't that difficult and realize she could handle going back and forth to school from here. She would only have to do it for four months. More wishful thinking. When we arrived, she gave me a hug, said goodbye, and went into the house as though nothing unusual was happening. I sobbed all the way back to my new home.

It was a bit scary going back to an empty house in a new neighborhood. Except for those few weeks in my studio apartment, before Buddy and I spent all our time together, I had never lived alone. The house's unfamiliar creaks and groans kept me awake. Despite that, I was grateful I had finally taken this huge step. Barking dogs nearby provided some comfort. If anyone was up to no good out there, I hoped the dogs would scare them away.

I prayed for protection and wrote in my journal until I could no longer keep my eyes open. I awoke before dawn with waves of sadness washing through me. I knew I wouldn't go back to sleep, so I got up and busied myself unpacking and rearranging closets.

Several friends had warned, "Don't make the same mistake I made. I wanted out so bad, I left with nothing. If I had to do it over again, I'd take better care of myself." Lynda, my counselor, continually urged me to protect myself financially. Following their advice, before my move, I had hired the attorney with the best reputation in Dayton. At the end of the week after my move, I filed for divorce.

That weekend, I visited Doug at the workhouse. Just driving onto the property unsettled me, but I wanted him to hear about my relocation from me. Emblazoned in my otherwise fuzzy recollection of that facility is being escorted into a large gymnasium-type space with glaring fluorescent fixtures. Visitors' chatter increased in intensity as it reverberated off the walls. It rattled my already frayed nerves. We took our places on cold metal chairs at metal tables bolted to the floor. Four armed guards ushered the prisoners in and stationed themselves around the perimeter.

When I saw Doug, my chest tightened. He looked around, spotted me, and sauntered over to my table wearing a silly grin. Some prisoners received smiles and hugs. Some laughed and seemed to joke with their visitors. To me, this was no joking matter.

Doug said, "Hi, Mom. Surprised to see you."

He sat down across the table and faced me. I crossed my arms and held myself. I shuddered and bit my lower lip. I could make no sense of Doug's behavior. When he dropped out of treatment months ago, I felt as though he had thrown cold water in my face. To me he seemed to be saying, "I don't care if I get better or not ... I don't care if others are hurt by my behavior. Tough rocks." Couldn't he see that thumbing his nose at his probation's requirements would lead to incarceration? I couldn't imagine anyone risking those consequences. Now here he was ... my son ... in jail.

I rubbed my arms against the chill, raised my head, straightened my spine, and looked him in the eyes: "Visiting you here is hard."

His grin disappeared and he looked down.

I continued, "I came because I wanted you to hear this from me."

He raised his head, his eyes full of questions.

"You know your dad and I are separating. I moved out last weekend. I no longer live with him. I filed for divorce on Friday."

Unfazed, he hurled questions at me: "Where are you living? Did Nicole move with you? What is your phone number?"

After I answered his questions, he launched into an upbeat account of jail life. He didn't seem as upset as I had imagined—about jail or the pending divorce.

When our time expired, we stood and moved to the end of the table. I gave him an awkward hug and choked out, "Take care of yourself." After a slight hesitation, I added, "I love you."

I drove home disheartened. Later, at my twelve-step meeting, I chose to listen rather than share the afternoon's events. That night I tossed and turned for hours, replaying again and again all our family had been through. *How did we get here? I want to do more than survive in my new life. I want to thrive. But how do I flourish while my children have so many unresolved problems?*

Survival Skills

1989

We each survive in our own way.

~Sarah J. Maas

Friends eased my transition into my new home. They told me to call anytime day or night. Whenever I needed help, someone came through for me. Before week's end, two friends had assembled and filled my waterbed while another hooked the antenna to my TV and configured my VCR and stereo system. My new abode began to look like home.

I loved my new home, but for days tears welled at unexpected intervals. I didn't want to live in the Kettering house anymore with all its painful memories, but leaving dredged up legions of grief and sorrow. I'd lost so much. Now I feared losing Nicole, the possibility I dreaded most.

I knew I'd be seeing her the next weekend. That was our arrangement—that she would spend weekends with me. But we hadn't made arrangements for phone contact during the week. I couldn't stand waiting until the weekend to see how she was doing, so I called mid-week. Nicole answered the phone, bubbling about events in her life. As I listened, I had mixed feelings. I was relieved she seemed to be adjusting well. However, I was scared she would never want to live with me.

She spent several weekends at my home, but her routine gave us little quality time. Nicole slept until noon or after, went to the kitchen to find something to eat, and left behind a mess. If I woke her early or asked her to clean up after herself, she grew cranky. I went along so as not to spoil what little time we had together. On the rare occasions she buzzed with enthusiasm about her life, I enjoyed her presence. Unfortunately, her visits disconcerted me almost as much as our separation.

I hadn't heard from Doug for several weeks when he called to tell me he had been thrown "in the hole"—solitary confinement. I no longer remember the details, but I remember being impressed while I listened to his story about how he had worked his way out. He must have mustered every ounce of internal discipline he possessed to do what they expected of him.

"Wow. That sounds like a difficult situation, and you handled it all by yourself. You should be proud of yourself."

In future calls, he sounded upbeat like he was at summer camp. While I listened, I agonized. *Will there ever be consequences severe enough for him to want to pull his life together?*

Nicole called to tell me she wouldn't be spending Palm Sunday and Easter weekends with me because she was going with Buddy to his brother's church. I was afraid to express my fear and disappointment because I didn't want to pressure her. I wanted her to want to spend time with me. I feigned acceptance and told her I looked forward to seeing her the weekend after Easter. But as that weekend approached, she said she had decided to begin attending church regularly with them. I imagined Buddy and his family turning her against me, but I bit my tongue. It was just another reminder of what little control I had over our situation.

Doug was released from jail on Easter Sunday, March 26. For the first time since his birth, I didn't know his whereabouts or whether he had a bed for the night. My twelve-step friends told me obsessing about him was easier than accepting my powerlessness. I knew they were right, but still I tossed and turned most of that night. I prayed for his Higher Power to protect him and finally fell asleep.

On Friday, he called me at work. I had suffered all week for nothing. He was doing fine. He stayed at the Gospel Mission the first night but objected to their prohibition against playing cards and watching television. He didn't like being required to go to bed early. So he made sure to secure a bed at St. Vincent's homeless shelter the other four nights. He learned he could earn laundry room privileges by volunteering there.

He sold his plasma twice, bought a bus pass, had his hair cut, and rented a locker at the bus station to store his few belongings. He went to the mall to watch TV and played pool at a high school friend's home. He said he had won a ticket to a rock concert and would be taken by limo to Cincinnati to attend, meet the stars, and receive a t-shirt with their logo.

His rock concert tale seemed pretty farfetched, but his survival skills dumbfounded me. Thus far he had done far better than I would have in his circumstances. I told him, "I'm impressed with the way you're taking care of yourself."

I began to sleep a little more soundly.

Then Doug phoned one evening. I could hear his excitement as he shared, "Mom, did you see me on the news tonight? They interviewed me about Medicare for homeless people."

I wished it didn't matter to me, but I cringed at the possibility of people in town knowing he was homeless.

Not long after, he phoned again. This time he told me he had seen someone from church. "Hey, Mom, I saw Henry Uy tonight. He volunteers at St. Vincent's. He served me dinner."

Full of shame, I stopped attending church. I didn't want to risk talking with anyone there about any aspect of my family life. I felt like such a failure. I was divorced with a homeless son who had been incarcerated. I imagined that they judged me behind my back and, if they said anything at all, would pity me to my face. I relied on my twelve-step lifeline for support. At meetings I could share the worst experiences of my life and receive love and understanding. We supported each other in handling whatever happens in as healthy a way as possible. I did my best to work the steps and apply their principles to my life.

When I filed for single status with the Internal Revenue, my income reduced. At the same time, a cold snap caused my utility bill to spike. My attorney asked the court to award me temporary support, but Buddy protested. I resolved to practice healthy behavior in response. When my insecurities were triggered by the financial threats Buddy made through his attorney, I took deep breaths and reminded myself to trust my Higher Power's care. My free-floating fear disappeared when the court awarded in my favor.

Doug called a few days after the temporary support hearing. "Dad told me you're getting a bunch of friends to talk against him in court." He burst into tears. "Dad says he might have me come to testify for him."

I swallowed hard. I didn't want to say something I would regret. I couldn't believe Buddy stooped so low as to pull our kids into the middle. I assured Doug what his father said was not true.

For months, my therapist, Lynda, had been encouraging me to connect with my anger. At my next therapy appointment, it burst forth into fury. I wanted to slap some sense into Buddy so he would stop making this harder on our children. She and I agreed I needed to let Buddy know my feelings. I called him at work, but he hung up on me, cutting my well-rehearsed speech short.

With every contact, Doug and Nicole would say, "Dad says this and this and this. Is that true?"

Each time, I responded, "That is between your father and me. It's not appropriate for me to talk about that with you."

They expressed outrage.

When I dipped into despair, friends from my past appeared and shared their divorce experiences. They relayed accounts of estrangement from their children, a common phenomenon during divorce. Their stories ended in reconciliation, bolstering my spirit and giving me hope.

As the court date approached, my emotions began to level out, and I felt on more solid footing. I had no control over the outcome, but I had done as much as I could to protect myself. I had located a document citing the amount from my teacher retirement fund, the money Buddy and his mother had made plans to spend so many years before. I researched the amount of my tuition to seminary and made a tally of my canceled checks, proof of the amount I had spent on our children and myself. My attorney expressed astonishment at the abundance of facts and figures I supplied to counter the false claims Buddy and his attorney made.

I wrote in my prayer journal, "I AM going to make it." I celebrated my growing ability to make choices from my higher self and gratitude filled my soul.

On May 18, 1989, my attorney, twelve-step sponsor, corroborating witness, pastor, and I arrived at the courthouse for the trial. We made our way down a long corridor toward our courtroom and waited on benches nearby. Shortly after we arrived, Buddy and his attorney came down the hall followed by Doug and Nicole. When they saw us, they found seats out of sight around a corner.

At my request, my attorney asked the judge to bar Doug and Nicole from the courtroom. They were twenty-one and eighteen, but I didn't want them dragged into the middle of their parents' nasty divorce. The judge denied my request.

I asked my attorney, "What happens if I refuse to give my grounds in front of my children?"

"You'll have to live apart for a year before the court will grant you a divorce."

"That's not acceptable. I don't want to give my grounds in front of my children, but if I have no choice, I'll have to do it."

Our trial started late, and while we waited in the bustling hallway, Buddy whittled away at the financial agreements already made. His attorney approached us repeatedly with new proposals. My attorney and I discussed each one and offered a counter. I hated that our children witnessed this disgrace.

I didn't know what to expect when we entered the courtroom. The judge, already seated behind his raised bench, avoided greetings. I couldn't imagine what it must be like for him to witness family devastation day after day. The room was bright because of the fluorescent lights on the ceiling. One tiny window on the wall to his right provided a little natural light.

My attorney and I took seats at a table to the judge's left across from the witness stand. Buddy and his attorney positioned themselves to the judge's right. My twelve-step sponsor, corroborating witness, Doug, and Nicole sat in the small gallery behind us. Buddy took the stand first and rattled on and on about all the cooking he had done. He claimed he paid for my seminary education and bought a new car to make my commutes safe. At the time I entered seminary, Buddy had voiced no objections, but now he admitted to giving up on our marriage at that time. *I knew it. I knew he only feigned support.* It was satisfying to have the source of his passive-aggressive behavior clarified at last. Buddy went on to say that he paid for all our children's expenses. He told about continuing to support Doug and Nicole financially.

My attorney asked Buddy, "Who tells you to financially support your adult children?"

Buddy paused, as though shocked by the question. His face reddened and puffed up like in our family counseling session years before. His voice pierced the air as he spewed out, "GOD," drawing out the "O" until his lungs drained of air.

I looked down and shook my head at the revelation. *He's sicker than I ever realized.*

When my turn came to take the stand, I reported that my teacher retirement fund had paid for one-fourth of my seminary education. I cited the facts and figures about my financial contribution to our children's welfare.

To my great relief, the judge cleared the courtroom before I gave my reason for seeking a divorce. My attorney, my twelve-step sponsor, and my corroborating witness remained.

When he asked for my grounds, I said, "My husband is addicted to pornography, and it has hurt our children. I've lost respect for myself for staying as long as I have."

After we all left the courtroom, Buddy, Doug, and Nicole were nowhere to be seen. My sponsor told me the judge looked out the window during Buddy's testimony as though bored. When I testified, he recorded the facts and figures I presented. When I gave my grounds, he lifted his bushy eyebrows. That seemed a good sign. I wouldn't know the judge's final decision for at least two months, but I had done what I could to take care of myself and was proud that I had stood up to Buddy and his attorney.

Two weeks after the trial, Nicole turned eighteen. She couldn't be direct in telling me, but whenever I tried to find a time to get together to celebrate her birthday, she was too busy. She did let me know the details of her high school graduation to be held two weeks after her birthday. But that evening, she ignored and excluded my parents and me. I didn't ask her what led to this estrangement, but I imagined she enjoyed her father's leniency. And Buddy no doubt painted me in the worst possible light. My face felt hot and tears stung my eyes as I watched her flash a smile and lift her diploma in the direction where her father and his family sat. Buddy smiled and waved back at her. He seemed to gloat over his victory.

Sometime during the week after Nicole's graduation, Doug phoned and told me I had asked for too much alimony. When I didn't react, he told me that he and Nicole planned to spend a day at King's Island, a nearby amusement park. He asked, "Are you angry we'll be alone together?"

Under the circumstances, my opinion didn't matter. If I stated my disapproval, it would just give Buddy something more to gloat about. Expressing my distress wouldn't make any difference. So I kept it to myself. *They've never worked through their issues. How will they ever heal? What will become of them?*

One evening, after sobbing myself to sleep, a signal that I would triumph over this came in the form of a vivid dream about a phoenix rising out of the ashes. When I awoke, I was awed at receiving a message through this vision of a mythical creature. Grateful to experience my Higher Power's care, I wrapped my arms around my chest and gave myself a big hug. I wanted to drink in this moment and remember it forever.

At a friend's suggestion, I wrote Bible verses, quotes from spiritual literature, and recovery slogans on small slips of paper, tucked them in a little pouch, and carried it in my pocket. Whenever anxiety welled up, reading these bits of wisdom calmed me and restored my trust. Tears filled my eyes every time I read these words from the Twenty-third Psalm: "Even though I walk through the valley of the shadow of death, I fear no evil; for thou art with me."

In mid-July, Nicole called to say she had a gift for my birthday but didn't have money for gas to bring it to me. I imagined she depended on her dad to operate the expensive car he helped her buy, and he wouldn't pay for her to visit me. I told her I would reimburse her.

I kept glancing out the front window as I paced the living room waiting for her arrival. When I saw her car pull into the driveway, I began to tremble. I opened the front door and ushered her in with a smile and a hug. She accepted but didn't return my greeting. She handed me the gift as though she had fulfilled her duty. The trinket cost less than the price of gasoline. She didn't have much to say and her visit was short. I focused on my best gift ... being able to see her and spend a little time with her. After she left, I closed the door and leaned against it, wondering what that was all about. I didn't know whether to celebrate her visit or cry at what seemed a gulf of unsaid feelings between us.

Ten days after I turned forty-seven, July 25, the divorce was final and I was single again. Lynda, my counselor, asked, "Have you given any thought as to why you stayed so long?"

I had asked myself that question a million times. The fear that I couldn't make it financially or handle being a single parent gave a partial answer. Nevertheless, her question continued to haunt me. Days later, a flier from a reputable school for problem children crossed my desk at work, forcing me to consider deeper reasons.

Years before, Anne Wilson Schaef had recommended this school as a possibility for Doug. In the flier, the school admitted to moderate success when handling impulse control problems. The word "moderate" jumped off the page. *What made me think I could turn him around?*

Exhaustion seeped into my bones at the memory of how hard I

had worked all those years seeking help for Doug—consulting professional after professional trying to accomplish the impossible. *What had kept me going? Was it arrogance? Was it refusal to accept the truth about my son? Was it an attempt to rid myself of shame? Was it an attempt to see myself as an adequate parent ... to avoid looking at how much I neglected my children?* I had no clear-cut answers.

Doug seemed content with the resources available to him as a homeless person. As far as I could see, he did nothing to find a job. Sometimes, however, his strategies didn't work. For example, one chilly November evening, I answered the phone around seven to hear Doug's panicked voice saying, "Mom, I couldn't get into St. Vincent's tonight. Can I spend the night at your place?"

Shaking all over, I hesitated, dreading the chaos he would bring and the hassle of forcing him out. If I agreed to one night, he would want more. Would he bring lice or bed bugs? Then I remembered the twelve-step meeting scheduled for 7:30. I hadn't planned to go, but now I needed to.

"Call me back at nine, and I'll let you know."

On the way to the meeting, questions swirled in my mind. *Am I selfish or is this self-caring? Is my refusal to enable him a loving action or am I back into my control issues? He is twenty-one. How long am I responsible for him?* I shared my dilemma at the meeting.

Parents shared their stories of similar quandaries with their children. They passed notes from all around the room: "No is a complete sentence." "What part of no don't you understand?" "When I say yes, you don't ask me why. Why do you ask me when I say no?"

When the phone rang at nine, I clutched those notes in my trembling hands. I willed my voice to sound resolute. "I'm sorry, Doug, I can't give you a place to stay."

He whined his familiar "Why?" routine.

I remained calm. "The answer is no, Doug. I'm sorry. I'm sure you'll find a way to handle this. You've been doing well taking care of yourself. I'm going to hang up now."

He didn't ask to stay again. I don't know where he stayed that night, but later I learned he sometimes stayed in the fathers' waiting room at the hospital. People thought he was an expectant father and asked no questions. His survival skills continued to astonish me. *Where in the world did he learn them? I would be terrified and immobilized in his situation.*

But he did possibly learn them from Buddy and me in an indirect way. As the problem child, he learned to manipulate us to get his needs met. Perhaps this gave him the ability to manipulate the resources available to him as an indigent. And he must have learned survival skills from those he met in homeless shelters. He seemed to have learned them well.

When Thanksgiving rolled around, Nicole made clear her intention to spend it with Buddy and his family. As Christmas approached, I asked her repeatedly when we might find some time to celebrate together. She didn't have the courage to tell me directly. Her avoidance told me she didn't intend to spend any time with me.

I dropped her gifts off at her father's house on my way home from work one evening. He answered the door and took them. He acted bright and cheerful and even invited me in, rubbing salt in my wound. Nicole was nowhere in sight. A part of me wanted to die.

My twelve-step group knew my situation. A few weeks before Christmas, I had told them about watching a television program that featured swimming with dolphins in the Florida Keys. "That looks like so much fun."

Almost in unison, they asked, "So when are you going to call and get the information?"

I telephoned Margie, my Living in Process friend from Georgia. I asked if she wanted to join me. She thought it sounded like great fun.

I spent Christmas at my parents' home in north central Florida. Margie joined us afterward and brought her camping equipment. She and I traveled to the Keys, assembled her tent at a campground, and roughed it for a week before our scheduled swim. My parents came to watch us participate in this wondrous experience. I had made the best of a sorrowful situation by creating a joyful experience for myself. For perhaps the first time in my life, I knew I would be okay no matter what the future held.

Meeting

1990

> *Out beyond ideas of wrongdoing and rightdoing is a field.*
> *I'll meet you there.*
>
> ~Rumi

Christmas without Nicole had come and gone. On a nippy February afternoon, a year after I moved and six months after the divorce, I was poking through the refrigerator to find something to prepare for dinner when a knock on the door startled me. *Who could that be?* I looked toward the front door, but the sheer curtains on the window revealed an amorphous figure. I closed the refrigerator door and headed through the living room to see who had come so close to dinnertime. As I swung the door open, my heart fluttered. "This is a surprise."

My smiling daughter stood on the porch. I tried to keep my emotions level—reserved. I swept my arm in welcome and said, "Come on in."

She stepped across the threshold into my living room and greeted me casually. "I got off work and thought I'd stop by."

She reeked of smoke so I held my breath while I gave her a big hug.

"Off work?" I pulled back and squeezed her upper arms, taking in her new look. She had permmed her dark brown, naturally wavy hair and dyed it black, lined her small eyes in black, and caked them with blue eye shadow. I helped her off with her jacket and hung it on the banister. She wore a red and blue uniform.

Nicole cashiering at a convenience store.

"Yea, I got a job at a convenience store close to here. Todd got it for me."

"Oh, what do you do there?"

"I'm a cashier, but I stock shelves and stuff like that."

I invited her to have a seat, pleased she selected the couch. I faced her on the other end at a safe distance. "Where is it located?"

She moved her hand and pointed her thumb over her shoulder. "It's over on Catalpa near Hillcrest."

"Is it full-time?"

"About thirty hours a week. I work four or five days a week."

"Do you like it?"

She shrugged her shoulders. "It's okay. I need the money, so it'll do 'til I can find something better."

I ventured into dangerous territory. "Are you still dating Todd?"

She shook her head. "Oh, no. They wouldn't hire me if we were dating. The owner had questions about that. We're seeing each other, but we don't date."

I gave her a puzzled look. "What's the difference between seeing each other and dating?"

She laughed at my confusion. "Tonya and me and a group of guys hang out, go to movies, stuff like that. But Todd has a girlfriend."

Glad for the clarification, I relaxed. I could stop worrying about a serious relationship with a guy who used drugs.

She updated me on her favorite soap opera, *General Hospital,* and her heartthrob, Jack Wagner. She seemed so relaxed and in no hurry to leave. "So, Mom, what have you been up to?"

Careful about how I responded, I didn't want to upset her or chase her away. I didn't say anything about how I spent Christmas. I didn't know whether I could trust her and didn't want my life turned into gossip fodder for her and her dad.

"Not much. Working and going to meetings. Nothing much new in my life." I leaned forward and changed the subject. "Hey, are you hungry? I was getting ready to fix dinner when you came."

"I wondered if you'd go to a movie with me tonight."

I leaned back and considered her surprise invitation. "Oh, I guess I could. Did you have something in mind?"

"Not really."

Wow. She is initiating time with me. We checked the paper and found an interesting one—*Stella* starring Bette Midler. She agreed to my suggestion to catch dinner at a nearby Mexican restaurant.

We could hear the mariachi music from the parking lot before we entered Pepito's through its ochre arches. The aroma of onions, cilantro, and peppers filled the air. Multicolor lights on green, red, and orange walls created a festive atmosphere. We made it through another hour of lighthearted, safe, small talk.

I had never been good at small talk, and Nicole despised the recovery-oriented conversations my friends and I enjoyed. My work didn't interest her. I wanted to know about her life but didn't want to sound like an interrogator. A recent phone call from my father, an avid follower of the space program, gave me a topic: "Grandpa called a couple of nights ago all excited about Columbia's safe return."

When she asked how her grandparents were doing, she opened the door for me to tell her about my Christmas visit. I didn't mention swimming with dolphins.

She changed the subject to the *Soap Opera Digest* award winners and the movies she'd seen. I did my best to show interest. As long as we stuck to her subjects, we were fine. I picked up the tab, and Nicole declared Chicken Enchilada Verdes, my Pepito's favorite, as her favorite, too. She said she'd like to do this again. I liked the sound of that.

The movie we chose proved providential. It portrayed a mother-daughter relationship and their separation as the daughter grew into adulthood. At the end, Stella, Bette Midler's character, stood in the pouring rain looking through a country club's window at her daughter's wedding. I couldn't stop my tears. I jabbed my fingernails into my palms to prevent noisy sobs. As we made our way out, I pulled tissues from my pocket and dabbed at my eyes. A huge knot formed in my throat.

Once in the car, my sobs broke loose. Nicole stayed quiet and handed me tissues from the box in the car. They piled high in my lap on the drive home. When we walked in the house, my sobs subsided. I grabbed a box of tissues, and we took our stations on opposite ends of the couch.

Nicole asked, "Why all the crying?"

"I've been so scared that's what would happen to us ... that you'd marry and wouldn't invite me to your wedding. You've been so angry with me."

Now she wept. I handed her tissues, reached out and touched her leg to soothe her. When she was able to speak, she referred to the couch where we sat. "I was just angry about you taking the couch and recliner. Dad was so proud of winning them."

She was almost nineteen and adult enough to understand the reasoning behind our property settlement. I longed for her to appreciate my perspective. But I upheld my resolve not to put her and her brother into the middle of issues between their father and me. I intended to behave in a healthy, adult manner. I empathized with her perception. "I can understand that."

Her next revelation stunned me. She said, "But most of it was my own stuff and had nothing to do with you."

My eyes widened, "Really?"

"Yeah. I'm sorry I hurt you. I've been lonely for you and Toshi. Both of you were always there for me."

To be considered as valuable as our beloved Siamese cat honored me, to say the least. Toshi died three years earlier in the midst of our worst family crisis.

"I'm relieved to hear you say that. I didn't know you felt that way."

I wanted to know what she meant by "my own stuff" but proceeded carefully so as not to push her away now that she had come closer. I moved toward her on the couch, put my arm around her shoulder, and pulled her to me. She rested her head on my shoulder.

I said, "I miss Toshi, too. He was a great cat."

She added, "The best ever."

"And I've missed *you*. I've been lonely, too. But I've been working on being okay being with myself."

I took a risk and hoped it was safe to be authentic: "I've been trying to learn the difference between solitude and loneliness. It has helped me learn a lot about myself." I gave her a bear hug and rocked her back and forth. "Oh, I love you so much."

"I love you, too."

"I'm glad you decided to stop by tonight. I feel so much better."

She surprised me again. "Me, too. Would it be okay if I stayed all night?"

Internally, I jumped for joy at her request but responded evenly, "Absolutely. You can stay as long as you like."

She stayed several nights. I didn't question her motives. I focused on my elation about the end of our estrangement. With the weight of grief and sadness lifting, I felt free to rebuild my life in earnest.

Evolving

1990–1993

> [E]ven through our limitations,
> we evolve rather than fail,
> the way a caterpillar becomes a chrysalis
> becomes a butterfly,
> and the succession of life's trials
> is precisely the unfolding we need
> to find our bliss and rightful place
> in the order of things.
>
> ~Mark Nepo

Buying my dream home ushered a period of bliss into my life. My friend Nancy agreed to make the rounds of open houses with me one April Sunday afternoon. I checked the newspaper real estate section and circled several possibilities. None of the selections thrilled me until our last stop—a renovated, two-story, reddish-brown brick Tudor. I glanced in every direction trying to take in every detail as Nancy and I strolled up the winding brick walkway amid an English garden of ivy, hostas, and redbud trees.

When we crossed the house's threshold, we spotted the real estate agent in the kitchen straight ahead talking to potential buyers. I motioned to Nancy to step into the living room on our left. We sank into a plush, moss green carpet covering the adjoining living and dining rooms. A massive oak mantel extended beyond the fireplace to form bookshelves and an entertainment center. The same warm cinnamon oak surrounded two large windows in each room. We were speechless as we stared out the dining room window into the backyard. A Zen garden surrounded a rectangular pond with a tiny frog-shaped fountain spitting water.

Nancy broke our silence. "Get out your checkbook."

"I'll never be able to afford anything this nice, and no other house will look good after this one."

We made our way upstairs and gasped again when we walked into the back bedroom. Outside the window overlooking the garden, two magnolia trees gushed in full bloom. I told Nancy, "If I could afford this house, I'd make this my bedroom."

The next morning, it took all my courage to call the bank. I had never taken a step like this all by myself. I tried to sound confident and mature.

When the finance officer gave the amount they were willing to loan me, I couldn't believe it. I didn't need that much to make this stunning 1930s Tudor my home. Apparently the reasonable price tag related to the house's proximity to a declining area. But some of my friends lived in that neighborhood, so I was comfortable there. The location near my beloved seminary drew me to it. I moved in June, not quite two years after the divorce, and felt proud to live in an integrated neighborhood amid this small enclave of stately old homes.

I couldn't wait to show my home to my parents. Mom and Dad

had distanced themselves for a bit during my divorce, perhaps fearing I would need them to support me financially. In August, they came to visit. I followed Dad as he walked through the house from top to bottom and all around the perimeter, checking it over thoroughly. "This is a nice house," he said. I beamed at his approval. My sanctuary embodied the beauty I held dear and was the nicest house I had ever lived in.

In July, new neighbors and friends from every area of my life came to my housewarming party. My home glowed with warmth, love, and laughter. Nicole declined my invitation, saying she had other plans, but Doug came and sat on the couch for most of the evening, covering his eyes with his hands and looking uncomfortable.

My heartbeat quickened when Monty walked through the door. I had been observing him across the room in my favorite twelve-step meeting. He was tall and sported thick silver hair and a mustache. He seemed laid back, his eyes crinkling whenever he broke into a big, toothy smile. More than his looks, the responses he gave to meeting topics attracted me to him. He seemed committed to personal and spiritual development.

My eyes followed his every move, impressed to see him talking and laughing with friends of mine he didn't know. When I approached him, he seemed calm and cool, his voice as deep and smooth as rich chocolate. He looked at me with intense curiosity as my hands trembled and my words came out all twisted.

After everyone left, I read my guestbook messages. My friends loved my home. Many conveyed how much they valued my friendship. My favorite read, "Your home is a reflection of how I perceive you: quiet and peaceful. With love, Monty."

Sighing, I gazed at his "With love." Holding the book to my heart, I leaned back, closed my eyes, and fantasized about a romance with Monty.

In September, a colleague from another hospital-based addiction treatment center phoned me. "We have an opening for a family therapist. Would you be interested in applying?"

Accepting this position would decrease my drive to work by twenty minutes and increase my wages, making my new expenses more manageable. They wanted someone who could craft a fresh and innovative family program. I felt excited about that possibility and had lots of ideas garnered during my twenty-eight-day treatment in Arizona. They hired me, and I began my new job on October 5, 1990.

My professional life took two additional leaps forward. First, my friend Chris, also an Anne Wilson Schaef trainee, recruited friends and organized an introductory meeting in hopes of forming a spiritual recovery group to meet in my home. His seasoned twelve-step friends worked various programs and wanted to address issues encountered in advanced stages of recovery. So many people responded that I began facilitating two groups, using Living in Process methodology.

Second, a psychologist friend offered to rent space to me in her office so I could work privately with couples and families.

Four months after he wrote "With love" in my guestbook, Monty asked me out to lunch. I said yes unsure whether he was asking for a date or for lunch with a friend. I hoped he meant it as a date, something I hadn't experienced in close to twenty-five years. Despite how awkward I felt, our conversation came easier than I anticipated.

He said, "I've wanted to talk with you for a long time, but I've been hanging back. I've been scared."

When he pulled a credit card from his wallet after our meal, I asked, "Are you treating me?"

His head tilted, and he said, "Of course."

After lunch, he walked me to my car. We had met at Jay's Seafood downtown because we both needed to report for the evening shift at the same hospital nearby where he worked in the lab. He asked whether it would be okay to drop by my house on the way home from work sometimes. Also, he suggested I come to his place to listen to CDs.

When I arrived on our unit and passed by the nurses' station, Helen said, "You're glowing. You look like you're in love."

"I just had lunch with a wonderful man." I beamed as I sauntered down the hall to my office.

I was happier in my personal and professional life than ever. Monty and I became an item. My new supervisor and coworkers expressed enthusiasm about the family program I developed. Some clients wrote thank-you letters to me. Others wrote to the hospital president and raved about how much the family program helped them. The groups meeting in my home reported their recovery and spirituality deepening. I worked with a few couples in private practice.

I walked a little taller and glowed with happiness as I fell in love with Monty. It was gratifying to know that I made a difference in my clients' lives. I wished I could wave a magic wand to help my children flourish. They continued to struggle as my life blossomed.

Nicole's sporadic contact with me after our reconciliation in February became more consistent when she started a new job cashiering at Meijer's, a grocery store chain, in October shortly after I began mine. She had quit her job at the convenience store when her dad arranged a job for her at his company in their Cincinnati location. He helped her buy an expensive new car to drive back and forth, but this temporary job had not resulted in being hired full-time. She spoke about her fear of making her dad angry. She didn't elaborate, but I imagined her fear related to being financially dependent on him. I hated to see her stuck but maintained my boundaries and stayed out of their relationship.

An average student, Nicole had expressed no interest in advanced education. I couldn't see how she would escape the minimum-wage trap. Doug's sporadic and short-lived employment in fast-food restaurants left him caught in that same trap.

I hoped that what someone told me about God considering a mother's prayers special was true. In my prayer journal during this time, I prayed for my children's protection, reminding myself of my limitations, and turned them over to their Higher Power's care. I prayed to trust the process of their lives, admitting I didn't know what was in their best interests. I did hope Nicole's new job would boost her self-esteem and give her the confidence to find a job paying more than minimum wage.

Doug continued to work the system. One day he called to tell me he had acquired stable housing. He had gained admission to a Salvation Army shelter downtown. I didn't tell him I knew their director. Jane and I had attended seminary together. If I had known that this shelter provided three months of room and board to homeless men who agreed to follow their rules, participate in their therapy groups, and cooperate to find a job placement and permanent housing, I might have asked for her help with Doug's problems a long time ago. But in my ignorance, I feared her judgment about my not allowing him to live with me. I hoped she wouldn't figure out she had my son living in her shelter. A couple of months later she did.

Doug called again. "Do you know Jane Benner? She wants to talk to you."

I didn't want to talk to her. I was reluctant to break the spell of bliss surrounding my life. But I began running into Jane all over town. First, I saw her in an office supply store, next in a musical venue. She didn't see me either time. Then I was sitting in Denny's waiting to meet a new friend for lunch. My friend didn't show, but in walked Jane. This time she spotted me. Unable to miss the synchronicity, I looked to the heavens and proclaimed, "Okay, okay, I get it. You want me to talk with Jane."

Instead of judging me, Jane applauded my boundary setting. She thought Doug acted like an active alcoholic even though he didn't drink, and she had encouraged him to attend AA meetings. Of course, he refused. Still, it meant a lot to receive her validation. I had long held this opinion about Doug's behavior.

She said, "Every social service agency in town has tried to help him without success. What makes you think you can?"

Her statement took me aback. I didn't know so many agencies had contact with him. Tears welled in my eyes. *No one has been able to help him? There goes my hope that somewhere, some way, someday, someone can help him get his life together and end this nightmare. That's a scary thought ... no one being able to help him.*

"I don't know. Part of me knows I can't, but he's my son. My first instinct is to make things better for him. I've been going to twelve-step meetings and practicing detachment, but dealing with a child being homeless is hard."

Her next statement relieved my anxiety somewhat: "He has survival skills you'd never dream of."

Many times Jane's words gave me pause whenever I was tempted to rescue Doug from whatever predicament he had provoked.

The first fourteen months of pure bliss with Monty started to fall apart as we began exploring the possibility of marriage, a second for each of us. We regressed from adolescent infatuation into the terrible twos, both wanting the relationship to be "my way." He needed his space; I wanted more togetherness. We found it difficult to negotiate these differences.

I called a Living in Process friend from Indianapolis for help. Micky recommended I read *Getting the Love You Want* by Harville Hendrix. In that book, I learned about stages in relationships and about the power struggle that follows the romantic love stage. I jumped for joy that Monty and I were normal.

I told Monty about what I read: "Hendrix says the conflicts in our relationships occur because our partner recreates our childhood experiences with our parents, especially our most painful ones. Will you read the book? Please."

He expressed skepticism, but I was thrilled when he agreed to my request. After he read the book, he was a little more open to the idea that we might possess some of our parents' worst characteristics. My hope for our relationship soared when he agreed to join me for a couples' workshop in Chicago led by Harville Hendrix himself.

At the workshop, Hendrix worked with couples to demonstrate how to move through painful, entrenched conflicts. Monty and I gripped each other's hands and wept silently during his work with one angry, highly charged couple. On the drive home, we developed a strategy to apply what we learned at the workshop to our relationship. We started filling out the workbook exercises and rendezvoused at Monty's house to share what we discovered about ourselves.

However, we were unable to find our way through our impasse's complexity. After two years, our relationship came to a painful and perplexing end. I was devastated at the loss of the love of my life, but after twenty-two years of trying to make my marriage work, I just didn't have it in me to keep trying with Monty unless I could see evidence that he was willing to work at our relationship as hard as I was.

I gave myself a year to grieve and then applied to enter the Imago Relationship Therapy training. I wanted to understand what went wrong for Monty and me and what each of us had contributed to the relationship not working. I wanted to make sure whatever I did to recreate this nightmare, I wouldn't do again.

As a therapist, even before reading *Getting the Love You Want*, I had tried to access these deeper childhood wounds under the clashes my clients experienced. Hendrix had developed a whole system to assist couples in making their conflicts work for them instead of against them. Despite the failure of the theory and methodology to work for Monty and me, it continued to make sense to me. I wanted to offer Hendrix expertise to my clients.

The training helped me understand my relationship with Monty. My complaints triggered Monty's sense of never having been accepted for himself, his core wound. When he didn't include me in his life as much as I wanted, he triggered my childhood neglect and isolation. I felt the same rejection I experienced when my mother stated her preference for my brother, my core wound.

Couples like us, wounded at an early age, require the guidance of a kind, gentle, nurturing therapist to move beyond our gridlock. Otherwise, we become overwhelmed by old emotions and memories surfacing. No Imago Therapists practiced in our area. It didn't occur to me to travel for the help we needed.

I will forever treasure the two years we had together and am grateful for what our relationship opened up for me. Our difficulties increased my empathy for my clients and my determination to learn from the experience made me a better therapist. My increased skill in relating to family came in handy as my daughter approached me with a significant request.

Acceptance

1993–1998

> *Acceptance is the answer to all my problems today. I can find no serenity until I accept a disturbing person, place, thing, or situation as being exactly the way it is supposed to be at this moment.*
>
> ~Paraphrased from the Big Book of Alcoholics Anonymous

Late summer 1993, Nicole called. "Hi, Mom. I have a favor to ask. Dad's getting married, and he told me I have to move out. Can I come live with you?"

My belly fluttered when I heard my ex was marrying again. I wasn't sure why I had any feeling at all. Because he wanted no contact with me, he was little more than the father of my children. *Interesting that now he wants Nicole to move out.*

Four years ago I had pined for Nicole to live with me. Now I felt torn. She thumbed her nose at recovery, and she certainly wouldn't have learned about healthy attitudes and behavior living with her dad. I didn't ever want to live in a toxic environment again. I didn't want her introducing chaos into my serene environment. I had to be clear with her about my needs, so I suggested she come over to discuss her request.

Nicole and I took our stations on opposite ends of the couch facing each other, our legs stretched out side by side.

To calm my nerves, I took a deep breath and started on a positive note. "I'm happy to have you come live with

Nicole as a young woman.

me. I don't need you to pay rent. You can be responsible for your food and your car."

"Thanks, Mom."

"I do have some needs, though. And you need to be aware of those. Okay?"

Nicole nodded.

"As you know, open, honest communication is important to me. I can't stand living with unresolved tension in my home."

"Yeah, I know."

"When we have differences about how things should go, I want us to find a solution that works for both of us. Since we haven't lived together for years, I think it would help to have weekly meetings for a while to work out any issues we encounter. What do you think?"

Her face screwed up as though she had swallowed a bitter pill. "I guess so."

"Is that asking too much?"

She gave a lukewarm reply. "I guess not."

"I need you to be sure. Think about it a minute. Can you live with that?"

She probably didn't believe she had a choice. She couldn't yet afford an apartment on her own.

I went on. "You know that we have different standards of cleanliness. I need you to respect me and my home, especially in the kitchen. You know how I resent cleaning up other people's messes. My kitchen is smaller than the one in Kettering, and I have less counter space. Any dirty dishes left sitting around makes preparing a meal difficult. I need you to clean up after yourself."

Without enthusiasm, she agreed to do as I asked.

I hated talking to a twenty-two year old this way, but I knew what I had tolerated in the past. I doubted much had changed. I intentionally said nothing about her bedroom. I considered that her space and not subject to my cleanliness standards. As long as she didn't stain the carpet, I could ignore her mess there.

"I would like our living together to be pleasant. I need you to keep the living room and dining room neat, too. I know you don't care, but it is important to me. I like my place to look nice when friends come over."

"Okay, Mom, I can do that," she replied with a tone of resignation.

Shortly after our conversation, she moved in. My schedule wasn't a typical nine-to-five, and Nicole worked different shifts each week. I had to chase her down to schedule family meetings. She avoided them if possible, and when we did get one scheduled, she barely participated.

I appreciated that she did at least try to keep the kitchen straightened, but she put dishes away dirty. When I pointed it out, she rolled her eyes and shrugged. Several months later, when I discovered mold on dirty dishes under her bed, I had no choice but to make a rule: no food in your bedroom. She started eating snacks in the living room and leaving behind a trail of crumbs on the carpet. She resisted my request to sweep after snacking and treated it as an imposition.

I longed for a friendship like some of my friends had with their adult daughters but couldn't find a way. I tried to show respect for her and wished she would make the effort with me. Instead of grumbling and complaining like I had done in the past, I made firm, direct requests. To her they sounded like demands. She complained I treated her like a teenager. I thought she acted like one. After a frustrating year for both of us, she decided to move out.

Her brother helped her find a run-down room where the absentee landlord collected rent but did nothing to improve the property. She seemed more comfortable living in squalor than living with me. I saw no alternative but to accept what I didn't like. As an adult, Nicole had a right to live life her way.

She called and visited occasionally and needed favors. One day she called and asked me to help retrieve stuff from her car. Repossessed the night before, it contained a lot of her worldly belongings. She had wrecked two cars before buying this one and couldn't afford another. I had one less worry. She wouldn't be injured in an accident ... at least not driving a car she owned.

For the next four years, she used the bus and moved from one deplorable living situation to another. One of the rooms she lived in flabbergasted me. Mice dropped from the ceiling onto her bed. *How can she be satisfied living like this?* I worked hard to mind my own business as my twelve-step program recommended.

In the mid-1990s, managed care efforts to trim medical costs forced our hospital to reduce the services we offered to addiction patients. Our staff experienced great stress at the downsizing of our treatment program, the closing of our inpatient unit, and the reduction in the services we offered to families. Where once I had provided therapy sessions for every patient with a family member willing to participate, now these sessions all but disappeared. Four family education sessions a week were reduced to two. I mourned the loss of the quality services I once provided.

After I completed the Imago training in 1993, a psychiatrist impressed with Imago's theory and methodology invited me to work with couples out of her office. I hoped to develop a full-time practice. I noticed my hospital supervisor's stress as he juggled finances and trimmed our program. I offered to reduce my hours to thirty a week which allowed me to retain my benefits and would give me time to build my Imago practice in the psychiatrist's office.

However, the clinical setting in the psychiatrist's office placed restrictions on my work with couples. These constraints diminished the quality of the service I provided. Fifty-minute sessions prevented the deep work with couples I had been trained to do in ninety-minute sessions. And I never grew comfortable giving mental health diagnoses. I viewed my clients' conflicts as resulting from their childhood wounds and didn't consider them sick.

In 1995, I attended a local contemplative retreat led by brothers from the Taizé ecumenical monastic order in France. I came to the retreat troubled about my professional life. In the midst of silence broken only by chanting, I received a vision of offering my services in a church. That possibility excited me. In that setting, I would be free to treat my work with clients as a spiritual process and take the time to allow them to go as deeply as they were comfortable. They would have the opportunity to experience the healing power of The Divine. I could even create a community of couples interested in turning their relationship into a spiritual partnership.

The still small voice within guided me to share my vision with Pastor Larry, the minister of St. John's United Church of Christ in downtown Dayton. He responded enthusiastically and went on to present a proposal to the church council. They offered me an office in a former Sunday school room. I could also schedule the church social room for educational programs. The way opened to me to offer my services as an outreach ministry of St. John's, a setting in alignment with my vision and values.

Money was tight, however, so in the spring of 1998, I considered renting out one of my bedrooms to help with expenses. My neighbor asked whether I had ever considered serving as a host mother for an international student. Amy worked at the University of Dayton Center for International Programs. She said a student could live with me for a year and, if it went well, I could request another student. I applied and was accepted. A month later, Jacqui, a Taiwanese student a year younger than Nicole, contacted me.

We met at Ben & Jerry's Ice Cream Parlor near the University of Dayton campus. She brought a friend more skilled in English to translate. I told her about my busy life, my nighttime work hours, and my fear she would be lonely. I told her to think about it.

A few days later, her friend called and said that Jacqui wanted to see my home. Unbeknownst to me, she had two conditions when selecting her host mother. I already passed the first: I smiled at our initial meeting. She also needed an orderly, clean environment.

When she later told me her secret requirements, I rejoiced. *Finally, I have someone who appreciates me and wants to live with me because of my neatnik qualities.*

Much later, Nicole admitted she thought a student living with me was weird because she had found me so hard to live with. As Jacqui and I grew closer, it bothered her that I seemed to enjoy Jacqui's company more than I did hers. Doug never expressed an opinion one way or another. Jacqui gave him another person to talk to, and he loved bending someone's ear. Jacqui treated my children with kindness but had little in common with them. She much later admitted her early judgment of me because I didn't rescue them, but as she learned more about the situation, she understood.

The development of my relationship with Jacqui had a significant effect on me. A couple of months after she moved in, we faced a major conflict and a cultural clash. I asked her to carry a laundry basket to the basement for me. I noticed her mood change noticeably. She did what I asked but grew sullen. When I returned after running an errand, she was gone. She left a note indicating she planned to move out. I couldn't imagine what all this meant.

When she came back, I asked her why. At first, she didn't want to talk about it. With time I came to understand her culture's requirement to obey her elders—no questions asked. Also, she was unaccustomed to talking about feelings. Slowly, as she came to trust me, she revealed that she had learned to hide hurt and anger when her parents abused her. My asking a favor of her seemed as though I would treat her like a slave, as her parents had. She decided not to subject herself to abuse again. Storming out in anger was the only way she knew to protect herself.

When she realized I would change my behavior to honor her concerns, she welcomed my approach. We didn't spend a lot of time together but developed a comfortable pattern. Most days, she left in the morning before I did. When I returned in the evenings, I found her studying in her room. We checked in about our day's activities. I helped her with homework or answered her questions about our culture. She listened to me talk about my frustrations at work or concerns about my children. After our initial conflict, our living together proceeded smoothly with only an occasional bump. She had no experience negotiating differences, but her willingness to learn touched me deeply. She respected my home as though it was her own. She filled a void in my life.

I admired Jacqui's spunk and courage. Without any parental help, she fulfilled her dream of coming to the United States to study English. Little by little, she revealed the extent of physical abuse she suffered at her parents' hands.

Jacqui, Linda and neighbor, Amy

More skillful in my parenting now, I comforted her, and we developed a close mother-daughter bond. Brokenness inside each of us began to heal.

It was gratifying to recognize my growth and to find my nurturing making a difference. At last I lived with someone who was willing to learn and practice the communication skills so important to me. I experienced joy at living with another human being in the harmony I had yearned for since childhood.

In September, Nicole called sounding giddy. She told me about her boyfriend, Dennis. They were living together in a half-duplex near my home. I collapsed into the recliner next to the phone and squeezed my eyes shut. I knew this couldn't be good. A couple of weeks later she called again to tell me about their engagement. I feigned happiness, not wanting to alienate her by objecting to how fast their relationship advanced. I hated to see her make the same mistake I made when I agreed to marry her father after only knowing him six weeks. We live a long time with decisions we make when we are young and naïve. However, at twenty-seven, she had a right to make her own decisions, whether I thought they were wise or not.

Despite the sun shining on crimson and gold leaves, I shivered at the chill in the October air as I drove the few blocks to where Nicole and her fiancé lived. I went to hand-deliver a congratulatory card, giving me an opportunity to see her and how she was living. I possessed no desire to be an interfering mother or mother-in-law, but I did want to meet my daughter's fiancé.

A TV blasted sound waves at me as a young woman wearing pink sweats opened the door. I shouted my introduction and asked for Nicole. Her long blonde hair swung as she turned around and yelled up the stairs, "Nicole, your mom is here."

Two guys appeared in the archway to the kitchen, peeked out, and disappeared.

"Come on in," the young woman said. She didn't give me her name.

As I stepped into the living room, I was welcomed by the smell of pizza and the feel of dirt and grit crunching under my shoes. I later learned the young woman was Dennis's sister. She lowered the TV volume, plopped on a dilapidated maroon couch, and continued to watch her program. Alongside an open bag of potato chips and two pizza boxes, several sweating pop cans formed rings on the coffee table. She grabbed a pizza slice and began eating.

A matching overstuffed chair with sagging cushions sat next to the couch. A floor lamp with a crooked, stained shade and a chrome kitchen chair with a red plastic seat completed the ensemble. Rumpled clothing, crushed pop cans, empty snack bags, and pizza cartons containing remnants of crust littered the floor. There wasn't a wastebasket in sight.

I shuddered as I heard Nicole bound down the steps. She gave me a hug, and pulling the engagement card from my handbag's back pocket, I offered it to her. She giggled as she opened and read it. She gave me another hug, turned around, and yelled, "Dennis, come see what my mom brought us."

He emerged from the kitchen and ambled toward us, looking like a shorter version of Sean Penn in *Mystic River*. She showed him the card and gushed, "Isn't that sweet of my mom?"

"Yeah." He rocked from foot to foot for a moment before disappearing back into the kitchen.

With no invitation to make myself comfortable, I remained stationed at the door. Nicole chattered about nothing I can remember and then an awkward silence ensued—my cue to leave.

"Well, I need to go." I gave her a hug and whispered in her ear, "Stay in touch, will you?"

On the ride home, I prayed. *God, grant me the serenity to accept the things I cannot change, the courage to change the things I can, and the wisdom to know I'm the only person I can change*—the adaptation of the Serenity prayer often used by the twelve-step program I attended. As bad as these living conditions appeared, they were an improvement over her previous, more appalling ones.

I resolved again to mind my own business and not inflict my need for order on my adult daughter. In twelve-step meetings, we laughed about our full-time job—changing our own controlling behavior. Today, I didn't feel like laughing.

To give Jacqui an American holiday experience, I hosted a family Christmas. My parents decided to attend—a first Christmas visit since they moved to Florida twelve years earlier. I planned my menu to include each family member's favorite food and chose special presents for each person. After dinner, we gathered before the six-foot tree in my living room to open gifts. I requested we share a favorite Christmas memory as we opened packages one at a time. Jacqui fascinated us with accounts of Taiwanese holidays.

Dennis sat silent and sullen on the sofa, glued to Nicole as though he wanted to fade away behind her back. After opening the gifts, the two of them vanished to the bathroom upstairs. When they reappeared a half hour later, Nicole announced they were leaving. My shoulders drooped as I stood at my front window and watched them disappear down the street carrying their stack of gifts.

After Christmas, Nicole and I talked on the phone several times, but when I tried to find a time to get together, she always gave an excuse. When I questioned her about it, she said, "Dennis thinks you dominate me."

I bit my lip. *Dominate her? Where did he dig up that idea? He doesn't know me. Why does she put up with that? Sounds like he's the one controlling her ... like a batterer does. Hope she doesn't get hurt.* I tried to stay in touch. But when their phone was disconnected, I had no way to contact her.

Friends told me they saw her downtown. "She doesn't look well," they reported.

Relieved to know she was still alive, I hated feeling so powerless. Acceptance didn't come easy. And so I prayed: *God, keep her safe. Please bring her to her senses. Or help me accept what I can't change and don't understand.*

The unanswered questions weighed heavily on my heart. Clearly, neither Doug nor Nicole was as alarmed as I was about the way they lived. Their lives could be falling apart around them, yet they remained cheerful and unconcerned—another part of the puzzle in the process of being solved.

Secrets

1998–1999

[S]hame is a great motivator for secrecy.

~Donna VanLiere

Pastor Larry retired three years after I began my ministry at the downtown church. Pastor Sharon, our new interim minister, and I met for a getting-to-know-you lunch. She talked at length and with pride about her children. She also revealed the way she planned to expand her ministry ... as a parenting coach. I gulped and squirmed.

No one at church knew much about my personal life. They knew I had adult children but didn't ask about them, and I offered nothing about their circumstances. To my relief, Pastor Sharon didn't ask. I avoided any mention of having children and stuck to safe topics—my relationship therapy and coaching ministry.

One Monday morning in February 1999, I stacked my breakfast dishes in the dishwasher and prepared to go to my upstairs office to work on a newsletter article when the phone rang. It was Pastor Sharon. I hadn't felt well and had missed church the day before. She asked how I felt, and then said, "I think your daughter was in church yesterday. What's going on?"

Shock waves coursed through my body. That was the last news I expected. I clutched my chest. *Thank God she's alive*—my first thought. *Oh my God*—my next thought.

Sinking into the recliner next to the phone table, I said, "I don't know." I gave minimum details—"engaged ... I don't have a good feeling about her fiancé ... haven't seen her since Christmas ... I've been worried about her."

"It's obvious they're living on the streets. She looks thin and pale. Fred [the church council president] invited them to the fellowship hour and saw to it they were fed."

Another shock wave. I stood and paced the floor. I tried to hold myself together, to remain calm and clearheaded. I looked out the front window at the sidewalk where I'd last seen Nicole and Dennis walking down the street carrying their Christmas presents.

Nicole living homeless. One child living homeless is bad enough. But two? Oh my God. What must Pastor Sharon think? What must the people at church think? I can see them all buzzing about this. How will I be able to face them? I can't explain this to myself much less to someone else. I have to hold myself together. I won't be any good to anybody if I fall apart.

Feeling cornered, I figured I might as well tell her. I rubbed the back of my neck and said what I hoped never to reveal: "Both my kids have had stints of homelessness. I've been through nightmares with both of them. I'm at a loss to explain it. I've spent years looking for answers. I'm going to a twelve-step program and practicing tough love. It's the only thing I know to do."

Pastor Sharon said, "I'm so sorry. How can we be of support?"

"I'm not sure. I don't know how to think about this. I'm relieved to know she's alive. She told me her fiancé thinks I dominate her. I wonder if they're trying to embarrass me, jeopardize my ministry."

"I wondered about that, too. How about we make a plan? If she comes again, you could head for my office after worship, and I'll bring her there. I can help you talk with her. We'll try to find out what's going on with her. What do you think? Would that work?"

"It's worth a try."

My mind whirled, but I didn't know what else to say. I thanked Pastor Sharon for her support and drank in her kindness. I told her I would call Fred. After we ended the call, I sank back into the recliner and let Pastor Sharon's revelation sink in. I held back sobs. *No, I can't cry. I have to stay strong. Breathe. Pull yourself together. I have to handle this. What is the best way to begin my conversation with Fred? Please give me the words.*

When Fred answered my call, I said, "I want to thank you for your kindness to my daughter yesterday."

"I wasn't sure what to do. I didn't feel I did enough for her."

"According to Pastor Sharon, you treated her like any other visitor to the church. That's all you needed to do. If she comes again, that's all anybody needs to do."

"Are you sure?"

"Yes, Pastor Sharon and I have a plan if she comes again. We'll handle it. This is embarrassing for me, Fred. I don't know how to explain her behavior. I haven't seen her since Christmas. Nothing I've done to help her has worked. I'm trying to give her responsibility for her choices. Does that make sense?"

"I guess so. Elsie [his wife] and I will keep both of you in our prayers."

After our call, I sobbed. He gave no hint of the judgment I feared.

The relief didn't last long. I steeled myself to face the members of the committee on which I served at our meeting next Wednesday. I had two days to prepare.

Deep breathing. Summoning courage. Bracing for judgment. Putting on my "professional face."

"Some of you may have heard my daughter was in church on Sunday ..."

They, too, responded with kindness, "We'll pray for both of you. We'll add your names to our prayer group."

"And I have a friend with a prayer group at her church. I'll get you on her list, too," Karen chuckled. "In fact, we'll see to it that every prayer group in town puts you and Nicole on their list. We'll cover all the bases." She gave me a reassuring hug.

Tears of relief ... so much support ... hard to take it all in ... overwhelming gratitude ... hugs all around.

Nicole and Dennis never came for a second visit.

Two months later, after seeing a client at the hospital treatment center, I left a therapy room carrying a patient chart and headed for my cubicle in the staff room to write notes. I turned left down the hallway. A voice I didn't recognize behind me said, "Hi, Mom."

I turned and squinted, trying to find recognition. Nicole was unkempt, pale, and gaunt, her hair long and stringy. Once my brain computed that this was indeed my daughter, I reached out and gave her a big hug. Before anyone saw us, I put my arm around her shoulder and ushered her into the room I had just vacated. I guided her to the loveseat at the far end of the room. We sat, held hands, and snuggled.

"It's so good to see you."

"I came to show you some pictures." She reached into her bag, pulled out papers, and handed them to me. "These are pictures of your granddaughter. I'm pregnant."

Time decelerated. I felt caught in a slow-motion dream. *Oh no, another nightmare. Not another nightmare.*

I reached for the ultrasound images of my granddaughter. A hushed gasp escaped from my mouth as I lifted the papers for a closer look. Overwhelming love swelled in my heart as I stared in awe. My trembling hands dropped to my lap, still holding the images of my granddaughter. I looked at Nicole and asked, "When are you due?"

"The first part of September."

She paused and searched my face. "I didn't think you'd be happy about this. It doesn't come at a good time."

"Not a good time?"

"No, Dennis doesn't have a job, and we can't afford it right now. I've been coming to the clinic here. I had an appointment today, and they did an ultrasound. So I decided to come and let you know. You can have one of the pictures if you want one."

Holding back tears, I murmured "Oh, okay. Thank you. Thank you for letting me know."

We looked at each other. I contemplated a moment about offering her advice or assistance. *She hasn't asked for my help. She's still with Dennis. It's not my place to interfere in their relationship. I wish she would break up with him. He's not providing for her or their baby's* needs. I don't know what to do. I'm not prepared to deal with this. These are not the circumstances I ever imagined for my first grandchild. I hate being put in this position.

We sat in awkward silence. Neither of us seemed to know what to say. Finally, I said, "I need to get back to work now. I hope you'll stay in touch. I've missed you."

We held each other in a long embrace. I told her, "I love you."

"I love you, too."

I watched her disappear around the corner at the end of our hallway. I spun around and returned to my cubicle in a daze. Hours later, back at home, the shock subsided and a flush of heat arose. *I taught her about birth control. I offered to go with her to Planned Parenthood. She refused. She never accepts my help. If only she had used birth control, she wouldn't be facing another damn crisis. And I wouldn't be in such distress, wrestling once again trying to determine my responsibility and the best way to respond. Having to let go yet again hurts so much. I hate it.*

I worked my twelve-step program to stay out of my children's business and to avoid trying to fix their poor choices and the chaos surrounding them—what I recommended to my clients. When I butted into their business, I made myself and everyone around me crazy. Still, as a fixer, turning my children over to a power greater remained a major challenge, especially when their lives weren't going the way I thought they *should*.

"Let go to give them space to learn their life lessons," I heard at meetings. So I worked at letting go, detaching with love, the ultimate goal. But I questioned my actions and motivations. *Is it love allowing Nicole to experience the painful consequences of her choices, especially with an innocent baby in the picture? Is it love when I refuse to rescue her? Is it self-care or selfishness, protecting myself from her chaos?*

I need to live with myself after this baby's birth. I don't want drama in my life anymore. Do I deserve a better life? Will it ever be possible?

Doubt about the wisdom of my choices hung over me like a shroud. The support I received at meetings helped me maintain my sanity.

A week later, I planned to leave for my spring visit to my parents' home in Florida. *What to tell Mom and Dad? I can see Mom's pursed lips and rolling eyes. Dad won't say anything, but he'll be as critical as Mom. I don't need their judgment now.*

I decided not to tell them. They would find out soon enough. Before I left, I made an appointment with my attorney and changed my will. If something happened to me, I would provide for my granddaughter. That gave me some sense I could be a constructive influence in her life—contribute to a positive future for her despite this despicable situation.

A couple of months later, in early July, Nicole phoned to tell me she had broken up with Dennis. "*He's* the one who dominated me. He tried to isolate me from you and everybody. He didn't even like it when I spent time with his sisters."

My hand covered my heart. *At last, she's coming to her senses.* I asked, "Are you okay?"

"Oh, I'm fine. I'm staying with some guys who helped me get away from him."

"How did they do that?"

"We've been staying at Daniel's, and he didn't like the way Dennis treated me, so he told me I could stay if I wanted to, but Dennis had to go. Dennis isn't allowed to come visit me here."

Holding my breath, afraid of what I might hear, not sure I wanted to know, I felt compelled to ask, "Was he ever violent with you?"

"He never touched me. I told him if he did, I'd leave."

My chest swelled with pride, "Good for you. Where is Daniel's place?"

"On East Third, not far from downtown."

East Third was the same riddled-with-flophouses street where Doug stayed years before. I wasn't comfortable with this part of town but had to admit Daniel's place seemed preferable to any option Dennis had provided.

With Dennis out of the picture, Nicole revealed the truth to me about their relationship. She told me he was separated but still legally married when they became engaged. Not long after Christmas, his domestic violence charge caught up with him. When the police arrested him, he lost his job. She didn't want contact with me because she didn't want to tell me she spent her time visiting him in jail. Without his income, they could no longer afford the duplex near my home.

After his release, they crashed for months anywhere they could find a place, sometimes in homeless shelters or on the streets. They didn't ask to stay with me. Jacqui still lived in my home, so Nicole assumed correctly I wouldn't allow it. My contract as a host mother didn't include subjecting my student to filth and lice. I wasn't in a position to provide Nicole with a home, even if I wanted to. And I had mixed feelings about that. I loved my daughter, but I detested the chaos surrounding her life. Besides, I would never, under any circumstances, allow Dennis to live with me.

When they crashed at Daniel's on East Third, the three guys living with him backed him up when he ordered Dennis to leave and not come back. The couple who rented the other half of the duplex befriended Nicole. Because they expected a baby, she had someone to talk with about her pregnancy.

With Dennis out of the picture, I wouldn't be interfering, so I had the freedom to ask, "Would you like me to come to your appointments with you?"

"Yeah, if you want to."

"I'm willing to be your birthing coach, too. That is if you'd like that."

She invited me to her next prenatal appointment, and we made plans to attend Lamaze classes the first week in August in anticipation of the baby's birth in September.

And so it was that on the morning of July 27 I found myself standing in a hallway outside an ultrasound room grumbling to God who seemed to have abandoned my daughter and me ... asking God to come to me with skin on and tell me loud and clear how to handle what looked to me like a deplorable situation. I needed an unmistakable sign because doing my best had not made a shred of difference in our family, and I felt hopeless and exhausted. When the nurse opened the ultrasound room door and told me Nicole was having contractions and needed to be sent to labor and delivery, I blurted out, "Oh no. This isn't good. She's not due for another five weeks. I'm supposed to coach her. We were going to start Lamaze classes next week. We're not ready."

I panicked and wasn't prepared for the about face my day had just taken. In order to give support to Nicole, I needed to secure coverage for my afternoon appointments and evening groups. I was due to report to work at three. I had kept Nicole's pregnancy a secret from my coworkers and cringed at the thought of telling them. Nicole had made no preparations for her baby's arrival. And I hadn't had time to do that. I felt totally unprepared for this turn of events.

While arrangements were in progress to transfer Nicole to labor and delivery, I trudged through busy walkways toward Turning Point on the other side of the campus. With bowed head and eyes focused on the shiny, tan-flecked floor and white shoes scurrying back and forth, I managed to avoid seeing anyone I knew. I didn't want to explain why I had arrived at the hospital early.

I opened the door to the meeting room where my new boss sat in a circle with four other hospital administrators. "Can I talk to you a minute?"

He frowned, narrowed his eyes, looked around at the others, and hesitated a moment before joining me in the bustling hallway. Elevator bells dinged, and the P.A. system paged and called out codes. I would have preferred meeting in private, but he seemed irritated, so I made my point: "My daughter's pregnant, and it looks like she'll deliver today. I need coverage for my afternoon appointments, and I might not be able to work tonight."

His face broke into a wide smile, "That's wonderful."

I burst into tears, "No, it's not."

At that moment, two coworkers exited the elevator and approached us. "What's wrong?" they asked.

The hallway roared with conversations as people rushed by in both directions. I stared at them. *No way am I going to say more here.* They reached out, one on each side, took my arms and swept me away down the hall to an empty therapy room as our bewildered supervisor returned to his meeting.

"What's the matter?" Joyce and Cheryl asked in unison as they stared at me with puzzled expressions.

My gaze dropped and I studied their feet standing side by side before me. I shook my head as though I could shake away having to reveal my secret shame. I heaved a sigh and said, "This is such a mess. Nicole became engaged to this guy with a history of domestic violence, and now she's pregnant. I've hardly had any contact with her until a couple of weeks ago when she broke up with him. I agreed to go to her prenatal checkups. That's why I'm at the hospital early. Now she's having contractions, so they've sent her to labor and delivery. She could deliver today."

"Is she on drugs?" Cheryl asked—a reasonable question from a chemical dependency counselor.

"I don't have any evidence of it. I wish she were. I'd know how to deal with drugs," I said—a reasonable response from a chemical dependency family therapist.

But none of my training had prepared me for this.

PART III – EMERGING

There is a hard truth to be told:
before spring becomes beautiful, it is plug ugly,
nothing but mud and muck.
I have walked in the early spring
through fields that will suck your boots off,
a world so wet and woeful
it makes you yearn for the return of ice.
But in that muddy mess,
the conditions for rebirth are being created.

~Parker Palmer

Living with mystery and paradox is the
birthplace of compassion and wisdom.

~Richard Rohr

Summoning Courage

July–August 1999

A more compassionate way to respond to those I love might be to allow them to face the consequences of their actions, even when it will cause them pain. ... Sometimes the most compassionate thing I can do is to let others take responsibility for their behavior.

~Courage to Change (a twelve-step daily guide)

With my secret out, I gathered my courage and held my head a little higher as I retraced my steps and headed back to the Berry Women's Center. When I entered Nicole's room, she had just arrived. I took a seat on the edge of the blue vinyl recliner and watched her nurse help her undress for a shower. From the shower room, I heard Marlene give Nicole instructions about how to use the special shampoo to kill the lice infesting her hair. I closed my eyes and dropped my head. Her nurse returned to the room where I sat.

"This is so embarrassing," I said.

Marlene stopped a moment and looked at me: "We see lots of

things in all kinds of families. No one is judging you."

She went on to tell me about a difficult situation in her family. I stayed perched on the recliner's edge but relaxed at her compassion, her willingness to share my vulnerability. Tension oozed from my pores. I prayed silently, *Thank you, thank you, thank you.*

Because Marlene seemed to comprehend my dilemma, I found the courage to speak what was on my mind: "Do you ever call Children's Services in a case like this?"

It grated on me, the thought of Children's Services involved in our lives again, but Nicole's baby needed protection. Just as Doug had needed to answer to an authority beyond his parents' so long ago, now Nicole needed this. I had hoped to break the chain of family dysfunction, but now another generation faced it.

Marlene didn't skip a beat and showed no shock. She said, "I'll have a social worker come talk with her." She gathered Nicole's clothing and stood before me holding the bundle. "For now, I need you to get her some clean clothes. These need to be burned. And while you're at it, you might want to pick up some clothes for the baby to wear home from the hospital."

Glad to be given a task, I headed out on a shopping expedition. First, I headed for a thrift store on Linden Avenue where I had purchased a dozen sweaters in good condition for Nicole at Christmas. I shook my head as I realized those sweaters were long gone. I found a clerk about Nicole's age and size. With her help, in no time we chose several matching t-shirt and short outfits.

K-Mart seemed a logical next stop to shop for underwear for Nicole and clothes for the baby. *Should I buy bottles and nursery items, too?* My mind ticked off a list of the baby's needs. *I can't deal with that today. I'll purchase some clothes for now and figure out how to handle the rest later.*

Employee laughter and the occasional cash register ka-ching didn't interfere with my late morning solitude. I strolled through the infant department, stroking the soft receiving blankets and selecting the cutest designs for drawstring infant gowns. I lingered over adorable smocked dresses with matching bloomers and booties. In my mind's eye, I saw endearing images of my daughter as a child, all gussied up posing for pictures in adorable dresses. She looked so cute with her long curly blonde ponytails bouncing on either side of her head.

Nicole at age 7.

What happened? Nicole was so happy as a child and resilient. She seems so passive now ... not the baby who wouldn't let a twisted thigh bone stop her ... who initiated hugs and kisses. Will I ever have precious moments like those with her again ... with my granddaughter? How did we get here? I wanted a better life for her than I've had. So much for that dream.

I rounded a corner and spotted a white satin dress with puffy sleeves that looked like a baptismal gown. Walking closer, I beheld its silky sleekness and flowing elegance as I fingered its soft, brushed polyester collar and cuffs. I couldn't resist succumbing to what might be my only opportunity to experience the joy of being a grandmother. I allowed myself this one small extravagance.

When I returned to the hospital, I encountered Marlene in the hall. She said, "I contacted the social worker, and she called Children's Services. They aren't willing to be involved at this point."

"I'm not surprised. I appreciate your trying anyway."

I had experience reporting a few Turning Point clients to Children's Services. Once they chastised me for overreacting. Years later the mother I had reported returned to tell me the steps she had taken to change her life's trajectory. I hoped a Children's Service intervention would produce a similar outcome for Nicole.

Marlene added, "The social worker warned Nicole if she delivers with lice in her hair, Children's Services might take her baby away. We put the fear of God into her. We told her the treatment for lice isn't good for her baby, and she'd better get her act together."

I hugged her and lifted another prayer of gratitude. *Thank you for this angel.* Disguised as a nurse, Marlene seemed the "God with skin on" I wanted and needed.

Back in Nicole's room, I pulled my purchases from shopping bags one by one and showed her my selections. I saved my favorite for last. "Look at this cute little satin dress."

We oohed and aahed over the dress. She approved the designs for the drawstring gowns and receiving blankets.

"Thanks, Mom, for getting stuff for us."

I gave her a hug. "You're welcome."

In the early afternoon Nicole's labor stalled. She still couldn't feel contractions. Marlene said it appeared to be false. We decided I might as well go to work.

Nicole was discharged on Wednesday, the day after she had been admitted. This gave me more time to explore better options for her baby. I had been praying for guidance for months and had some possibilities in mind but hadn't had a chance to investigate them yet.

Nothing in me wanted to rear another child. I hadn't done such a great job with my children, but still, I seemed the best option. I talked with a twelve-step friend who had taken custody of her grandchild when her daughter was on cocaine. She gave me the name of the attorney she and her husband had used. On a blazing hot Saturday, July 31 morning, three days after Nicole's discharge, I consulted their attorney. He thought I had a good chance to obtain custody.

During the twenty-minute drive home, the air conditioner's hum put me in a trance. Oblivious to my surroundings, I replayed the attorney's words again and again. I imagined if I was granted custody, Nicole would be angry and get pregnant again to spite me. My potential life flashed before me as one reduced to crisis intervention and turmoil as I rescued one grandchild after another. I shivered with a bone-chilling fatigue.

At fifty-seven, do I possess the stamina to rear another child? How can I rearrange my life to include a baby when I work with clients in the evening? Oh God, what would you have me do? Do you want me to take custody of this child? Am I to take responsibility for raising my granddaughter? Is that what is right for me to do? Please speak to me. Give me a sign I can't miss.

The still small voice within spoke—as clearly as it had so long ago when it told me Buddy and I were not a good match for each other.

This time the voice said, "You are not to take custody of this child. You are to be an oasis of light in her life."

An oasis of light. Wow. What a beautiful image.

Scenarios danced across my mind as I envisioned special times together. I would read to her and introduce her to the arts. We would go to parks and arboretums and marvel together at flowers and trees and butterflies. An oasis of light—this image both delighted me and made me sad. I doubted the scenes I visualized would become a reality. My experience with my children had been nightmarish for so long, it would take a miracle for my dream to materialize. I couldn't imagine how that could ever happen at this late date.

The phone rang as I walked toward my front door. I rushed to answer it.

"Hi, Mom, it's me. My water broke this morning. I'm back in the hospital."

My heart skipped a beat. With no hint of the anxiety surging within me, I asked, "Do you want me to come?"

She still couldn't feel the contractions, so we decided she would call if her labor sped up. I assured her, "I can be there in minutes if you need me."

The next morning, Sunday, August 1, Nicole called again. this time seeking my advice. "The doctor talked to me about a study they're doing. They're worried about me getting an infection because my water broke. They're giving me antibiotics, but the study is about inducing labor, you know, so I don't get an infection. But there's a problem because my baby's lungs aren't developed enough. She'd have a better chance in a couple more weeks. He wants to know if I want to be in the study. What do you think I should do?"

It still seemed surreal—Nicole having a baby. I collected my thoughts—how best to advise her. "If I were you, I'd let nature take its course. If they decide to induce, it's on them if the baby's hurt."

"Okay, that's what I was thinking."

At about nine the next morning, Monday, August 2, Nicole called to say they decided to induce labor. "I'll be there as soon as I can." Before I left for the hospital, I made a telephone call to explore one last option. The oasis-of-light image anchored me and gave me purpose in the midst of my powerlessness as my granddaughter's birth approached.

All the way to the hospital I rehearsed what I would say and how I would say it, praying to be given the right words. My heart broke, knowing what I must do. Grateful to have Nicole back in my life, I didn't want to do or say anything to push her away again. I hoped she would recognize my love for her and her baby. I prayed for her openness to the suggestion I was about to make.

I exited the employees' parking garage, the shade between the tall buildings protecting me from the blazing sun as I headed across the street to the main entrance. I pushed the round revolving door and left the humid August heat behind as I entered the cool Berry Women's Center. The dome skylight illuminated the circular rotunda decorated in elegant redwood panels. I shivered in the air conditioning and donned my sweater against the chill.

I looked at the two upper floor walkways surrounding the rotunda and tucked my anxiety deep inside. On a mission, I wouldn't allow nervousness to disrupt my focus. With determined steps, I entered the elevator and exited onto the top floor, the birthing room location. I wound my way past a nurses' station and to the right down the hallway to Nicole's room.

Open blue curtains revealed a soothing view of emerald green treetops covering East Dayton's rolling hills. A blue vinyl recliner sat in front of the window and several others lined the wall at the end of her bed. A blue zigzag border at the top broke the wall's off-white neutrality.

I moved toward Nicole's bedside. Red pimples splotched her pale face. Her long, dark, shiny hair had been chopped short. She combed it straight back. Her belly ascended from her emaciated, anemic body's middle in a mound. My hands trembled as I attempted to make a loving connection before initiating my conversation. She still couldn't feel the contractions. They hadn't given her any idea how long this might take.

"How are you dealing with this?"

"I'm doing okay."

She is always doing okay ... no matter how dreadful the situation. I'm the one who carries all the anxiety and angst. I seem to remember being told that isn't good for any of us. God, please help me.

I reached out and touched her arm, heaved a big sigh, and said, "I have something important I need to talk with you about. This may not be easy for you to hear, but I'm saying this because I love you, and I'm concerned about you and your baby."

"Okay," she replied warily.

"This morning I talked with a woman who's adopting a baby through Catholic Social Services."

"Mom, I don't want my baby winding up in foster care. It was horrible for Dennis."

I tried to reassure her about this different option. "The process at Catholic Social Services is a whole lot better than the way the public system handles adoptions. You would be able to choose who gets your baby."

Nicole blinked back tears and turned her head away from me.

About this time Julie, her nurse, entered the room. "What's the matter?" she asked.

"I'm having a difficult conversation with my daughter."

"Oh," she replied as she scurried out to give us privacy.

I turned back toward Nicole. She wiped her nose with her hand. "I know this is hard." I said. "It's hard for me, too."

Her chin trembled.

I went on, "The people adopting have to write a story about their lives and tell about what's important to them. You would get to read the stories and decide who you want to raise your baby. I think this is something you should consider."

Nicole's lashes grew heavy with tears. I handed her tissues, but she wadded them in her fists. Tears ran down her face.

"I'm going to leave the room now and give you some time to think about and pray about what's best for your baby. When I come back, I'm not going to say another word about it. It has to be your decision."

With a squeeze to her arm, I paused a moment, full of love and pain as my daughter attempted to hold back sobs. All we could do now was await the birth of this baby... and continue to pray to a power greater than our own: *Please give us a miracle.*

Surrender

August 2, 1999

God is humble and never comes if not first invited, but God will find some clever way to get invited.

~Richard Rohr

Relieved to have completed my mission, I sought out a quiet corner and found an alcove off the birthing center's circular walkway. I sank into a loveseat, leaned back, closed my eyes, and felt the exhaustion I had been carrying for weeks ... for years really. Doubt and guilt lashed me with dark thoughts and condemning questions.

Was this my fault? Have I been such a bad mother? Did the atmosphere in our home produce this? Was Buddy's parenting and mine this bad? Is this punishment? Why are both our children following such self-destructive paths?

One more time, I faced the challenge of turning my will and my life over to a power greater than myself. Part of me resented having no other option. I leaned forward, shoulders hunched, head down, fingers twisted together between my legs. Like it or not, I couldn't stop this baby's birth. I sighed and murmured a prayer. "Okay, God, you know if I could, I'd stop this baby from coming into the world. I've done everything I know to do."

Still alone in that alcove—no one around—I straightened, looked up, stretched out my arms, turned my palms toward the heavens, and surrendered. "I turn it over to You."

A deep calm descended on me as I experienced the serenity of full surrender. I took it in. With it came trust in my Higher Power to work our circumstances out for the best, even if I couldn't see how. Curiosity about how the day would unfold accompanied the peace.

To my surprise, humor emerged. I chuckled and chided myself at the hold my controlling ways had over me, convincing me the world would fall apart if I didn't orchestrate everything. "Things have to become pretty drastic for you to surrender, huh. An ordained minister you say you are? This is a major spiritual lesson, you know—surrendering."

I called Kathy, my former coworker who had expressed concern about my lack of self-care so many years before. "Today's the day. Can you come?" She had offered to be with us on the day of the birth. Nicole knew and liked Kathy, and her great sense of humor would lighten the tension between my daughter and me.

Aware of the many challenges I had faced with my children throughout the years, Kathy had served as my confidante during the months of no contact with Nicole. She listened to my fears for my daughter's safety and my lamentations about her pregnancy.

She hesitated at first when I told her about my wish Nicole would consider adoption. As Nicole's due date approached, she suggested I talk with her sister who had adopted a child through Catholic Social Services (CSS). As my fears grew more intense, she said, "If Nicole does become willing to put her baby up for adoption, maybe Dan and I could be the adoptive parents. I could talk with Dan about it."

Kathy's inability to get pregnant again left her longing for another child. I loved her idea because it would be possible for Nicole and me to continue to be a part of the baby's life. But we didn't know whether CSS would go along with such a plan. Kathy and Dan had not made application. Kathy was a Roman Catholic, but Dan was not. Would that make a difference to the agency? We had little time to obtain answers to all these questions.

Kathy's sister and I scheduled a time to talk. Because Nicole's water broke five weeks early, our conversation occurred on the day the doctor decided to induce labor. That meant I had to ask Nicole to consider adoption on the day she was giving birth. I hated having to do it then, but I wouldn't have been able to live with myself if I didn't at least tell her about this agency's humane approach. We needed a workable solution to protect her baby.

As confident as I might have looked on the outside, I doubted that I navigated any of the challenges I faced as a parent well. And this situation was new terrain. When I called Kathy to tell her the doctor had decided to induce labor and to ask if she was available to come be with us, I filled her in on my tearful conversation with Nicole and my belief I had done all I could.

On my way back to Nicole's room, I encountered Julie. Her intense blue eyes looked straight into mine: "I talked with your daughter after you left. I told her you love her, and you're concerned about her and the baby."

I gave her a hug and thanked her. Another angel disguised as a nurse had entered our lives. Julie exuded confidence, giving no doubt she was an excellent nurse. I felt grateful she was a compassionate human being as well.

When I walked into her room, Nicole was still in tears. "I called Dad. He won't come. He says he told me not to get pregnant, and he doesn't want anything to do with this."

I flinched and swallowed hard. *What an ass. Best he doesn't come. He'd only make this more difficult than it already is. Still, how can he be so crass to our daughter?* I ached for Nicole. I held her hand and said all I knew to say, "I'm so sorry."

Kathy, an upbeat extrovert with a gift of gab, arrived about one in the afternoon. I was grateful she filled the spaces between Nicole and me. Only fourteen years older than Nicole, she could talk about Rick Springfield and Jack Wagner in a way I had never been able. Kathy was conversant in 1980's music and musicians, the kind of conversation Nicole loves but bewilders me.

Julie buzzed in and out of the room and joined our banter. We compared this hospital to *General Hospital*, Nicole's favorite soap opera. As the hours passed, Nicole's labor made minimal progress. We avoided any mention of the gravity of her situation.

At about five-thirty, Kathy and I decided to take a dinner break. The cafeteria hummed with the chatter of staff and visitors and the clank of silverware. Amid the noise and mingling smells of food, I told Kathy about the most recent events.

She said, "You've been through so much, Linda, and you've come so far. I remember when you were a basket case, losing weight, looking haggard. Remember that?"

"Yes, I remember. You've seen me at my worst. You've been a good friend for a long time."

"You're a different person now. You're here supporting Nicole, and you're calm and composed. Nicole is lucky to have you for a mother."

"Thank you. I wish she believed that."

"It's going to be fine. It's going to work out. You wait and see."

I yearned to believe her. "It would be wonderful if Nicole agreed to allow you to adopt her baby. It may be selfish, but I think it would be great for both of us. We could still be a part of the baby's life."

"Yeah, but we'll have to take it one step at a time and see what's possible. We don't know yet what's best for everybody concerned."

"I know. I've turned it over, and I'm not going to take it back now. It would be nice, though."

We thought we had plenty of time, so we took a swing through the hospital gift shop before heading back through underground tunnels to the Berry building. We were gone for about an hour. During that time, Nicole's cervix dilated from two centimeters to eight.

When we returned to Nicole's floor, we found Doug and his best friend Rob in the waiting area. Doug said, "They took her to the operating room."

"The operating room? Why an operating room?"

"I don't know. That's what they said."

I whirled around in a panic to search for Julie, finding her charging down the hall toward us. "I'm supposed to be with Nicole."

"Follow me," Julie signaled as she turned down another hallway. "They've just taken her to the operating room."

"Is it okay if Kathy comes, too?"

"She's really not supposed to." She turned around and paused a moment, looking into our imploring faces. "Oh well, come on," she motioned as she turned around and continued down the corridor.

"Why is she in an operating room?" I asked as Kathy and I rushed headlong after her.

"They want to make sure everything goes okay. There's more equipment in an operating room." Later I learned this is standard procedure for a premature birth.

Julie led us into a room and helped us don surgical gowns, hats, and masks. At about six forty-five, she escorted Kathy and me into the operating room.

My eyes took a moment to adjust to the brilliant light. I searched for my daughter in the midst of the crowd. At least eight men and women adorned in scrubs attended to her. The resident, his ruddy complexion almost as red as Nicole's, urged her, "Push. Push."

She was strapped to the operating room table, hooked to monitors and an IV, her face scrunched from the exertion. Kathy and I stationed ourselves on either side of her but found it difficult to move close enough to hold her hand much less provide coaching. Nicole resisted the resident's charge to push. She disliked this man because, during her prenatal examinations, he dismissed her complaints about the roughness of his stubby fingers. She must be resenting his presence now.

I assured her, "Women have been doing this for thousands of years. You can do it, too."

She stared daggers at me and shot back, "Oh, shut up." My coaching technique seemed to leave a little to be desired. We could have used those Lamaze classes.

The resident inserted forceps. An older doctor, a huge man with a head full of snow white hair, burst into the room. He looked around as though assessing the situation. Without warning, he slapped the resident's hands and exclaimed, "Get back." He removed the forceps, set them aside, and examined Nicole manually.

Others moved forward to assist. I stepped back to make room. One assistant turned to me and pointed to a nearby instrument tray, "Would you hand me ..."

My eyes widened. "I'm the grandmother."

"Oh," he replied with a surprised look. A woman, another assistant, came forward and handed him the requested instrument.

Nicole turned toward me, her eyes welling with tears. "I'm not going through this hell and then give my baby away. Will you support me in that?"

All eyes turned toward me awaiting my response. Knowing this was not the time or place for such a conversation and unsure what to say, I replied, "We'll talk about that later."

Grace Unfolding

August 2–3, 1999

Grace is the breath of God – an invisible essence beyond intellect that moves swiftly amongst us. It is not only possible to become a living conduit of this powerful force, grace is immediately accessible to us along with the courage to follow divine guidance.

~Caroline Myss

Alexandra no sooner emerged from her mother's womb than an attendant whisked her away into an adjoining room. The clock read 7:17 p.m. We didn't hear her cry.

"Mommy, find out what's happening to her," Nicole begged.

Because I was barred from entering, Julie went for us. She returned, shaking her head and looking down. "She's really sick. There's a whole team of doctors working on her."

At around eight o'clock, a doctor asked me to leave the operating room while they sewed the rips and tears Nicole received during delivery. Kathy had left earlier to join Doug and Rob in the waiting area. Julie, who had started work at seven that morning, continued to serve as a courier, giving us updates on Alexandra until nine-thirty when she gave herself permission to go home. Her reports remained the same. Sometimes unable to find words, she shook her head with a pained expression on her face.

A delivery room resident agreed to take over as courier. We sat vigil, waiting for news about Alexandra and for Nicole's transfer from recovery to her hospital room. I remained serene as I observed the events around me and my own response to them. My curiosity about how this would unfold persisted. I displayed uncharacteristic patience with Doug's constant prattle and felt grateful that Rob met much of his attention-seeking needs. Kathy continued to lighten the mood.

Buddy called around nine. A nurse summoned me to the nurses' station and handed the phone to me. I gave him a straightforward account of Alexandra's birth. I felt relieved I would be able to tell Nicole her father had called. At some level, he loved her and was concerned about her and curious about his first grandchild.

At ten-thirty, orderlies wheeled Nicole back into her room. Kathy, Doug, and I joined her, taking our places in the blue recliners and continuing our vigil. I glanced back and forth between my son and daughter, pondering our history together. Nicole slept in her hospital bed, still groggy from the anesthetic given to stitch her episiotomy. She remained unaware of what was happening around her as her jovial brother chattered away. Doug's presence instead of a loving husband's seemed incongruous. I still couldn't fathom how Doug and Nicole continued to relate to each other as though nothing traumatic ever happened between them. They seemed closer than ever.

At around eleven, the resident courier appeared. "They're concerned about the baby's muscle tone. Are there any muscle problems in your family?"

I hesitated a moment before "muscle problems" registered in my brain. "My children have myotonia in their hands."

His eyes opened wide. "Oh. I think that's significant." He bolted out the door.

About a half hour later, he returned to explain, "I wasn't able to tell the doctor about the myotonia. When he comes to talk to you, be sure to give him that information. I have to leave now."

Close to midnight, Alexandra's pediatrician, a medium-built man in his late thirties, arrived with two residents in tow. He looked exhausted. Dr. Peppard introduced himself and them. One resident pulled up a chair for him. He dropped into it, leaned forward with his elbows on his thighs, crossed his hands between his legs, and surveyed the scene. The residents stationed themselves behind him.

After I introduced our crew, I told Dr. Peppard, "One of the doctors came in earlier asking whether there were muscle problems in our family. He told me to tell you my children both have myotonia in their hands."

"That's what I thought," he said. His gentle eyes magnified through light-rimmed glasses. "It's myotonic dystrophy. It's genetic ... a rare form of muscular dystrophy. It plays havoc in families. Children with this disorder usually have lots of difficulty in school."

For me, the heavens opened. *That is what this is about. This baby is the answer to our prayers.*

I said, "You wouldn't believe the nightmares we've been through with schools, especially with my son. He was abused by teachers."

Dr. Peppard said, "I understand. I have a developmentally disabled brother, and I know what you mean." *Dr. Peppard, our third angel.*

The room seemed to shrink into a tunnel of soft radiance that surrounded my children and me. A transcendent moment, I saw Doug and Nicole as I had never seen them before.

I'm seeing my children, really seeing them for the first time. I'm in awe. I feel closer and more connected to them than ever. Now I understand why they're so bonded with each other.

Dr. Peppard broke my spell. "How'd you know about the myotonia?"

"Years ago, I took Doug to see a pediatric neurologist in Indianapolis. He found myotonia in Doug's hands and tongue. We knew Nicole experienced that, too, just not as bad. He didn't say anything about muscular dystrophy, though."

"Do you remember the doctor's name?"

I looked at Doug. He shook his head.

I looked back at Dr. Peppard. "It was so long ago. I'd probably remember if I heard it."

"Was it Bradford Hale?"

My eyes widened. "How did you know that?"

"I used to practice in Indianapolis."

Goosebumps broke out on my arms. *This doesn't seem a coincidence.*

"I wanted help for Doug's behavior problems. His hand and tongue stiffening seemed minor compared with his behavior. I'd lost hope of ever knowing what was going on with either of my children."

"I understand," he said with those same gentle blue eyes. "Yes, their problems directly relate to this condition. And it's not unusual for people to find out like this—when a baby's born."

That's why this baby came. Without her, we'd never know. The breath of God is blowing. We're being visited with Divine grace.

Dr. Peppard said, "The baby has pneumonia in both lungs. Her diaphragm on the right side is too high. Even if we can clear the pneumonia, she probably won't be able to breathe without a ventilator."

A sinking feeling came over me. *She won't survive. But at least she won't have to suffer the way we have. This, too, is Divine grace.* A fearful thought flashed through my mind. *I hope Nicole won't be faced with a decision about whether to take her off the ventilator.*

Dr. Peppard mentioned two tests that could give him information about Alexandra's condition. One, a blood test, he worried would become lost in the system. He wanted Nicole to give permission for a muscle biopsy to confirm the diagnosis. Nicole, still groggy and unable to take in all Dr. Peppard said, was awake enough to give permission. That proved fortunate because the blood test did get lost.

Dr. Peppard told me I could see Alexandra soon. Emotionally spent, Kathy needed to return home to her family. I called another friend, Karen. Despite the late hour, she offered to come. I wanted someone with me when I visited Alexandra because I feared I would faint. I felt light-headed in the past while making hospital calls on parishioners. Karen lived close and arrived within minutes.

She and I waited on a bench outside the neonatal intensive care unit. At around twelve-thirty, a nurse appeared to usher me in. She wouldn't allow Karen to accompany me because she wasn't a blood relative. NICU rules didn't take into account families of choice.

Karen gave me a hug while I whispered a prayer: *Give me strength; give me strength.*

She said, "I'll be waiting for you when you come out."

Fire Walk

August 3–6, 1999

Sometimes the elements of our life present us with a challenge that is an initiation in disguise, a fire walk that burns your lower nature right out of you so that you are able to adapt to a higher level of consciousness.

~Caroline Myss

A nurse escorted me into the NICU. The fledgling nurse who attended Alexandra watched me intently as I approached. Tani was gorgeous, with long dark hair and big blue eyes. She whispered, "I'm sorry."

I responded, "This baby has blessed us so much. Alexandra gave us information we wouldn't have received in any other way."

Her eyes softened as she reached out to give me a hug. "I'm glad to know her name. I'll be with her all night, and I'll call her by name so she comes to know it."

"Thank you. Her full name is Alexandra Danielle." I squeezed Tani's hand and moved to the side of Alexandra's crib. She was long at nineteen inches but so tiny at four pounds nine ounces. Her dark skin was reddish and mottled. She had thick black hair and her ears sat lower on her head than normal. Tubes emanated from every orifice.

The next few minutes seemed an eternity.

I placed my left index finger under her left hand. Her tiny fingers curled around mine. My right hand caressed and stroked her head. "Thank you. Thank you so much for coming. You're such a gift to us. You've eased years of pain. You've helped us understand. You've given us information we wouldn't have received any other way. We love you so much." Despite her impaired muscle tone, she responded. Her right arm moved across her body toward me.

She knows ... she knows. I gazed at her in amazement. *This tiny gift from The Divine has been sent to us for a purpose—to ease our suffering.* I continued stroking her head and beaming love at her. I had no words to express the huge difference this little miracle made. My heart filled with wonder and awe.

"Alexandra, I love you so much. You're a miracle. We got your message. We understand now. Thank you so much for giving us this information. We appreciate it more than you'll ever know."

I continued stroking her head and beaming love at her. I knew what I must do next. I must give her permission to go. "If this living thing is too hard for you, it's okay for you to go. You've fulfilled your purpose. We'll be okay now."

I lingered a little longer, still astounded by the miracle of it all, before bidding her goodbye. "It's late, sweet angel. I need to get some sleep. I'll see you tomorrow."

I gave Tani a hug and returned to Karen waiting on the bench outside the NICU door.

Karen wanted to hear the whole story, and I needed to share it. She grasped the miracle. She pulled a Bible from her bag and read the 139th Psalm. It had never held such profound meaning.

O Lord, you have searched me and known me ... and are acquainted with all my ways.

Such knowledge is too wonderful for me; it is so high that I cannot attain it.

Where can I go from your spirit ... or where can I flee from your presence?

In heaven ... in hell, you are there ... darkness is as light to you.

For it is you who formed my inward parts; you knit me together in my mother's womb.

I praise you, for I am fearfully and wonderfully made.

Wonderful are your works; that I know very well.

My frame was not hidden from you, when I was being made in secret, intricately woven in the depths of the earth.

Your eyes beheld my unformed substance.

In your book were written all the days that were formed for me, when none of them as yet existed.

How weighty to me are your thoughts, O God.

How vast is the sum of them.

I try to count them–they are more than the sand;

I come to the end–I am still with you. [5]

We left the hospital at two in the morning. I was exhausted and also wired. Despite the hour, as soon as I arrived home, I phoned two close friends. I couldn't wait to tell Marvel and Barbara about the miracle. Both visited distant cities awaiting the births of grandchildren. They had agonized with me about the circumstances surrounding Nicole's pregnancy. They were grateful I called and wanted to hear every detail.

Afterward, I wrote out the whole story to send in a letter to friends around the country who had been praying for us. Around four-thirty, my adrenaline waned and sleep overtook me.

At six forty-five, the phone rang. "Mommy, Alexandra's going downhill fast. Please come."

"I'll be there as fast as I can."

Before leaving, I called Pastor Sharon. "Nicole's baby was born yesterday, and it looks like she's going to die. Could you come to be with us?"

When I arrived, Nicole sat slumped in a wheelchair next to Alexandra's crib surrounded by several women—the chaplain who had baptized Alexandra, Tani and Marlene, and other nurses not familiar to me. When Nicole saw me, she stretched her body toward me. They all looked in my direction as I rushed to Nicole. When I reached her, she whimpered, "Mommy, she's going to die."

I knelt down and looked into her tear-filled eyes. "Nicole, Alexandra has been a gift and a blessing to us. She came for a purpose. She came to help us understand why you and Doug have so many problems. She came to help you get your lives together, and she has fulfilled her purpose. Now she doesn't have to suffer anymore."

Nicole slumped back in the wheelchair. Tears spilled down her cheeks.

The nurses had waited for this moment before removing the tubes. When they disconnected the ventilator at 8:10 a.m., they pronounced Alexandra dead.

I noticed Tani and walked over to give her a hug. "This must have been difficult for you."

"I've never been through anything like this," she said. "I know what I'm going to do when I get to my car."

Pastor Sharon arrived. Marlene placed Alexandra, wrapped in a blanket, in Nicole's arms. She escorted us across the hall to a room where we could say our goodbyes in private.

Nicole rocked her daughter in her arms as she told Pastor Sharon and Marlene about her miracle baby. "She came to bring my mother peace from years of torment and to help my brother and me understand why we have so many problems."

Marlene gave us all the time we needed to recount the story of our miracle and say our goodbyes. When Nicole indicated she was ready, she gave Alexandra back into Marlene's care. Marlene collected the gown I'd purchased and dressed Alexandra. She attached a bow

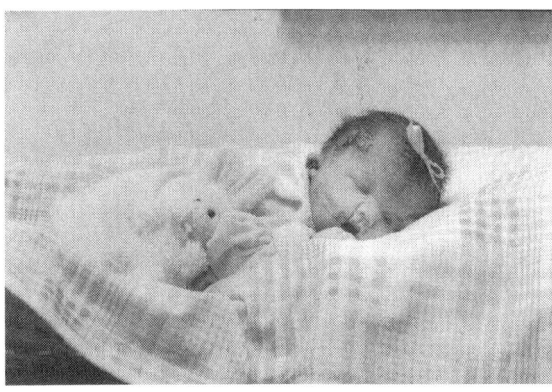

Alexandra

to her hair and placed a ring on her finger. A photographer took keepsake pictures. Later Marlene gave the pictures and Alexandra's ring to Nicole.

Nicole, Sharon, and I returned to Nicole's room and began planning Alexandra's funeral. When Marlene overheard the name of the funeral home we were considering, she intervened. She spoke to Nicole. "I'll ask a social worker to help with this because there are funeral homes that work with people without money when there is an infant burial. Now, Nicole, this is your responsibility. This is not your mother's responsibility."

I smiled, bowed my head, and offered up a prayer of gratitude. This angel disguised as a nurse seemed to see into my heart and sense my need for support and Nicole's need to take responsibility in a way no other professional ever had. I was in awe of her insight and compassion.

Nicole looked at me and proclaimed, "She's my baby, and I want to pay for her funeral."

She turned to Pastor Sharon, "Since you are the only pastor who has met her, I'd like you to do the service."

She turned to me and added, "And I want you to do her eulogy."

I hesitated, not sure how to eulogize an infant. Then it dawned on me. Of course, Alexandra's tribute relates to her mother's story and her uncle's story.

Nicole called her father to tell him about her baby's death. His response hurt. "I'm sorry to hear that. Keep out of trouble and call me tomorrow." He wouldn't promise to come to the funeral.

The birthing center transferred Nicole to a different floor. On

Wednesday evening, Julie came to visit at the end of another twelve-hour shift. She stayed an hour and listened to Nicole tell the story of her miracle baby. She looked back and forth in awe between Nicole and me.

I knew Nicole needed to come back to live with me. In the midst of planning a funeral, many preparations needed to be made. Jacqui wouldn't return to Taiwan for another two months, but I needed her bedroom for Nicole. I couldn't think straight through my exhaustion, but friends and neighbors appeared to help. Padrick lived across the street and offered his spare bedroom. Jacqui could continue living in my home until evening when she went to his house to sleep.

Rachel, my former neighbor, appeared on Thursday morning with a bag full of clothes she and her daughters no longer wore. In the bag was a nice dress and shoes for Nicole to wear to the funeral. Rachel helped keep me focused on preparing the house for Nicole to move in later in the day.

Friday morning, Nicole and I met Pastor Sharon at the funeral home. The funeral director, Teresa Davis, helped us plan the ceremony. As we four women sat together, images of the nurses at the hospital and my women friends floated into my mind—all strong women supporting each other. We planned a liturgy to celebrate Alexandra's short life and to affirm that every life matters.

Nicole called her father to give him the details about the funeral. He still wouldn't commit to attending but did agree to let his family know.

We needed frames to display pictures of Alexandra next to her closed casket. Nicole wanted an angel birthstone necklace to wear with Alexandra's ring. With my exhaustion and Nicole's weakness, I didn't know how to manage this last-minute shopping. Karen offered to chauffeur and prop us up for the task.

Later that evening after Nicole went to bed, Karen and I talked about Buddy's refusal to agree to come to the funeral. We debated about whether I should call and encourage him. After some deliberation, we decided, despite his aversion to hearing my voice, it seemed the right action to take.

I trembled as I made the call. When he answered, I said, "I want to encourage you to come to the funeral."

"I don't know."

"You're missing out on a miracle. There's a reason why our children are the way they are."

"I have to think about it."

To my dismay, he hung up.

He did, however, attend along with the rest of his family. I hadn't seen him in ten years and couldn't help but notice how much he had aged. I didn't yet know the origin of the dramatic change in his appearance, but much about Buddy and our children would be explained in the years to come.

My eulogy focused on the miracle baby who had helped us understand the struggles our children experienced growing up and finding their way as adults. Buddy didn't look at me, but he did shed tears. I finished by saying, "We don't know the origin of this disease. It's genetic. It could be on their father's side of the family. It could be on mine. We're still searching for the source."

When the service came to a close, the funeral director asked everyone except family to wait outside. My friends, closer than family and the only ones there supporting me, walked out. I stood there, alone again, as Nicole and Doug joined Buddy's family on their side of the room. After a few minutes, I took a few faltering steps in their direction.

My former sister-in-law approached me. "You need to talk with Estelle." I looked at her puzzled. "Chip had this disease. She has lots of information about it."

Chip was Buddy's cousin. Estelle was married to Peter, Chip's brother. How I wished Buddy's family had informed me earlier about this genetic disease. Did they not consider the possibility this could be the source of Doug and Nicole's problems? Was their meager communication more than a lack of skill? That they withheld this information until now seemed thoughtless at best and uncharitable at worst. Still, finding the answer to this puzzle at the funeral saved me another long search.

Nicole reached out to her father for a reassuring hug. He stiffened and refused her. He and his wife were among the first to leave.

Nicole, Doug, and his friend Rob rode with me to the cemetery. Teresa drove the hearse following my car. Pastor Sharon accompanied her. Rachel, my friend who helped me prepare the house for Nicole to move in, followed the hearse. We buried Alexandra thirty-five miles north of Dayton in a family plot my father had purchased before he and Mom moved to Florida.

After the graveside service, Teresa approached and gave me a hug. She said, "You have been a special family to work with." I never expected to hear these words spoken in reference to our family.

I smiled. "Thank you so much. I can't tell you what it means to me to hear you say that."

On our way home, Nicole shared her hurt about her father's refusal to give her a hug. Doug commented on how fast he left after the funeral. He asked, "Why is Dad acting like this?"

I told them, "Your dad has a disability. He loves you, but he's not able to show it. You need to think of it as his disability." Much later I learned the enormous truth contained in those words. Myotonic muscular dystrophy explained the dramatic change in Buddy's appearance and, at least in part, his insensitive behavior toward Nicole during her heart-wrenching ordeal.

My explanation for their father's behavior seemed to lift our spirits and rouse our hunger pangs. We stopped at Pearson House, a small diner in West Milton known for its homemade pie. I treated us all to dinner and dessert as we continued to celebrate Alexandra's thirteen-hour life.

Surrendering and being present to the unfolding of grace gave me my most profound spiritual experience. A long awakening, I recognized the work of The Divine in the midst of what others viewed as a tragedy. Without a doubt, I rose to the challenge of mothering with love. I succeeded in extending love to my daughter and granddaughter—my finest and most fulfilling moments. Helping my daughter embrace Alexandra's life and death as a gift transformed me into a mother and grandmother for whom I could hold respect. At last, the disparity between my personal life and my professional life dissolved. Hard won, finally I became a person with integrity.

Mama Bear

1999–2000

> Your inner mama bear is a powerful, protective parenting instinct.
> The challenge is to channel it effectively
> without completely losing the growl.
>
> ~Jen Klein

After a twenty-two year search, receiving a muscular dystrophy diagnosis in August 1999 made my children eligible for vocational rehabilitation services. I intended to see they received them along with any other services for which they might qualify.

Nicole wanted to return to work after a two-year absence. She needed a job she could handle with her muscle weakness. In the past, while she cashiered at the grocery store chain, she wrenched her back pushing carts in the parking lot. I contacted the Bureau of Vocational Rehabilitation and scheduled an appointment for August 26, not quite a month after Alexandra's birth. After a lengthy evaluation, BVR accepted Nicole, and she entered their training program.

Doug had set a record by working as a McDonald's crew member for two years straight. However, minimum wage with no benefits offered no security. Missing work with a common cold or the flu meant he might not be able to pay his rent. The threat of eviction always hung over him.

With Doug's muscular dystrophy diagnosis and a stable work record, BVR agreed to give him an opportunity to prove he had changed. He entered a probationary evaluation period before full entrance into the program. I hoped his training would lead to improved compensation and benefits.

The week after Alexandra's funeral, I contacted Estelle. She gave me the name of Chip's neurologist, a Wright State University Medical School professor who practiced at the Veterans' Administration. I scheduled an appointment for August 31—Doug's thirty-first birthday.

I researched myotonic muscular dystrophy (DM) on the Internet. I didn't find as much as I would have liked. I already knew myotonia described an impairment in the relaxation of muscles. This symptom manifested in Doug and Nicole when their hands froze in a claw-like position after a firm handshake and when their tongues froze, slurring their speech for a few seconds.

I learned DM, one of forty neuromuscular diseases, had no treatment and no cure. A British study astonished me: The researchers found their subjects by driving around neighborhoods identifying houses and yards in deplorable condition. When people with DM arise in the morning, they feel as though they've already put in a full day's work, giving them little energy to attend to the upkeep of their homes or living spaces.

I located a man in California whose wife and nine-year-old son had DM and contacted him by e-mail. He said his wife slept most of the day. Excessive daytime sleepiness is another symptom.

When we arrived for our appointment with Dr. Matthews, he asked a favor. Because he took every opportunity to educate students about this rare disease, he asked whether we would be willing to share our experience with medical students before the examination. Doug and Nicole pleased me when they agreed to his request.

Dr. Matthews ushered us into a room where a dozen or so medical students in white coats sat in a circle chatting. When we entered, they came to attention. At his request, the students added three more chairs. Dr. Matthews took his seat and introduced us. He gave information about DM along with some details about it being a slow-progressing genetic disease that becomes worse with each generation. He opened the floor for questions.

Doug, glad to be the center of attention, demonstrated his hand cramping and answered questions about how his muscle deterioration affected his day-to-day life. I attempted to coach shy Nicole to share her story, but she only shared a little before she deferred to me. I told the students about how Alexandra provided the missing information after our long search for answers to Doug and Nicole's life challenges. We probably spent about thirty minutes with the students before Dr. Matthews escorted us to his office.

After he examined Doug and Nicole to determine the progression of their muscle deterioration, he explained that the symptoms tend to be more severe when passed through the mother. Later, I learned it is common for a mother carrying a baby with DM to have more amniotic fluid than normal, as Nicole did.

I also learned anesthesia is dangerous and sometimes deadly for people with wasting muscles. That explained why it took Nicole so long to regain alert consciousness after the administration of general anesthetic for her episiotomy following Alexandra's birth.

Dr. Matthews said, "The younger the person is when symptoms begin to manifest, the more severe the symptoms will be." He indicated Doug and Nicole's father and grandfather had to have the disease. Their milder form would not have produced symptoms until they were adults. Alexandra's severe case related to onset at birth. Dr. Matthews recommended all children in the family seek genetic testing. I sent a letter to Buddy's brother and his wife informing them of this recommendation. I received no response.

Dr. Matthews explained other characteristics: DM progresses slowly with muscles weakening and wasting away at a variable degree of severity. Because it manifests differently in different people, DM is hard to diagnose. Some affected people experience low intelligence with aggressive and demanding personalities while others do not. Some have difficulty in school while others do well. Chip, in fact, graduated college and performed successfully in his early career.

Dr. Matthews showed us a video of Chip. Before his death in his early sixties of a heart condition related to the disease, Chip allowed Dr. Matthews to videotape interviews to provide ongoing education for medical students.

I hadn't seen Chip in over ten years. I flinched at how much Doug looked like him. They shared the same body type, had both put on considerable weight, and were balding. A pattern of early balding is a common symptom in men. Their sagging muscles gave their faces the same square shape. Their bodies drooped. Doug's shoulders hunched, and when he walked, his arms hung forward in simian fashion.

Doug and Nicole showed no interest in continuing to educate medical students. They could have either been videotaped or interviewed in person. To me, it would have been a way to save other children and families the devastation we went through. I learned their lack of motivation, apathy, blunted emotions, emotional detachment, self-centeredness, and cheerful attitude when everything around them falls apart are aspects of the disease.

Before we left, I revealed to Dr. Matthews that Doug had sexually abused Nicole. He replied, "He didn't know any better." His words burst my balloon of hope. I didn't want to believe him. If Doug truly didn't know any better, he might hurt someone else the way he hurt Nicole. My nightmare would never be over. After that appointment, caution tinged all my efforts to help him get his life together.

Next, I addressed Doug's housing. With his sociopathic-type behavior, I could have maintained no quality of life if he lived with me. After learning about the protracted waiting list for low-income housing where rent fluctuates with income, I contacted Jane Benner for ideas about stable housing. She continued to direct the Salvation Army program Doug had participated in years before. She pulled some strings with the director of a St. Vincent DePaul homeless shelter. This shelter served homeless men who worked on increasing their education. The director agreed to consider Doug's

BVR training as his schooling.

For his probationary period, BVR placed Doug in a downtown Goodwill Store and gave him management training, which had the potential to lead to stable employment and housing. I relaxed.

Nicole received several months' training as a data processor. A company that manufactured firefighter uniforms hired her. A year after Alexandra's birth and death, Nicole and I rejoiced when she regained her independence and moved into her own apartment.

One caregiver refers to DM as a "thief." This disease robs those who carry it and their caregivers of a normal life. Caregivers often grow depressed and frustrated from dealing with their loved one's apathy, lack of vitality, and inability to connect in a meaningful way. Scarce resources to help with the day-to-day trials make living with DM overwhelming. Some drugs help marginally manage symptoms, but the disease remains incurable. Progress in understanding this disorder as a form of muscular dystrophy emerged in the early 1990s. Euphoric after Alexandra's birth in 1999, I couldn't yet comprehend the no-end-of-obstacles associated with DM that my children and I had yet to face. Many more challenges lay before us in the years ahead.

Doug's Story

2000–2008

> *Your children are not your children.*
> *They are the sons and daughters*
> *of Life's longing for itself.*
> *They come through you but not from you,*
> *And though they are with you*
> *yet they belong not to you.*
>
> ~Kahlil Gibran

At first, Doug seemed to do well in his job, at least as far as I could tell from a distance. However, his self-sabotage pattern reasserted itself. The Goodwill Store where he worked noticed missing merchandise. The surveillance camera identified Doug as the thief. He lost his job and his housing. He was back on the streets.

When I learned of his situation, I winced, feeling as powerless as ever. Having a diagnosis and people willing to go the extra mile for him wasn't going to change Doug as I had hoped. I didn't want to live in a constant state of alarm, but now I couldn't help but dread what might happen next. Accepting reality and letting go of unrealistic aspirations for my children challenged me at every juncture.

Doug began to spend most days hanging out at the downtown library, using its computers to participate in online matchmaking. He sometimes crashed at Nicole's apartment, stealing checks from her checkbook to buy flowers for an online heartthrob. He seemed unconcerned that he ruined his sister's credit rating. He found a girlfriend across the state and brought her to meet me. I liked her more than I expected to.

I counseled him, "Looks like you've found a good one. Better treat her right."

In October 2003, four years after the diagnosis, Doug and Mindy married, and he moved across the state to Jackson. He had burned his bridges in Dayton. I became a step-grandmother to Mindy's six- and four-year-old daughters. Her four year old was born on the exact same day as Alexandra.

Doug knew I was concerned he might sexually abuse Mindy's children. He assured me he had been honest with her about abusing Nicole. As far as I could tell, he treated Mindy and her children well. If true, I give myself partial credit. I summoned the courage to give him tough love during his time in the psychiatric hospital. Even though the doctor confused me and I struggled with guilt, I held firm. I believe my tough-love actions caught his damaged brain's attention, giving him the message that sexual abuse is forbidden.

While he and Mindy lived together, he appeared to have more stability in his life. That propelled me up the roller coaster of hope once again. She seemed to love him; he seemed serious about being a good stepfather. Mindy was on Medicaid and knew the system. She helped him fill out the paperwork and Social Security at last approved his application for disability insurance. He developed kidney stone attacks, psoriasis, and a sleep disorder. The sleep disorder required sleeping with oxygen. With his SSI, he received the medical attention he needed.

Then, two years after they married I received a call at work. When I answered the phone, Doug was sobbing and begging me to send him $60 for bus fare back to Dayton. Mindy had kicked him out. My hopes plummeted. He didn't say why, and I didn't ask. I didn't want to get sucked into his chaos. I bought him a bus ticket.

Back in Dayton, he resumed trying to manipulate the system, but because of his reputation, he was less and less successful. He continued to take financial advantage of his sister. Despite my encouragement that she set boundaries, she continued her bond with him. "He drives me crazy, but he's the only one I have to talk with about our disease." She adamantly refused to attend support groups through MDA.

In June 2004, I sold my beautiful home. No longer able to handle the upkeep by myself, it seemed time to simplify my life. I moved to a two-bedroom condo in a south suburb, Centerville. Shortly after I moved, my dad called. "I've finally convinced your mom to come back to Ohio," he said. "Find us a condo."

After my brother's death in 1995, I was my parents' only child. We had explored options for how I could be available to them during their declining years. Mom didn't want to leave their home in Florida, and I couldn't afford to move there. A condo close to me seemed the best alternative, and I found one similar to mine in a neighboring complex. In October, they moved.

Two years later, my dad phoned sounding distressed, "Do you know where Hollow Run is?"

I thought he was asking for directions. "I have no idea."

"Well, I do. It's right around the corner from us, and Doug's moving there."

His renting a room so close to us unnerved both my parents and me. I told Doug how frightened we were. He asked, "What do you think I'm going to do?"

"I have no idea. That's part of the problem. I never know what you're going to do next. The way you live is painful for me."

"Mom, I like my life."

Perhaps having a cheerful attitude despite negative circumstances is a positive trait. Personally, I couldn't imagine being happy in the face of conditions like his.

Doug maintained the boundaries my parents and I requested. He and my dad even started having some fun together. But before long, his landlord asked him to move out. I don't know why, but he did take it upon himself to find Doug a room in a house of his friend across town.

In early May 2008, my friend Karen and I were driving home after a training event for Imago therapists in Detroit. We listened to music, chattered, and marveled at the popcorn clouds hanging over Toledo's overcast sky. I didn't hear my cell phone ringing in my purse on the car floor.

When we arrived at Karen's, I noticed several missed calls and a voicemail message. Mindy, Doug's ex-wife, had left a frantic message: "I received a call that Doug died in a house fire. Please call back, and let me know if it's true." Shock waves coursed through me for a split second and the world seemed to stand still.

I told Karen about the message and said, "I'll call Nicole and see if she knows anything." When I reached her, Nicole told me she had ignored several calls because she didn't recognize the number. We hesitated and tried to figure out what to do next. I told her I would call her back when I knew more.

Karen suggested I call the coroner's office. She found the number, and my whole body shook as I made the call. The person who answered the phone confirmed Mindy's message: "Yes, he died this morning from burns. There was a fire sometime after midnight." I gasped. Another flush of adrenaline surged despite my long-term suspicion that, given his lifestyle, he might experience an early and possibly a violent death.

"I should call Nicole."

Nicole had contacted the coroner's office at about the same time I did, so she had already received the news. "How are you doing?" I asked her.

"I can't believe it." No tears came. We were both in a state of shock.

I asked if she needed me to come over or if she'd like to spend the night with me. She said she was okay and preferred staying at home. She said she would call her dad, and let him know.

We talked later in the day, and she told me her dad had a life insurance policy on Doug and could help with funeral expenses. I was surprised by this information and grateful to hear it.

Nicole and I checked in with each other the next morning. Neither of us slept the night before. My mind had whirled with the best way to handle Doug's funeral. Thrown together to finalize plans, Buddy had little to say but agreed to my ideas. During the week as we prepared, I kept a previously scheduled cardiology appointment. My blood pressure, which usually runs low, surged off the charts.

In 2005, after two weeks of chest pains, a stress test revealed that my left anterior descending artery contained ninety-eight percent blockage. The doctor sent me straight to the hospital for I wasn't sure what. While I awaited his arrival, I laid on the treatment table asking myself how I got here. Then it dawned on me. *I've had so much heartbreak in my life. That is why I've developed a heart problem.* I was relieved that open-heart surgery was not necessary. The doctor inserted a stent.

Doug's housemate asked to meet with me. I agreed despite my fear of what he wanted and what he might say. He seemed to need to assuage some guilt as he told me what happened the night before the fire. He said that he and Doug came home and sat in the living room talking about each other's activities that day. He lit a candle while they talked. "I did that because Doug smelled so bad," he confessed. Shivers rolled down my spine. He went on to say that he forgot to blow the candle out before heading upstairs for bed. It was left burning in the living room next to Doug's bedroom.

If understanding and forgiveness was what he sought, I gave it to him. I hoped he could come to the harder task of forgiving himself. He was not to blame and blame solves nothing. I told him he was welcome to attend the funeral if he liked. Sadly, but not surprisingly, Doug's poor hygiene, a symptom of his disease, had contributed to his death. After our conversation, I returned to my car full of sorrow for what might have been.

Doug in his twenties.

We invited those present at the funeral to share an experience or story about Doug. Several spoke, including his best friend Rob's mother. She recalled positive experiences with him and spoke with affection, telling us how much he loved her buckeye candy. She said she would never make buckeyes at Christmas without thinking of him.

I knew from experience how important it is to have surrogate parents when your biological parents are unable to provide the nurturing you need. Her sharing filled my heart with gratitude. Those who spoke revealed facets of my son I missed because I looked at him through eyes clouded by pain.

People consider losing a child to be a parent's worst nightmare. However, I had experienced worse than death with Doug. I had lost him years before. While he lived, I rode a roller coaster of emotion.

I lost hope, recovered it, and then lost it again. I loved my son, but I hated his behavior.

I had tried to overcome the constant fear I lived in about what he might do next. I froze in place when the nightly news reported on molestation or rape. I held my breath until I learned he was not the perpetrator. I worried about whether I should do more to protect others from his behavior. It is no way to live.

My nightmare ended on May 3, 2008, with Doug's death. I found it hard to admit to those expressing condolences for my loss that I experienced relief—and guilt and sorrow for my relief. I had done my grieving a long time before. With his death, I buried my constant fear about what would happen next.

Doug at thirty-nine — 2008.

Families living with DM founded the Myotonic Dystrophy Foundation (MDF) in 2007, but I didn't learn about the organization until after Doug's death. At their 2011 national conference, carriers of this disorder urged researchers to go beyond their focus on finding a cure for muscle wasting, something they felt they could deal with. On the MDF website, I watched them implore the researchers to address the executive function deficit symptom, the symptom that frightened them the most. I hoped the researchers would listen to them because the most profound effect on our family had been the damage to the brain.

Shannon Lord, one of the MDF founders, had a mild form of adult onset DM. I listened to her plea as she spoke of passing the disease to both her sons and explained her son's symptoms, especially those connected to executive function deficits. When she described her youngest son, she could have been describing Doug.

"A small subset of those with juvenile onset DM lead lives of addiction, unemployment, homelessness, and jail. These young people have difficulty finding steady work and are frequently fired for showing up late or not working fast enough. They struggle with many symptoms from childhood, including fatigue and lack of motivation, which interfere with their ability to function. Even those with high IQs often fall short of others' expectations and are unable to support themselves or live independently as they prefer."

Shannon's presentation explained so much. I replayed her words several times, allowing their impact to sink in. I sat back in my desk chair and stared at her picture on the screen. Six years after his death, all the pieces of the puzzle came together and, for the first time, I could see clearly the origin of Doug's aberrant behavior. Dr. Matthews' words, "He didn't know any better," made sense. I finally understood what it meant when I was told something organic was going on, that he was born with an inability to cope. And best of all, I was not alone. I found a mother who understood as no other could. Decades of shame and guilt lifted from my shoulders.

I had long admired parents of disabled children, especially those wise parents who know enough not to lower their expectations. I viewed with awe their children's achievements. I thought of myself as incapable of parenting an intellectually disabled or wheelchair-bound child. I soothed myself with, "At least I'm not dealing with that."

And all the while I held to this perception, I mothered two children with intellectual and physical disabilities. Perhaps it was to their advantage I didn't know their problems' origin for so many years. I might have pitied them and lowered my expectations.

Perhaps my failure to fully grasp the implications of what professionals told me about Doug contributed to his doing as well as he did. I didn't coddle either of my children. Because I expected them to behave as normal children, they were forced to draw on their own resources. I didn't understand the severity of their limitations. Even though their ability to overcome their misfortunes was severely compromised, they learned to adjust and survive.

Nicole's Story

2004–2013

> [O]ur children have to have their own story,
> no matter how far it strays from what we wanted for them.
>
> ~David Richo

Nicole phoned. "Mom, I have some bad news. I've been laid off. But don't worry, I've already contacted unemployment." Her data entry job lasted four years. I didn't know what to make of her lay off. Did that mean they fired her for not performing well on the job? Because her employer hired her through BVR, they knew of her disability. I worried about her capacity to find another.

BVR reevaluated her and identified cashiering as her only capability. They moved at a snail's pace in their responsibility to find her another job. I grew frantic as her unemployment compensation neared an end. I didn't like the idea of her living with me again, but I didn't want her living homeless.

At the last minute, a synchronicity occurred. My coworkers Joyce and Cheryl invited me to join them at the hospital's health fair. Obsessed with Nicole's situation and in a foul mood, I declined. After they left, I couldn't concentrate on my work, and something told me to check out the health fair.

I went through the motions, making my way around the various booths in the gymnasium, collecting pamphlets and information. I froze in astonishment when I came upon a BVR table. I hadn't expected to find them there. I poured out my frustration to the two young people working the booth. I complained about the slow process and Nicole's unemployment running out. The young man sitting on a folding chair behind the table leaned forward and calmly asked, "What kind of job is she looking for?"

Nicole in 2016.
Photo credit: Rick Guidotti of Positive Exposure.

"She's been told cashier work is all she's capable of doing."

"I have a job for her. We have a convenience store looking for a cashier. Sounds like she'd be a perfect fit."

I stared at him slack-jawed.

In my opinion, Nicole's new job was the best job she had ever held. She cashiered for E's Express, a convenience store located inside

Elizabeth Place. After St. Elizabeth Hospital closed, it was converted into office space for medical personnel and social service agencies. Over time, Nicole earned her employer's trust, and he gave her responsibility for stocking shelves, doing inventory, and some light bookkeeping. During her seven years there, she became a trusted and valued full-time employee, greatly reducing my stress.

Turning Point, our chemical dependency treatment center, moved to Elizabeth Place shortly before my retirement in 2007. Nicole and I worked in the same building. Parents of challenging children rarely, if ever, hear them described in glowing terms. Before I retired, several such opportunities blessed me. The first came when I offered to give her a ride home from work.

We decided to grab a bite to eat before we headed home. While we walked through the Elizabeth Place lobby on the way to Subway, we encountered Wright State University medical interns arranging health fair displays. Nicole approached a table and joked with five young, bright, energetic women. She introduced me to them.

They exclaimed, "You're Nicole's mother? We love her." They surrounded her and gave her a group hug. I pulled my shoulders back, filled with pride and gratitude, and smiled from ear to ear.

Over dinner, Nicole told me about her relationship with these interns. She knew the price of every item in the store and thus could help them make the most of their E's Express stipend. She also remembered all their names and initialed the tracking sheet for them, saving them time going through the line. She enjoyed their light-hearted banter.

Whenever E's Express customers learned I was Nicole's mother, they exclaimed, "She's your daughter? She's great."

She thrived in this supportive community, the structure gave her stability, and her self-esteem rose as she received positive evaluations from her bosses, coworkers, and customers.

After Nicole moved to an apartment ten minutes from my condo in January 2006, I noticed the progression of her muscle wasting and executive function deficits. She had been able to clean her former apartment and get her deposit back. However, each year the condition of her new apartment deteriorated drastically. She didn't take out her trash, and it piled high.

Proud of her determination to work full time, I realized it sapped all her energy. Her disease contributed to her being too tired to attend to her living conditions. I worried about her being evicted. Should I intervene? Once more I struggled with whether to stick my nose into my adult daughter's business, but barely had time to worry about or deal with it.

In May 2008, I was dealing with my son's death. Then, the day after Thanksgiving, my mother died. Thirty-six days later, on January 3, my father died. I was in the process of settling their estate when I was diagnosed with lymphoma. I had to focus on taking care of myself. Between May 23 and December 17, eight rounds of chemotherapy and seventeen radiation treatments had put my cancer in remission.

By Thanksgiving Day 2010, I had regained most of my strength. Nicole and I sat together on my couch after dinner and recounted our blessings—gratitude for my eleven months of recovery, her work, and our perpetual thankfulness for Alexandra's gift. I smiled and said, "She came to help you get your life together."

Nicole replied, "I don't have my life together. My apartment is a disaster." Tears ran down her cheeks. I was surprised she was so bothered and seized the opportunity to intervene. She didn't know where to find help. Of course, I did. We hired an organizer who specialized in working with hoarders.

On a frigid Saturday in January 2011, I helped Donna remove at least fifty bulging trash bags from Nicole's three-room apartment. We started at eight in the morning and stopped at five in the afternoon. The job wasn't finished. Donna confided to me that Nicole's apartment was the worst she'd ever seen. Nicole resented Donna's attempts to teach her organizing skills. She was especially upset that Donna disposed of extra items that created clutter. Nicole only wanted the trash removed. She refused to hire Donna to finish the job. Once more, I forced myself to accept what I couldn't change.

On Mother's Day 2012, I found it strange Nicole hadn't called, a sure sign something was wrong. By late afternoon, I couldn't stand it any longer. I phoned, and, when she answered, I asked, "Is there something you're not telling me?"

She said, "Yes."

"Are you going to tell me?"

"E's Express is closing."

I shuddered. The one bright spot in Nicole's life was coming to an end. To make matters worse, our country's worst economic downturn in modern history created soaring unemployment. Finding a job wouldn't be easy. I went into Mama Bear mode again.

BVR had tightened its belt and made qualifying criteria more stringent. Nicole was required to go through the application and testing process for the third time. I collected information on the MDF web page and accompanied her to her appointments. I gave her case manager printouts documenting executive function deficit symptoms—difficulty in long-range planning and maintaining living spaces. I brought pictures of her apartment and shared my alarm at behavior changes I noticed—how fast her disease progressed following E's closure.

At the end of her previous data entry job, she had contacted unemployment before informing me. Now she couldn't figure out how to access the system. Because I had never used it, I wasn't much help. She had savings so she wasn't concerned. She stayed home, slept, and watched TV, rarely checking her mailbox. Unemployment correspondence and her W2 form went missing. In previous years, she had received sizable tax refunds, extra money she could have used. I found her apathy and lack of motivation maddening.

I made frantic attempts to find help, researching and following every lead. She had no health insurance, so she relied on her Muscular Dystrophy Association (MDA) doctor, our only DM resource. I questioned him about why her appointments focused only on her muscle weakness progression but neglected to address executive function deficits. I used the same routine with him as I had used with BVR. I described her behavior, gave him the MDF documents, and showed him the pictures of her apartment.

He tried to help. He wrote a letter to accelerate the BVR application process. He referred Nicole to a psychologist to be evaluated for depression. He suspected a sleep disorder and referred her to a specialist to evaluate her erratic sleep pattern.

Nicole denied being depressed and refused to seek the counseling the psychologist recommended. She refused the proposed sleep study, saying "I'll never get used to wearing a C-pap." I sat back and watched with interest as those professionals' initial enthusiasm dissolved in the face of her apathy and disinterest in receiving their help. *They're as powerless to help her as I am. God, I need your help accepting what I can't change.*

I found it difficult to accept Nicole's rapid deterioration and the possibility she might no longer work full-time. I wanted her to retain the structure and self-esteem her job provided. *Am I holding on to unrealistic hope for her just as I did for Doug?*

I told her BVR case manager, "I may be advising her incorrectly. Maybe she needs to apply for disability. I worry about what will happen to her after I'm gone."

"All our clients' parents worry about that," she replied dispassionately.

Nicole pulled a packet from her bag and threw it on the desk in my direction. It contained an application filled out and ready to mail to a company that advertised on television about helping people secure Social Security Disability (SSD). Her BVR case manager told us about someone else on her caseload who had gained approval.

As I look back, I view these interactions with her case manager as the kick I needed to let go of another layer of hopes and dreams for

Nicole. On October 5, more than three months after she lost her job, I took the SSD application to the post office. This action brought me out of denial about her symptoms' severity. I let go of seeing her alive and vital and valued as when she worked at E's Express, another step in accepting my powerlessness over her disease.

Because of its inflexible protocol, BVR took three months to complete her evaluation before it accepted her into its program to help her find a job. While we waited, her money dwindled away.

I followed every lead to find resources to help keep Nicole in her apartment. The last straw came when I contacted a federally mandated program responsible for advocating for and protecting the disabled. The attorney told me the economic downturn forced them to transition from a state agency to a nonprofit. She said, "Two years ago resources existed to help Nicole. Today there are none ... unless she's homeless. If she were homeless, she'd be eligible. You'd probably like to be proactive. So would I. But that's impossible." She recommended I allow Nicole to lose her housing so she would be eligible for services.

Once more I was faced with the terror of Nicole being homeless. I railed at God about everything involving my children being so hard. I didn't know if I could live with myself if I followed the attorney's advice. I cycled through apprehension, overwhelm, powerlessness, and resignation. I tried to accept my lack of control over her disease, the state of our economy, the growing disparity between the rich and poor, and the attitude that disabled people are disposable.

I tried to accept that Nicole has life lessons to learn. I turned her over to her Higher Power again. Her situation seemed more than I, her only support, could bear.

I invited Nicole for dinner on Easter Sunday, March 31, nine months after she stopped working. When I arrived to pick her up, she came out of her apartment wearing pink house slippers, no socks, baggy fleece NASCAR pants, and one of her nicest sweaters. Her bangs had grown below her chin, so she combed her greasy, stringy hair straight back. When she climbed into the car, her odor overwhelmed and choked me. I held my tongue for a moment before rolling down the windows. "Nicole, you smell so bad I can hardly breathe." She said nothing. I drove as fast as possible to my condo.

When we arrived, she remained silent as I ordered her to undress and get into the shower. I gave her an outfit from my closet, laundered her clothes in hot water, and cut her hair before I prepared dinner. She babbled about the lives of this or that celebrity. I tried to participate, but my heart wasn't in it. After dinner, we watched a movie on DVD. She maintained her cheerful mood while I continued to count the hours until the time arrived to take her home.

After I dropped her off at her apartment, I dipped into depression. I wished I could move away and disappear and start my life all over somewhere else—not a new fantasy.

A week later, Nicole phoned and matter-of-factly stated, "Looks like I've got a job."

K-Mart hired her part-time at minimum wage. We tempered our relief while we waited to see whether she would make enough money to pay her bills. With so much awry, any one thing going wrong could begin a cascade of dominos falling.

On Monday, May 13, 2013, Nicole received her first paycheck. She called around dinner time to tell me, "Mom, it looks like I'll be able to pay my bills."

"That's good to hear."

We sorted out her finances and went over them several times to make sure we didn't miss anything. "I guess you're right. Looks like you've got enough to cover your expenses this month."

Before our call ended, she said, "I have a voicemail message, but I can't get it."

"Call the cable company, and they'll help you."

I doubted she would follow through. She neglected so many details these past weeks. However, a couple of hours later, Nicole called back and sounded excited. "Mom, you know that voicemail message? It was from Social Security. I've been approved for disability."

I burst into uncontrollable sobs.

She remained silent until I regained my composure. I said, "This is such a relief. You're going to be okay now."

The Mystery

*I do not at all understand the mystery of grace—
only that it meets us where we are,
but does not leave us where it found us.*

~Anne Lamott

At times, I become rattled beyond rationality or stymied with lethargy when faced with DM's overwhelming obstacles. While we wait for a cure, DM families cope as best we can. In my worst moments, I have been known to spew out on my children my frustration over the complications inherent in obtaining services. I find maddening the dearth of resources and guidance in dealing with DM's behavioral manifestations.

In the old days, I lectured Doug and attempted to shame him into responsibility. The twelve-step program taught me to accept what I couldn't change. Yes, letting go of control and turning him over to his Higher Power nurtured my spiritual growth but didn't give me the loving feelings of connection I desired. And so I stand in awe at my last conversation with my son before his death.

Doug called several times a week to rattle on and on about his pet topics. He showed no interest in my life. I found these interactions difficult. Most times I tolerated his intrusion and listened to him a reasonable length of time before giving a reason to end the call. Despite my knowledge about his disease, questions persisted after any contact.

Is there anything I can do to make a difference in his life, a difference that takes my nightmare away? What is to become of him? How responsible am I for protecting others from his intrusion into their lives? How responsible am I for protecting him from himself?

Doug ended our last conversation sooner than usual, perhaps because he received what he needed from me.

"Hi, Mom. Guess how much it cost for the tickets to the concert at The Fraze."

"Oh, I don't know, Doug. Twenty-five dollars?"

"Fifty dollars. You know they're having ten bands this year."

I didn't express the thoughts whirling in my brain. *Oh my God, where is he getting fifty dollars? Did he bilk his sister out of it?*

Instead, I said, "You know, you can listen to all those bands outside The Fraze without paying a penny."

"But, Mom, we like to be in on the action. We like to see the bands, joke around with Jeff and Kristie Leigh [local radio personalities], and get a chance to win the prizes."

"Oh, I know. I remember how much fun you all had last year. I can understand how you'd want to be in on all the action inside."

He finished by telling me how much fun he anticipated having. We didn't know this would be our last conversation. Doug's death came before the concert he so looked forward to attending.

While pondering his life after the funeral, I experienced gratitude at the recognition of the gift contained in our last conversation. At the end of our journey together in this life, grace enabled me to be a loving presence. My Imago skills—leaving behind my world of pain to be present to his world of excitement—came naturally. I'd grown in my capacity to act in a loving way despite the absence of warm, fuzzy feelings, the principle involved in "Do unto others as you would have them do unto you," the compassionate response at the heart of all world religions and spiritual paths.

Not long after K-Mart hired her, I pressured Nicole during a phone call to follow through on some important action. She grew quiet. I interpreted her lack of response as resistance, which triggered a frustrated reaction in me. This time I became curious instead. That opened the way for clearing the air and healing old wounds. I invited her to share her world.

"What goes on with you when you grow quiet?"

She whimpered, "I feel like I'm a disappointment to you ... that you regret ever having children."

I gulped, lamenting my inappropriate words in the past. Years before, while consumed with guilt about my inadequate parenting, I had expressed regret at ever having children. I can see how she would have interpreted that as disappointment in her and her brother. After all, why would I be wishing I had never had children if they were thriving?

It was a cruel thing to say... to her and to me. I was doing the best I could and so were they. But nothing was going well in my children's lives and I couldn't figure out why. I blamed myself and my ill-chosen words scarred my children.

Now I needed to help Nicole understand my meaning. I paced the living room floor and reminded Nicole of a recent conversation where I'd expressed pride in her. I repeated, "I'm proud of you for doing such a good job working full-time for seven years. I know that wasn't easy for you, but you did it, and you did it well."

Sniffling now accompanied her silence as I continued, "When I badger you about something you need to do, it's not because I'm disappointed in you. It's because I'm scared. I love you and don't want anything bad to happen to you. I'm scared you'll be homeless."

More sniffling.

"I'm sorry I told you I regretted having children. I said that not because I regret having you, but because I don't have good parenting skills and I have to live with the guilt of that every day."

We went on to have a conversation about whether she feared becoming homeless. She said, "Sometimes I think I should give up my apartment and get a room somewhere. It would be easier."

The next day I gave Nicole a ride to work. I told her, "I owe you an apology. My guilt is causing me to do things that bring you pain. And my guilt is not your problem. It's something I need to work on. I intend to do that. I'm sorry I've hurt you." When I dropped her off, I told her, "I love you."

Through her tears, she responded, "I love you, too."

After that, she relaxed in my presence. She didn't take my frustration as personally. Laughter emerged, and the air between us lightened—gifts of grace.

Social Security appointed me as her payee. We became a team. We strategized and explored options for allocating these funds in the best possible way. I acquiesced to her wishes, letting go when I thought another option would be better.

In the process of revising this memoir, I dug deeper into my failings.

Just before Nicole's forty-fourth birthday, I asked her to share with me what it was like having me for a mother while she grew up. She responded honestly, and I found our conversation painful. I listened to how Doug receiving all the attention affected her. At one point, she said she quit trying to be the "good kid" doing her best in school. She didn't care anymore.

My pain turned to awe at Nicole's next revelation. She said, "You weren't nurtured, so you didn't know how to nurture. And when kids get to be a certain age, parents expect to be able to leave their children alone. They don't know the signs of sexual abuse. They don't know what to look for."

While I appreciated her gracious forgiveness, I questioned whether I deserved it. The first incident of molestation had warranted more vigilance than I gave.

It became clear my words about wishing I'd never had children had hurt her deeply to the point she couldn't remember my meaning. Explaining again wasn't enough to diminish her core wound. And so I sent her a birthday letter.

In the letter, I expressed my love for her and admitted to my limitations in showing it. I explained that my hurtful words come from my guilt at lacking the nurturing qualities a mother needs. I assured her I have always wanted the best for her. I confessed that my perfectionist personality tends to see problems that I am responsible for fixing. Coupled with my fear something bad will happen to her, I communicate disappointment. I apologized, took responsibility for my need to work on my guilt and perfectionism so as not to hurt her further, and told her my intention to do better in the future.

I went on to highlight the hugeness of her heart, a sign of advanced spiritual development and thanked her for her understanding and forgiveness. I pointed out that since she was a toddler, she freely gave hugs and made people around her feel cared about.

I gave my reasons for being proud of her and admitted that since I did have children, I am grateful she is my daughter. I pointed to her difficult life, acknowledging her tremendous losses. I noted how she endures her disease cheerfully. I told her how I ache at her suffering and of my wish that she had been born healthy.

I asked her to keep this letter so when I screw up in the future, she can read what is really in my heart—always wanting the best for her. I admitted I would never adequately be able to communicate the extent of my love for her.

Later, she told me she'd read it four times and cried every time.

Parents of disabled children carry intense grief. Our chronic sorrow is a normal response to living with ongoing loss. I am not immune. We lack opportunities to express pride in our children because they aren't intelligent, successful, and attractive in the world's eyes. Many perceive our children as disposable and pity us for our lot in life.

As I deal with the sorrow, frustration, and exhaustion in the chasm between "what is" and "what could have been," M. Scott Peck's definition continues to inspire me: "Love is the willingness to extend yourself for the purpose of nurturing your own and another person's spiritual growth."

I grew in my ability to experience being accompanied by a compassionate spiritual presence in the midst of myriad life challenges. Even in our darkest moments, we were never abandoned. We were strengthened to meet every obstacle, and I was graced with strength to extend myself with wisdom and love. "Once I was blind, but now I see." These words to the hymn Amazing Grace take on new meaning.

My daughter's pregnancy brought me to my knees and forced me to surrender—just the opening I needed to awaken to the power of Divine grace. Grace helped me see my granddaughter's short life as a gift instead of a tragedy and transformed me into a grandmother who could extend love by letting her go. As I continue opening to its alchemy, grace transforms me into a kinder, gentler, more loving human being—a mother capable of listening with empathy to her children's suffering, apologizing for her shortcomings, and changing her behavior—a gift all children deserve and few receive.

While I neared the end of reworking this manuscript, life sent me another opportunity to grow in wisdom and the ability to love. Nicole's gynecologist recommended surgery to treat her increasingly painful fibroids. When she entered the hospital in May 2016, her oxygen level was 78. Normal levels are 98–100. Her DM had progressed so slowly, she didn't know her increased fatigue was abnormal. A consulting pulmonologist gave approval for surgery, and two days later she underwent a hysterectomy.

Between May 11 and June 16, Nicole spent fifteen days in the hospital, nine of those in ICU, and then twenty-one days in rehab. During her first rehab, she developed pneumonia and had to return to the hospital. The doctor prescribed oxygen and fitted her with a machine similar to a C-pap called a Bi-pap. When she sleeps, it applies pressure as she inhales to assist with oxygen intake and as she exhales to eliminate extra carbon dioxide from her body. She will need to use this machine while sleeping for the rest of her life.

Being on oxygen full-time meant she could not continue working, and without a job, she could not afford to pay rent. She needed to live with me for the foreseeable future. A friend helped me clear out her apartment. I took pictures of her belongings so Nicole could tell me what she wanted to keep. She moved in with me on June 16, a huge change in both our lives.

Technicians overwhelmed us when they descended on my home with her oxygen tanks and breathing machine, configured their settings, and taught us how to use them. During the first couple of months, doctor and home healthcare appointments filled our schedule. Grocery shopping and cooking for two consumed most of the time I had previously spent writing and socializing.

We both struggled to adjust to living together again and dipped in and out of depression. It took about five months for us to accept our new situation, settle into a workable routine, and find enjoyment in each other's company. This year when we shared our Thanksgiving blessings, Nicole expressed gratitude for being alive, having a place to live, and "for my mommy."

I added many other blessings: the Affordable Care Act's Medicaid expansion providing medical coverage for Nicole, her referral to Ohio State University Wexner Medical Center doctors who specialize in DM, visiting physicians taking over as her primary care doctor, working with a wonderful editor, and being almost finished writing my memoir.

Living with me is not a viable long-term arrangement. Nicole will have more stability in an independent living facility. We have applied for a Medicaid waiver, which if approved, will give her the physical and financial assistance to make such a move possible. It will give her a case manager to advocate for her once I am no longer able to do that. We try once again to be proactive, though we learned recently that approval can take years. If she does not receive authorization before I die, my death will create a crisis and hopefully propel it.

While we both would prefer that she live independently, living with Nicole has provided me with an opportunity to give her the love and attention I neglected to give her during the years I focused on finding help for her brother. That I have succeeded revealed itself recently during a FaceTime conversation with Jacqui where she described a recent visit to see her mother in Taiwan.

On the first day of their visit, Jacqui was touched to hear her mother share about the abuse she had received as a child from her mother. It was no surprise to learn that Jacqui's mother had been physically, emotionally, and verbally abused. Through her tears, Jacqui then described the continuation of this generational abuse. On the second day of their visit, Jacqui's mother proceeded to verbally and emotionally abuse her. Nicole looked at me and said, "I'm glad you don't treat me the way your mother treated you."

I celebrated her validation. With the help of a power greater than myself, I am at last the loving mother of my aspirations. Nicole and I are closer than ever ... another gift of grace.

Linda and Nicole — 2016. Photo by Rick Guidotti.

Epilogue: Awakening to "The Better Way"

[T]there are no wrong turns, only unexpected paths.

~Mark Nepo

Inseparable friends since seminary, Sharon, Kathryn, and I took our theological studies and personal and spiritual growth seriously. "I don't feel I have a choice," I would tell them. "It feels like I was born with a mandate to grow."

They recognized the same directive in themselves. We all strove to do and be our best. Kathryn dubbed us "Quality Butterflies."

During my unconscious years, quality meant the better way to be family, an ideal that had fascinated me since I was ten years old. Under my fascination was a yearning to experience love, the greatest of spiritual gifts. Because I was not awake to the spiritual significance of my longing and love didn't come in wrappings I recognized, I distorted it throughout a good part of my life.

I pondered love's rough edges in childhood and searched for love's balm in every relationship. I studied love intellectually and entered experiential training programs to learn about it empirically. Love's expression encompassed my calling and ministry as a family and couple's therapist.

Monty taught me the vast difference between being "in love" and "loving." Living in Process and twelve-step programs taught me the importance of loving myself if I am ever to truly love another and opened my eyes to the wisdom of letting go with love.

The training in Imago Relationship Therapy taught me deep listening skills that required me to suspend my viewpoint to be in the other person's world—allowing empathy and compassion to emerge. I grew in my capacity to extend love.

In the process of writing this memoir and being present to the world of my younger self, grace gifted me with forgiveness and love of self. As I relived my early years through more mature eyes, compassion assuaged shame, guilt, and self-hatred. Empathy deepened for the young woman who buckled under the weight of family and cultural forces and betrayed herself; for the young wife, still stinging from her parents' confusing messages and bewildered by her sexual experiences; for the mother unable to protect her children from sex's more tawdry expressions; for the theology student and ordained minister who struggled to experience the love of The Divine.

Admiration grew for this woman's strength and her strong determination to grow and evolve. She never gave up despite numerous failures and no reason to hope; she never stopped seeking teachers and resources to help her children and to become the person she aspired to be. I beheld with awe the way her childhood longing transformed into a call to ministry in service to others as a healer of relationships.

And then one day while writing in my prayer journal, these words emerged from my pen: "Thank God for my pain ... it transformed me, broke me open, awakened me to grace, infused me with trust in the inherent goodness and wisdom of life." I awakened. My very existence proves that I am loved and valued just as I am. At the same time, I am invited to continue growing and evolving to an expanded level of consciousness. I experience this invitation as both a challenge and a privilege.

Another day while writing in my prayer journal, I awakened with awe once again as wisdom flowed from my pen. I saw for the first time that my imperfect children were my greatest spiritual teachers. They gifted me with profound spiritual lessons. Our painful circumstances provided the context for my spiritual journey. Perhaps an easier life would not have provided the imperative to grow and evolve. My life made sense.

No longer a victim of circumstances, I now see myself as a heroine—that butterfly in flight Phyllis envisioned for me with her birthday gift and message so many years ago. I embrace a profound truth. In the heart of The Divine, I am cherished. And so is Nicole. And so was Doug. And so was Buddy, who passed away on January 3, 2015, at the age of seventy-seven from complications of myotonic muscular dystrophy.

I found *the better way*. It just doesn't look like I thought it would. I never imagined this would be the path to my awakening to grace.

Acknowledgements

"One night, a little child cried out from the bedroom across the hall. 'Daddy, I'm scared!' Daddy responded, 'Sweetie, don't be afraid. God is watching over you.' The child cried out again, 'But Daddy, I want God with skin on.'"

~Sermon Illustration

I owe a debt of gratitude to many angels who entered my life as God with skin on, especially:

Alice Hegemier and Phyllis Wacker who loved me and opened new vistas for me;

Anne Wilson Schaef who gave me my first glimpse of *a better way*;

Julie Beck who listened to my daughter tell our story and told me to write a book;

Shannon Lord who inserted the last piece of the puzzle.

Special thanks goes to my greatest cheerleaders:

Nita Leland, my writing partner. After listening to me read several drafts, she said, "I believe I was chosen to hear your story." I have no doubt that we were brought together by Divine guidance. Thank you for your consistent affirmation and encouragement.

Judy Plazyk, a Story Circle Network Sister who took a special interest in my memoir. Thank you for praising my writing, for eliciting clarity with probing questions, and for your sustained guidance toward publication.

April (Wilson) Barnswell, a local author and publishing mentor. Thank you for generously taking me under your wing, believing in my project, and helping me launch my memoir into the world.

Thanks also to the communities who provided depth of wisdom and practical skills for moving forward in life: Living in Process, Twelve-step, and Imago Relationships International.

Thanks to friends who bolstered me to continue writing when I was ready to give up: Karen Nelson, Danny Manglesdorf, Nora Dorris, and Amy Scheer.

Thanks to early readers who gave me invaluable feedback and companionship on the long journey to publication: Sharon Everhart, Kathryn Damiano, Kate Johnson, Penny Peterson, Jim Brooks, Christina Consolino, and Ani Nadler Grosser;

To the Cincinnati Contemplative Writing Group who provided practice in honing my skills;

To Jude Walsh Whelley, who introduced me to the extraordinary Works in Progress group through the Story Circle Network. The support and encouragement this group of women writers give to each other is enormous. Thank you all for your willingness to share your vast knowledge of the writing world, your wisdom and practical suggestions about the art of writing memoir, and your support for making outrageous requests. Most of all, thank you for the hugeness of your hearts. You are the best of the best.

To my teachers Nancy Pinard through the Mad Anthony Writer's Workshop Master Class; Erin Flanagan through Antioch Writer's Workshop, Marge Piercy, Ira Wood, and Maia Danziger through Omega Institute's writing workshops; Katrina Kittle through Dayton's Wordsworth Writing Center; and Lisa Dale Norton through Story Circle Network's 2016 conference;

To my many supportive friends... I couldn't have done this without you... you know who you are;

And to my readers. I am humbled and honored that you chose

to read my memoir. My fervent prayer is that my story enriches you and gives you hope for transcending any struggle you may be facing. Knowing we are not alone in the darkness may be just the flicker of light we need to find the way to our buried treasure, our gift of grace. At least, that has been my experience.

Footnotes

1. Paulus, Trina, *Hope for the Flowers*, (New York: Paulist Press, 1972), 75

2. Peck, M. Scott, *The Road Less Traveled*, (New York: Touchstone, 1978), 15

3. Cloke, Dr. Bill, Care2 Healthy Living, (Los Angeles), *Five Things Couples Should Never Do*, May 23, 2012, http://www.care2.com/greenliving/5-things-couples-should-never-do.html

4. Rohr, Richard, *Daily Meditations*, (New Mexico: Center for Action and Contemplation), My Wisdom Lineage, January 2, 2015, https://cac.org/my-wisdom-lineage-2015-01-02/

5. Psalm 139:1, 3b, 6-8, 12c, 13-18 (The New Revised Standard Version)

Resources

Big Book of Alcoholics Anonymous, The, AA World Services, Inc.

Black, Claudia, *It Will Never Happen to Me*, (Minnesota: Hazelton, 1981, 2001)

Bourgeault, Cynthia, *The Meaning of Mary Magdalene: Discovering the Woman at the Heart of Christianity*, (Boston & London: Shambhala, 2011)

Brans, Jo and Margaret Taylor Smith (research), *Mother, I Have Something to Tell You*, (New York: A Signet Book, New American Library, 1987

Caroline Myss Books: www.amazon.com/Caroline-Myss/e/B000APAWW6

Caroline Myss website: www.myss.com

Courage to Change, Al-Anon Family Group Head Inc.

Hendrix, Harville and Helen LaKelly Hunt, *Getting the Love You Want*, (New York: Henry Holt & Company, 20th Anniversary Edition, 2001)

Ilg, Ames, and Baker: www.amazon.com/Child-Behavior-Classic-Institute-Development/dp/0060922761

Mark Nepo Books: www.amazon.com/Mark-Nepo/e/B0001JOVBDG

Mark Nepo website: www.marknepo.com

O'Connor, Elizabeth, *Call to Commitment*,
(New York: Harper & Row, 1963)

O'Connor, Elizabeth, *Eighth Day of Creation*,
(Waco, Texas: Word Books, 1971)

Richard Rohr quote (Part II Awakening): https://cac.org/self-critical-thinking-2015-02-16

Schaef, Anne Wilson, *When Society Becomes an Addict*,
(San Francisco: Harper & Row, 1987)

Schaef, Anne Wilson, *Women's Reality*,
(Minneapolis: Winston Press, 1981)

Spock, Benjamin M.D.: www.amazon.com/Dr-Spocks-Baby-Child-Care/

Wile, Daniel, *Couples Therapy: A Non-traditional Approach*,
(New York: John Wiley & Sons, 1981, 1993)

Author's Biography

Linda A. Marshall's contemplative writing is reflected in her blog, "Emerging Grace," which can be subscribed to on her website: www.LindaAMarshall.com. She is known for giving voice to difficult topics in a heart-felt, vulnerable, and courageous manner. She has been a member of Story Circle Network, a non-profit organization for women with stories to tell, since 2011.

While earning her master of divinity degree at United Theological, her academic writing was praised for its clarity and depth. One of her papers, *A Systems Analysis of the Apostle Paul*, was published in two University of Dayton academic journals, *New Testament Perspectives* and *Explorations: Journal for Adventurous Thought*. Linda was thrilled to be considered an adventurous thinker.

For seven years, as director of Couples' Programs at the Relationship Coaching Institute, she wrote articles for and edited an online newsletter. She served for four years as Dayton's Relationship Coach and wrote a monthly column for the periodical *Single Source News*. She was a contributing author to *Sophia's Table: Women's Wisdom in Five Voices* (2013).

In addition to her most important role of mother, Linda wore many professional hats: business education teacher, ordained minister, retreat facilitator, family therapist for those caught in the pain of addiction, Imago Relationship Therapist, and couples' coach trainer. These experiences gave her an appreciation for the indomitable spirit present in all people's stories and struggles.

Linda enjoys reading memoir, historical fiction, and educational non-fiction, walking in the local arboretum, and spending quality time with her daughter and friends. She participates in several spiritually-oriented groups. She and her daughter enjoy watching movies portraying true life stories of real people. They live with their Siamese-mix cat in a suburb of Dayton, Ohio.

You can contact Linda through her website: www.LindaAMarshall.com

Linda A. Marshall

Made in the USA
Columbia, SC
18 December 2017